D1525257

TRUTH IS IN THE PARADOX

LEARNING TO THRIVE
IN A FRACTIOUS SOCIETY

KATHRYN LISS

❧❧

"Truth shares the same Indo-European root as 'trust' and 'tree.' It's like trust and truth are grounded in the solidity and dependability that we associate with great oaks, redwoods, cedars, and baobobs. We might also reflect that trees—and, metaphorically, trust and truth—are living things that can thrive and grow— or be damaged and die. We are in a period that is sometimes called the 'post-truth era,' with a disturbing subtext that it might also be post-trust."

- Tom Atlee

꧁꧂

PROLOLGUE

THIS IS A BOOK ABOUT TRUTH; ABOUT SEEKING TRUTH, finding truth, being disillusioned, blaming hypocrisy, and eventually discovering that truth is in the eye of the beholder. Even if my parents were still alive to tell me their story of how things happened, it would still only be their version of the truth.

"Meet my conservative daughter, Kathy," said my anti-war mother to her colleagues. She was speaking to the young men and women who worked with her at the National Conference for New Politics in 1967. I was completing my undergraduate degree at the University of Wisconsin. She was disappointed that I had no more attraction to the tall good looking young man she was working with than I had for her politics. I could see that the political views they shared were worthy, but they weren't compelling to me and the folk I would have had to hang out with lived in a world of righteousness.

I can see from reading *Red Diaper Babies: Children of the Left* that I was like many of my peers raised by left-wing parents in feeling that my values and outlook were shaped by my parents' views and not really based in my own understanding of the world. It took many more years of experience and the death of both my parents before I felt free to shape my own political thoughts and find my own path.

This is not a polemic. I seek truth; to tell my true feelings, to seek spiritual truth and to act in integrity knowing I cannot judge others. I can only discern for myself the next right thing to do, as I listen to the still small voice within. One thing I learned over the years that was transformational is that truth is in the paradox and the spectrum is a more accurate representation of reality than duality. Any attempt to choose between dualities will inevitably result in hypocrisy. As a philosophy major in college, I learned to seek the Hegelian synthesis which then creates its own contradiction. (Hegel said that for every thesis, there will be an antithesis and then there will be a new synthesis, generating another antithesis.) Thus my life has been a series of paradoxes and learning opportunities. A tribute to Hegel.

The conflict in my life is a result of the mixed messages I received as a Jewish child—get out and fix the world, (tikkun olam), and watch out, as a Jew, you are marked. And then the messages from my mother—you will never be as good as I am and you are inadequate because your commitment to peace isn't progressive enough. You are "not good enough" but you had better put your shoulder to the wheel and do what needs to be done. Only by walking your talk can you justify your existence.

My mother said my father was committed to mankind, not to individual people. In truth she, too, had more passion for social change than for raising children. As bell hooks observes in her book *All About Love*, just because parents call it love, doesn't mean it is loving!

Trees are enduring. Their roots plant them firmly in Mother Earth while the branches strive to reach Father Sun. No matter how battered they are, if they can still suck some nutrients from the earth, they will grow up. Always up away from mother, toward father. Away from the trunk and bigger, more branches going into every nook where sunshine can be found to be drawn into the leaves or needles and transformed by the miracle catalyst chlorophyll into nourishment. I, too, began believing everything my mother told me only to discover that love and nurturing came from my father. As I grew toward that sun, I reevaluated my life lessons and became increasingly my own person.

In deciduous trees the nutrients are stored over the winter when the leaves with their transforming power have dropped to the ground to become fertilizer for future growth. Nothing wasted, these recycled nutrients get absorbed again with the sap in the spring to provide energy for new growth, new leaves. I, too, have used the shed leaves of my life to create new growth in myself. I have spent hours and days and years in reflection on my life. I have used writing in my journal and this memoir to grow myself from the fertilizer of my hurts and disappointments as well as joys and successes.

One of my favorite trees was on the land I owned in North Georgia. Along the path from the house to the cascade on that property I looked to the right and always was surprised to notice the tree that had formed a complete circle on itself. Something must have leaned on it to turn it to the side and then instead of going back toward the light in an S way, it completed the circle and grew up from there. It always exemplified for me the perseverance of trees in seeking the light and finding the path of least resistance no matter how it looks.

I, too, seek enlightenment without resistance, my own hesitation to believe what seems not believable. Yet I have faith— faith that the universe is benign, harm only comes from harm done and nature is neutral. This planet is evolving and we can be its consciousness if we choose. I have been very influenced by Jean Houston, Barbara Marx Hubbard and other Culture Creatives. I have come to believe what Reevaluation Counseling says about the "upward trend," that humans are overall moving toward a better society. And I believe that the earth will continue whether or not humans as a species continue. I hope we will transform to be able to consciously create society and culture that will sustain us as a species in harmony with nature.

I am struck by how a tree will adapt to its circumstances. Unlike me, it cannot move away when conditions become unwelcoming. Forced by its nature to accept the conditions that prevail, it finds a way to fulfill its purpose. It demonstrates flexibility to move with the wind and not be broken. Whatever small seed it started from continues to manifest exactly what it was designed to be. A cedar doesn't suddenly turn into a pine or an apple into an orange, no matter how much grafting man may do. I, on the other hand, had the freedom to move and change my environment whenever I found the one I was in too inhospitable or something new attracted me. You will learn that I have done this often!

I will always be a New York Jew no matter how long I live in the South. I will never like grits and collards nor will I stop finding a tongue sandwich on rye comfort food. I will continue to make White Southerners uneasy when I know what I want when they are not allowed to. My bluntness of expression and enthusiastic presentation of new ideas scares them. No matter how much I tone myself down and let men open doors or walk on the street side, no one will ever mistake me for a Southern Belle. I may learn to say "y'all" and "bless her heart." But I still call someone I appreciate a "mensch" and someone I don't like a "schmuck." I still kibbitz and kvetch and seek nuchis for the successes of my son.

Born in the sign of Cancer I spent every childhood summer at the beach. I am as comfortable in the water as on land and generally happier. I prefer a thundering ocean or tumultuous river to a placid lake. I feel most alive rafting on the Pacuare River in Costa Rica or diving through the waves on Long Island. I spent my adult life as a professional mediator and I have often said that my image of peace is surfing in the ocean, not reading a book under a tree by a lake. I have chosen mediation as a career because I am familiar with conflict, the tension doesn't scare me. I ride the wave and shift to keep my balance, moving from peak to trough. Water is fluid, shifting, changing course. My understanding of reality is also, not choosing between either/or rather exploring the space between and coming to understand how the same picture can be interpreted very differently, finding the mandorla, the shared space, the common ground.

This memoir traces the events of my life as I have evolved from the values and upbringing I received in a family where my father's near fatal encounter in the 1950s with political hypocrisy turned my young sapling away from the light and ended my innocence. Many of these experiences involved living with illusions, having those illusions shattered and then reconnecting myself with reality. I believe the essential truth is that we are all born loving, brilliant, competent beings eager to connect with one another and then we are twisted into various shapes by our experiences. I have learned spiritual lessons about willingness and willfulness. I have learned that given the opportunity, we can all reemerge into the benign reality and work together to build a world that works for everyone, finding in the shifting waters that stable common ground underneath. After a life of wandering I have turned into a tree that has many roots buried in soil and water while my branches reach for the sky. I am Artemis, the huntress, happiest in the forest, looking for the place where I can most effectively influence movement toward a more just society.

"What makes a good American, what do you have to be?

Am I a good American?

Let's take a look and see.

I like democracy; I'm for equality;

I say be neighborly.

Do I practice what I preach?

I don't care where you are from.

I go by what you are.

I stand up for my rights, but do I stand up for yours?

Am I a good American and by the way, are you?"

From "Little Songs on Big Subjects"
written by Hy Zaret and Lou Singer that was used
in the early 50s for public service animated
TV commercials that promoted "brotherhood" and tolerance
in our changing post-WWII society.

I had a 78 RPM recording of these songs,
which I listened to repeatedly.

CHAPTER ONE

I'M A "RED DIAPER BABY" BORN BY C-SECTION AT 12:01 A.M. on the Fourth of July, 1946. My mother chose this time because she wanted me to be a "good citizen." But perhaps we really were in critical condition and needed a Caesarian in the middle of the night. Whose truth?

What is a "red diaper baby?" Children born to parents who in the late 1940s and early 50s were progressive, members of the Communist Party, or fellow travelers are called "red diaper babies." We were the ones born into "red" families during the period of American history when our parents faced prejudice, discrimination, and blacklisting because of their political beliefs. I was born nine months after my father came back from serving in the U.S. army, helping to set up labor unions in defeated Germany as part of the military government and after my parents had been married for ten years.

Mother's idea of a good citizen was someone who held the country to the stated principles of democracy, freedom of speech and belief, valuing all people, self determination. Mother had a clear sense of what was right and what was wrong in the world. I have learned that many things are not that clear cut.

Most of the time I have chosen to be happy rather than being "right," although I have a deep desire for discovering the truth. Uncovering the truth can be a challenge. I have also learned that for meaningful change to happen, it is most useful to find common ground and build on that foundation, rather than pushing an unrealizable agenda. Much of my life has been about trying to live up to my mother's expectations while also trying to get out from under her shadow.

One of the confusions of my life has been whether "my people" are the true patriots, committed to the principles our country claims to stand for or if our beliefs and activities are subversive. Whose truth?

❧

I have very fond memories of living in Chevy Chase. The house on Shepherd Street was the second alphabet out from Chevy Chase Circle—the DC line. The streets are named in alphabetical order starting at the Circle where the public library is. We went there often. There is a picture of me at three years old with a librarian reading to me. The picture was published in the Washington Post with a caption describing me as the youngest patron. It was the first of many times I had my picture in the paper. My father framed that photo and hung it on the wall of his home office when I was in college. He called me "Chip" because he said I was a "chip off the old block."

The house was warm and comfortable. My room had windows on three sides covered with green patterned drapes that matched the green of the waste basket my mother painted with a flowered design in red. They matched the bedspread. The small lamp with a red design had a white girlish shade that directed the light to my bed so I could look at a book as I lay in bed.

Upstairs was my father's study. That was where the television was when we were the first on the block to get one. My father's brother worked for Philco Playhouse so we got a Philco television as soon as they came out. The room smelled like my father's pipe tobacco and had an afghan on the couch that my mother had knitted.

I keep a photograph on my dresser now of me at about four years old. I am hanging over the rail of the back porch outside the dining room which my parents had added on to the house with a patio below. My belly is braced against the wood, feet in the air, arms draped over the rail so I won't fall. My father must have held the camera below on the back lawn.

In that picture I am radiating joy. The broad smile on a wide warm mouth reaches out to the viewer. There is only delight on my face. I am loved and loveable. No harm will ever come to me. I completely trust my father's love and protection, feeling safe and sure that I won't tumble onto the ground. The universe is on my side, supporting me even as I trust my own small arms to attach me to that railing.

I am wearing a jumper over a blouse. I don't care what you put on me. I am still me, playful, kinesthetic, enjoying my strong healthy body. My long blond hair is in two braids. The one thing my mother did to take care of me every day till I was thirteen was to brush and braid my hair. It was often a struggle getting through the knots tangled by my tomboyish activities, but I treasured that time of being cared for. She told me stories to keep me still while she worked. I reveled in my coarse, wavy hair and still enjoy the blissful sensations when someone runs their fingers through the tangles and massages my scalp.

The sensory pleasures of being a child, free to roll on the lawn, run naked through the sprinkler, jump in puddles, touch, taste, and experience all that newness. Joy is in the senses and on my beaming face in that snapshot now fading from many years of exposure to the light of life. I still love sensuous experiences and seek opportunities to enjoy the outdoors.

∽✧∽

My mother grew up in a family of privilege. Her father was a very wealthy man. Among other properties and businesses, he owned hospitals in New York City. I was born in one of my grandfather's hospitals although my parents were living in Chevy Chase, Maryland at the time. My mother went to New York after running a large fund raising dinner in June and hung out with John Kulscar, her father's personal physician until she was ready to have her baby. It was hot and humid and she went to the air conditioned movies during the day. Dr. Kulscar went along to keep her company. He was probably as glad as she was to have the baby, me, born and over with.

When I was four, my grandfather died and my parents decided to adopt a child. My mother felt that she could not have gotten through that time if she hadn't had the support of her siblings and she wanted to be sure I had a sibling to depend on when she died. So they were very excited when they found that that they could do a private adoption through the hospital that her brothers now owned. The family story was that at that time, Jews couldn't adopt publically because there was no cross-religion adoption. However, I have learned since (watching the movie Three Identical Strangers) that there was actually a Jewish adoption agency in New York City at that time. Whose truth?

I wasn't excited about having a brother. As it turned out, his arrival foreshadowed substantial changes in my family. Yet, while we still lived in Chevy Chase, I enjoyed wheeling him around in the baby carriage on the concrete floor in the basement and pretending I was Annie Oakley on my tricycle. The basement stairs came down in the middle of a large open space, and I rode around and round. My father had a work table with tools hung on a pegboard wall– all neat and organized, just like Ozzie Nelson, or any other conventional dad of the 50s.

There was also a playroom in the basement, connected to the room where Ginny slept. She was the housekeeper who came when I was five and my brother, Ricky, was adopted. She left her daughter who was my age so that she could earn a living by taking care of us. I thought Ginny was beautiful; warm mahogany skin, quiet and reserved, she was always there, providing meals and a clean house. She shared her basement bedroom with our playroom, where Ricky and I stored our toys on bookcases that outlined our area. There was also a washing machine and ironing board, but Ginny was the only person I ever saw using them. Outside the basement was a patio.

Beyond the patio was the lawn with a clothes line on a pole

with four arms making four sides with parallel ropes. I watched as Ginny hung the wash out there. I wanted to be tall enough to reach it myself and put on the clothespins. On the other side was the garage. Next to it stood a tall tree from which hung a swing. I loved to have my dad push me on the swing. Flying higher and higher. Also in that backyard was a strawberry patch that my mother took care of. It was covered in cheesecloth to keep the bugs off. Those strawberries tasted like captured sunshine and I still today seek fresh picked strawberries to recall those years of comfort and safety.

There was a mulberry tree in the front yard that was easy to climb. I remember my father boosting me up into its branches where I clung to the tree feeling safe because he was below. I felt loved and part of a protective family. Suddenly one spring, hordes of locusts came eating the leaves off the tree, leaving it bare, naked and vulnerable. The fruit which used to drop to the ground was replaced by their discarded shells.

My best friend, Betty Hughes Reeside, lived across Shepherd Street. from me. She was a little older than I was, and we loved playing together. We sometimes let Cornelia, Sidney Dines or some of the other children on the street join us, but mostly it was just the two of us. We'd climb trees, swing on the swing in the backyard, run under the sprinkler or pretend to be cowboys shooting the guns from our holsters. Sometimes Jessie, the daughter of my father's best friend, Ben, and her family came to visit. They were always there for my birthday parties. Even though my birthday is in July, we always celebrated in June before leaving for our summer vacation on Long Island so I could have my winter friends at my party.

Betty Hughes' family was rather strict. They insisted she call my mother "Aunt Terry," even though we weren't related. Hardly! Her family was so WASP they belonged to the Chevy Chase Country Club.

One day when I was visiting, Betty's mother said, "Tell Kathy she must go home now." Betty asked "why?" Her mother said, "We are going to the Club and they don't allow Jews there." I looked at her my brow wrinkled with confusion.

I was completely perplexed. How was I different from Betty Hughes that kept me from joining in her activity? I was hurt that I couldn't join my friend in her activities as she joined me in mine. I went home and Betty Hughes went to the Club. I hardly knew what it meant to be a Jew, but they were clear that I didn't belong.

I never could figure out what to call her parents because I was taught to call adults by their first names. Was this pattern part of being a "red diaper baby" where people didn't use last names to protect each other's identity? Or was it just the casual nature of adult/child relationships in my family?

Betty Hughes and I walked from our house to school without a parent, even crossing four lane busy Connecticut Avenue. My first grade teacher, Ms. Marshall, wrote on my report card, signed by my father, "Kathy makes many worthwhile contributions to her class. ...Kathy's reading is coming along nicely. She uses her time and materials wisely. Kathy takes a great deal of interest and pride in her work. She is a very dependable and responsible member of her class... [She] has made excellent progress in First Grade."

My memory of the school is of running through the undeveloped wooded area behind it during recess and leaping over the roots of the old trees. I had a crush on Bobby McLaughlin who lived across the street from the school and was in my class. He came to visit at our house and I told him I had a couple of baseball mitts.

He said, "Where's the third one?"

I said, "A couple is two, not three."

He said, "It can be three."

"No, it can't," I replied.

He rolled his eyes and never visited again. It was more important for me to be right than to get along, even with this boy I had a crush on. Already I was testing what was right and what was wrong.

I came home to our house from elementary school and found my mother in the dining room playing Scrabble with a woman friend while Ginny made dinner. Good smells emanated from the kitchen and murmured conversation came from the dining room. Soon dad came home and we all sat around the cherry dining table while Ginny served us dinner.

ৰ৶৵

August 28, 1951. The day after my brother, Rick, was born and my father had gone out to celebrate the birth of his son with his best friend, Ben. Although I wasn't there and was only five years old when it happened. I can see my father, Sam Liss, returning home from his day of work as an agricultural economist in Farm Security Administration at the Department of Agriculture in Washington, DC. He is dropped off by his car pool buddies in front of 114 Shepherd St. and walks up the concrete path to the front porch of the small grey house. Turning the key in the lock, he feels hot, sweaty, tired. The house is silent. It is empty. His wife and daughter are away for the summer months on Long Island and he has a long dark night ahead.

My father was tall (5'10"), blond and athletic. He was proud of his ability to keep his weight at 165 pounds and he exercised regularly. He had been captain of the basketball team in City College in New York when their Jewish team had won the national championship and he is in the Basketball Hall of Fame. Tonight he is not feeling like a winner. He enters the living room and notices the furniture, all wedding gifts from his father-in-law. A matching pair of uncomfortable high backed upholstered chairs, another large head of the household chair and one more feminine, the latter two that he and my mother, Terry, usually each sit in if they are not on the couch. A lot of furniture for this small room. All well-made to last.

There is the fireplace, surrounded by the tiles made by Terry's artist friend, Dante. Over it, a mantel piece where Sam likes to sit his small daughter so she can jump into his arms. A hand knotted Oriental rug lies on the floor: red and green flowers on a brown and tan background. Another part of Terry's trousseau.

He goes down the hall into the bedroom and hangs his suit jacket in the closet. There are twin beds with a night table between them. His bed is closest to the door so that if his daughter awakens in the night, she will find him and not wake her mother. On the night table is a phone. He knows he will have to use it soon to call Terry and see how her trip into New York City to pick up their new son went today. Although they are both very pleased to be receiving the child they are adopting, he will have to tell her his news. He decides to wait until he has had something to eat.

Sam walks back through the living room and into the kitchen. In the refrigerator he finds the makings of a sandwich and some cold borscht, a reminder of his childhood in the Ukraine and growing up on the Lower East Side of New York City where his father had a printing business. Fixing his sandwich he wonders how he is going to break the news. Is this a day to celebrate or to mourn? What will become of his growing family if he doesn't have a job? What kind of work will he be able to find with the reputation his wife's political activities have created for them?

Sitting at the cherry dining table with its matching custom made side board (more gifts from her wealthy family), he imagines the conversation and decides to start by asking about her day. She will just assume his was another ordinary day. How much money will this long distance call cost? Money may become a big issue now. How much should he tell her of his fears?

He goes to the phone and dials the number for the cottage in Springs, New York a farming and fishing village on the east end of Long Island where Terry is vacationing with her daughter, Kathy, and her niece, Judy. Sam only has two weeks' vacation each summer but Terry doesn't have a job and can spend two months at the beach. Terry answers cheerfully. Sam asks about the baby she has gone to pick up from her family's hospital in Manhattan (the same one I was born in). The baby's biological mother worked at the United Nations right down the street from the hospital and his father was an Indonesian diplomat.

Preparing for the phone call, Sam lights up his pipe, sits down on the bed and dials the phone. Wanting to start on a positive note, he asks about how his new son looks.

Terry excited to share about their new baby, says, "He does look rather Asian but his skin isn't any darker than mine."

Sam, still trying to focus on the delight of having a new son, asks, "How was the drive? It is a long way to drive into the city and back to East Hampton in one day."

"I didn't mind. I had Kathy and Judy along. I left Judy with my sister and just came back with our children. I was so excited to have finally gotten the baby I didn't really notice the drive. Kathy sat in back with the baby and helped keep him quiet."

"Are we still planning to name him Frederick Louis Liss?" he asked. "I know it will be good to give him the name Louis just after your father's passing, but Frederick is a rather unusual name for a Jew."

"I like it; we can call him Ricky."

Sam, pauses to draw on his pipe and being his usual agreeable self says, "It's okay."

It's time for Terry to think about how things might be back in Chevy Chase and she asks, "How was your day?"

With trepidation and taking a deep breath, Sam replies, "Well,

I have some bad news. When I got to my desk this morning there was a note that said, 'Resign or be investigated.'"

The shift from the delight of having finally gotten the child she has been waiting for to pure fear happened instantly. "Oh, my God, what are we going to do with a new child to care for and you out of a job?"

"Well, no one said anything more to me today so I guess I will just not resign and see what happens." Sam has been thinking all day about what alternatives he might have. "Meanwhile, I guess I need to start looking for something else. I don't think I will be able to work anywhere else in government, but maybe I can get back into academia, even finish my Ph.D. and teach economics."

Feeling panicked, Terry says, "You've already been through a loyalty board investigation and been determined 'eligible on loyalty.' Why do you think it will be different this time? What has changed?"

"I don't know if I can continue to concentrate on my work with all the pressure of another investigation. They may try to make me name our friends. I am not going to be an informer!"

"Of course you can't name other people to the loyalty board, but you have to be able to earn a living. We have two children to support now."

Now the fears Sam has been feeling all day emerge, "Who will hire me? What if they decide to deport me? I know we have never been members of the Party, but I am still a naturalized citizen."

Terry, still thinking mostly about her growing family asks, "How can we be facing this now? With another mouth to feed and my father only dead a year, I just can't cope with more change."

"Well, for the time being, I'll just keep going to work each day and see what it brings. You and the children will be home in a week and we can talk about it more face to face. In the meantime, we need to be thinking about what other alternatives there are for work for me and who might be willing to help us."

"I really don't know how I will be able to sleep tonight worrying about all this and with a brand new baby in the house! We'll talk again tomorrow evening and see how things look then. G' night."

"G' night."

With that Sam hangs up the phone and retreats to the bedroom to put the rest of his work clothes away and get ready for bed. He wonders if either of them will be able to sleep this night. What will the future bring? What should he be doing to continue to provide for his wife and children? Where will they be in a year or two? A restless night is ahead and possibly many more.

Eventually it became clear that someone saw Sam that night with his best friend, Ben, getting a drink to celebrate the new baby. The FBI must have reported to the loyalty board which was investigating if any government employee's loyalty could be doubted. Ben was already labeled a Communist and association with "a known Communist" would overrule the fact that dad had been cleared three years earlier and declared "eligible on loyalty." The Loyalty Boards were established by Harry Truman in 1947 "to inquire into the loyalty to the government of the U.S. of persons employed or considered for employment by the U.S. government or by international organizations of which the U.S. is a member and to make usually advisory determinations in such cases." (Merriam Webster)

The "Happy Family" life we lived was lost when my father was threatened with losing his job. It affected me deeply. I overheard conversations among the adults when I was supposed to be asleep at night as they worried about what would become of our family if my father was fired. I had many dreams after that of running down Shepherd Street on fire, a five year old's image of being "fired." I could see the houses on our street in my dreams and fire rained from the sky. There was nowhere safe to hide. If he was fired, I must have been also. I always associated the changes in our family with my brother joining our family.

I also learned to distrust our government. Later I realized that what the government says about freedom of speech and association was theory and not practice. This was a powerful lesson that contradicted what I learned in school and left me with a cynicism about the U.S. such that I am rarely moved by other ways in which the country doesn't walk its talk. I was not surprised when I arrived at the realization that the wealth of this nation is built on the stolen land and stolen labor of people of color.

The 1950s was a period in American history called "the McCarthy Era." Senator Joseph McCarthy, junior senator from Wisconsin from 1947, created a reign of terror in the U.S. After World War II, America turned from its fear of fascism in Germany and Italy to a fear of Communism in Russia. We had been afraid of Russian Communism since the Russian Revolution and had sent troops into Russia in 1918 to try to turn the tide against communism there. However, during WW2, the Russians were our allies in stopping the spread of Hitler's power in Europe. This changed immediately after the war.

Enter McCarthy, blowing cold winds on the frozen fear that held America in its grip after the war. This was the start of the Cold War which paralyzed Americans for decades. The fear was that we would be infiltrated and subverted from within and McCarthy used that fear to subvert American freedom to dissent and to inflate his own power. He is best known for his claim in 1950 that 205 communists had infiltrated the U.S. State Department. Soon after, he held up a piece of paper claiming to have the names of 57 State Department employees who were members of the Party. The people he accused of being communists were subpoenaed and the only way you could keep your job was by "naming names" of others. This became a phrase used to indicate informing on your colleagues.

McCarthy took it upon himself to expose anyone implicated by anyone else or anyone who refused to "name names" and to see that they were never able to obtain another job. This created a purge of all government agencies. Many people today remember the Hollywood Ten and others in the movie industry who were blacklisted, but there were many others in other occupations, particularly government employees whose lives were destroyed by the blacklist.

Roy Cohn was McCarthy's chief counsel. He was instrumental in advising McCarthy how to pursue his reign of terror. He was largely responsible for sending Julius and Ethel Rosenberg to the electric chair for their alleged espionage. Later, Cohn became lawyer to Donald Trump during his early career. The New York Times on June 20, 2016 details the influence Cohn had on Trump. They cite "the gleeful smearing of his opponents, the embracing of bluster as brand" as indicators of that influence. My cousin Victor Kovner, a lawyer who had known Cohn for years, was quoted in Daily Kos as saying "You knew when you were in Cohn's presence you were in the presence of pure evil." Daily Kos went on to say, "Cohn's power derived largely from his ability to scare potential adversaries with hollow threats and spurious lawsuits. And the fee he demanded for his services? Ironclad loyalty."

The vehicle for ensuring that there were no Communists in government was an institution called the "loyalty boards." These committees were installed in every department of the government and they reviewed any cases of apparent "disloyalty." Each employee had to sign an oath of loyalty to the U.S. government in order to continue employment. Many people refused on the grounds that it was un-American to be required to do this. They lost their jobs. My father signed the loyalty pledge because he was loyal to the U.S. government and still he lost his job. Dad was declared 'eligible on loyalty' in 1948 but was threatened with another investigation in 1951 and forced to resign in 1953.

Senator McCarthy's activities were preceded by other committees of Congress and continued by the House Committee on Un-American Activities (HUAC) which was formed in 1945. HUAC was a House of Representatives committee and McCarthy was a senator so they were separate investigations. Immediately preceding HUAC was another congressional committee investigating disloyalty and subversive activities, the Dies Committee (1938 – 1944). My mother was very proud of being a "premature anti-fascist" and having been called before that committee in 1942 apparently for association with the American League for Peace and Democracy of which she denied being a member.

I have researched my parents' stories. I obtained and read both their FBI files, General Services Administration files, newspaper articles about them. I have learned a great deal from reading what the FBI informants had to say about my parents' activities. These documents stir up the feelings of confusion and fear that have followed me throughout my life. I have felt like an outsider, not really conforming to the norms of any place I have lived, although I have lived up and down the east coast and a pivotal year in Kenya and travelled Europe, and parts of Africa, Asia and Central America. I kept trying to find a place where I belonged.

According to my mother's FBI file, in that Dies committee interview she was asked: "Do you know of any reason why anyone should, in your opinion, suspect you of being a member of the Communist Party?"

She replied, "The fact that you say 'anyone' makes it a little difficult to answer. Mr. Dies always claims I am, considering his definition of the word and his way of making those claims, I have very little to say. I have never done anything that should make that possible. I believe in democracy and if Mr. Dies considers that 'left' or whatever term you might give it, I can't help it."

Next question: "Do you now or have you ever advocated the overthrow of the form of government we now have in the United

States?"

Reply: "I never have and I doubt I ever will. We are all trying now to fight to keep it—awfully hard."

This philosophy of my mother's was in stark contrast with the beliefs of the time. The fear of Communism was so great that freedom of speech and belief was suppressed by the government. Anyone who questioned the value of capitalism was considered to be dangerous. From my point of view, it is only in the last few years that we have been able to say that perhaps capitalism is dangerous for our world, causing much of the ecological damage that is threatening life on this planet. Americans have been taught that there are only two possibilities—capitalism or communism and these economic systems are identified with the political systems of democracy or totalitarianism. The progressives who supported Franklin Delano Roosevelt saw the possibility of democratic socialism—a political system that is inclusive matched with an economic system that addresses the needs of all the people. Once World War II was over and Franklin D. Roosevelt was no longer in office, such beliefs became labeled as "dangerous."

&⁊&

My mother at 5'4 with dark brown hair, olive skin and a very deep voice lived her life for causes. Before I was born, much of her volunteer work was with the Friends of Spanish Democracy. She was honored for her work raising money for the Lincoln Brigade (the Americans who fought for a Republican Spain in opposition to Franco's takeover) by being given a metal replica of the famous statue of La Passionaria (Dolores Ibarrui) which I eventually was able to donate to the Abraham Lincoln Brigade Archives with great relief. It took me until 2016 to remove this part of the shadow she cast over my life.

She was also sent to Mexico after Franco won as a delegate to the conference on how to help the Spanish refugees. I have a copy of the letter she wrote in 1940 requesting donations for the Spanish Refugee Relief Campaign of which she was the Executive Secretary.

Reading from the stationary I can see that the national honorary chairman was Harold Ickes, Secretary of Interior, and there were many distinguished people as national sponsors including Mary McLeod Bethune, Mrs. Louis Brandeis, Albert Einstein, Mrs. James Roosevelt and several well known authors. Was this a "subversive organization" as was implied by my father's FBI file? Whose truth?

Her social justice work began when she first came to Washington after her graduation from NYU in 1935. My parents met each other at a gathering to create a labor union for civil service workers. They married in 1936. She received her Masters' degree from American University two years later. She credited her husband with helping her get through graduate school. This allowed her to work for the government for several years as a statistician in various departments although she most liked her time with the Railroad Retirement Board.

She participated in social change activities throughout her life. While still in Washington, she raised money to start Georgetown Day School, the first integrated private school in Washington, DC which is still operational. This was during a time when schools were segregated by law. She helped to desegregate the lunch counters in DC. In 1945—46 she was director of community relations for the Downtown Community School in New York City. She was very proud of working with Leonard Boudin and Margaret Mead on this project. She also met Eleanor Roosevelt through her fundraising. She was active in initiating the Washington Bookshop which seems to have been a store that sold left wing books and was mentioned several times in the FBI reports.

Informants quoted in her FBI file say that she was always loyal to the American government. One "described her as a normal middle class individual who was 'reasonably liberal in her thinking but not liberal to the extent of advocating revolutionary ideas.' He advised that Mrs. Liss was a very energetic person, a hard worker and the type of individual who was not happy unless she was working....

'definitely not a radical' and intensely loyal to the United States and would be willing to give her life if necessary to preserve the existing democratic form of government in this country." Someone else described her as a "social climber" who might have been led astray by efforts to meet prominent people. Whose truth?

In 1948 government employment records show these activities of my mother were cited in the investigation of my father who was called before the loyalty board in the Department of Agriculture and was "determined to be eligible on loyalty." However, in 1949 the U.S.S.R. exploded its first atomic weapon and the fear in the U.S. ratcheted up several notches. In 1950 the trial of Alger Hiss, the first identified spy for Russia, brought increased attention to the alleged activities of "subversives" who might undermine American government. Thus, when my brother was born in 1951 the standards had changed and my father being seen with his best friend, Herb Benjamin (Ben) made him vulnerable to discharge and possibly to deportation.

This statement was written in *Jewish Currents* when Ben died.

"A MAN TO REMEMBER

"On May 10, 1983 Herbert Benjamin died, aged 85. Do you know this name? If you have received unemployment insurance or social security you should. Nowhere does his name appear in history books. Yet it should. Only a small obituary in the New York Times; only a handful of people mourned his passing, but it should have been a day of national mourning. He led the unemployment movement of the 1920s and 1930s that ended in the victory of unemployment insurance and social security for working people. He did more for the people of the United States than most famous Americans.

"Can you imagine the suffering today without these benefits? Remember his name. Honor his memory. Continue the struggle."

On the other hand, this is how the FBI describes Ben (who

was the Communist dad was seen with on August 27, 1951).

"In August, 1950, Confidential Informant [redacted] of known reliability, advised that [redacted] was a member of the Communist Party as of 1949. Informant stated that he believed [redacted] was dangerous to the United States and that [redacted] would carry out any assignment given to him by the communist Party, even including espionage or sabotage. Informant stated that he based this opinion on his personal knowledge and belief concerning [redacted].

"The *Washington Times Herald* for [redacted] in an article entitled [redacted] in part states that [redacted] a key figure of the Communist Party for more than twenty five years was one of the group of men arrested here for [redacted]. Concerning [redacted] background, this article stated he was in charge of the St. Louis Office of the Communist Political Association in 1944, that in 1942 he toured the state of Utah for the Communist Party."

Ben's daughter, Jessie, confirms that this describes Ben. Whose truth?

&&

One may wonder what an agricultural economist who studied migratory labor and helped start the first racially integrated farmers cooperative in Missouri could do to "subvert the U.S. government." However, it is true that one of my father's bosses seems to have been a spy for the U.S.S.R. His name is Gregory Silvermaster and according to Wikipedia his FBI file is 26,000 pages of documents compared to the 150 pages of my father's. Like my father he was also born in Odessa, Ukraine and he worked with Farm Security until 1944. Silvermaster took a job with the War Production Board during the war where he had access to classified information and was implicated by Elizabeth Ullman whose story is told by Kathryn S. Olmsted, in *Red Spy Queen* (2002). He was forced to retire from government in 1946.

As it happens, Silvermaster died when I was in college and my father wrote to me about him in one of his letters that I have kept,

"I was greatly saddened a few days ago when I learned that Greg Silvermaster, with whom I spent many happy and constructive working years at Farm Security Administration in Washington, died at age 65. As you may remember my mentioning it, he was Director of the Farm Labor Division when I was Assistant Director. He was hounded out of Washington in about 1950 via the HUAC and the Senate McCarran Committee during the period of the political witch hunt and the Loyalty Oath procedures that followed W.W.II even prior to the McCarthy period of the early 1950's. Seeing Greg go was like losing a very important part of my intellectual life and then carefully and deliberately reading it in the *New York Times* left me with an empty feeling that brooked no solace. To me he personified that very exciting and crucial period of anti-fascism that pervaded the minds, hearts and actions of thinking and politically-literate people in the early 1930's—the people who fundamentally were responsible for the defeat of fascism and Nazism. He also remains my personal symbol of the New Deal as FDR is the national symbol."

Whose truth?

Our neighborhood was a very small and intimate one. One time my paternal grandmother was staying with us. I wanted to go to see Betty Hughes but she insisted I could not cross the street alone. That seemed very strange to me, since I did it all the time. It was not a very large street. In winter when it snowed, all the children rode sleds down the middle. The road went down a hill in front of our house that looked steep to me as a child, but as an adult I can see it is small.

Next door down the hill lived the Robertsons. They had two children somewhat older than me. The girl, Judy, babysat for us. Her brother, Don, went into the Navy. Our backyards shared a fence, but our yard was full of gardens and theirs was full of equipment. Were they the neighbors who reported to the FBI that we often had gatherings of people at our house?

I felt very connected in that neighborhood. I feel confused now reading the FBI file on my father in 1948 which led to his being declared "eligible on loyalty." Who were we to those neighbors? There are comments about our family made by neighbors whose names are blacked out. People saying that my parents were suspicious because they had visitors who spoke foreign languages (was it Yiddish like they grew up with or Ukrainian, the language of my father's birth?) Neighbors were reported to have said, "They are the only Jewish family on the street." Or "Regular meetings of some type were being held at the Liss residence. No information was obtainable as to the nature of these meetings but neighbors indicated they suspicioned (sic) these meetings were possibly meetings of a Communist nature." (April 19, 1948) Some people seemed to think there was nothing suspicious, but others took note of the many gatherings of friends – backyard barbeques and Scrabble games in the dining room, from my point of view.

Whose truth?

Another effect of the anti-communism of the '50s was that the U.S. asserted that Communism was "godless" and that the U.S. was a more moral nation because of our respect for God. That was when "under God" was added to the Pledge of Allegiance and "In God We Trust" was added to our printed money. That got perverted into a belief that the U.S. is a Christian nation. The founding fathers were actually not Christian, but theists and they carefully wrote into the Constitution that the government should never be dominated by one religion or another. As a Jew, this is very important to me. I have found a great deal of enlightenment from the freedom to learn from other religions than Christianity. I am concerned that we are very confused by assertions that the government should regulate our bodies based on Christian principles or that we should not allow people who follow a different religion to enter our country. Not only did my family lose political freedoms and economic opportunity due to the purges, but as a nation we have given up many freedoms as result of McCarthyism.

What is clear to me after all these years is that my father

decided he had to find other work. I believe he applied for several academic jobs during the twenty months between receiving that note on his desk and actually leaving government employment. No one would hire him. Other red diaper babies I have talked with over the years have told stories of their blacklisted parent getting support from other members of the Party to find work. Since he was not a member of the Party, there were no fellow Communists who had connections to lead him to the kind of academic or research job that would have been appropriate for his skills and abilities. For some reason that I will never know, he decided to look for a summer camp to run. We had friends on the left who ran summer camps for red diaper babies and I guess he thought he could, too. (I attended two of these summer camps which were very influential for many of the children of the left.)

In any case, the family story was that he was looking for a summer camp back on the east end of Long Island and found a large building with twenty-four small cottages in the back and decided to buy it with money that my mother had inherited from her father who was recently deceased. It turned out that this was the Elm Tree Inn and they decided to continue to run it as a bar, restaurant and motel. It opened in spring of 1954, a year after he left government service. I say that my father got blacklisted and the family moved to hell.

"You have to accept whatever comes
and the only important thing is
that you meet it with courage
and with the best that you have to give."

- Eleanor Roosevelt

CHAPTER TWO

AMAGANSETT WAS A SMALL FARMING AND FISHING VILLAGE at the end of Long Island in the 1950s. Beautiful beaches began attracting a mix of artists and theater people to this previously isolated bit of heaven. The clash of cultures engendered much tension. I was in the middle of it. Fatso-Lisso, a third grade girl displaced from her comfortable middle class world of suburban Washington, D.C. I drowned my unhappiness, fears, and despair in chocolate.

Who were those benighted people—my family? A communist, a kike, a chink, a nigger, a faggot and fatso; that's what they called us. So many maligned identities. All alien to children whose highest ambition was to own their own fishing boat so they could supply the meal factory at Promised Land. The leader of the present day volunteer fire department (a high status among the local Bonikers) was in my grade of sixteen students. He inherited his father's plumbing business. A good way to make a living from those "summer people."

Much of who I am today was shaped by the five years I lived year round in Amagansett. I was challenged by living in a place where so many of the values and norms with which I was raised were out of step with others in the community. I experienced repeated attacks and acquired many scars.

Until I was seven, we spent every summer in the house we rented from Jack Conklin in Springs on Long Island just a mile from Gardner's Bay, near my father's brother's house. Mornings I woke to the warm sun flowing in the window. Scratching mosquito bites on my ankle, I anticipated the day to come. Who would we meet at the beach? Would this be a tennis day or a bike riding day?

For my fifth birthday, my parents bought me a bicycle. The road in front of the house was not used a great deal although it connected Springs to Amagansett. My parents decided that it was a good place for me to learn to ride. The road was paved and smooth with black tar and had few speeding cars.

When I awoke on my birthday morning I was excited. I put on my blue cotton pedal pushers and a striped blue and white tee shirt with my black and white saddle oxford shoes. I ate a breakfast of cereal and milk and fresh strawberries. Mother braided my hair in pigtails as she did every morning. "Mama, ouch, you are pulling it too tight!"

Continuing to tightly twist the strands of my long wild hair, she said, "I'll tell you a story about a little girl who hated to have her hair braided. Her mother told her a story about a little girl who hated to have her hair braided and she sat still and listened while her mother told the story."

As soon as she was finished, I cried, "Where is my new bicycle? I want to ride!"

Running outside to admire the red Schwinn bike, just the right size for me, I was jumping up and down eager to get on it. But I had no idea of how to ride it. Dad said, "Just sit on the seat and pedal. I promise to hold on to the handle bars and to you so you won't fall off."

We moved slowly as he walked alongside of me and I pushed hard on the pedals. Eventually, he had to run to continue to hold on to me as we moved faster and faster down the road. It felt good to move that quickly. I could feel the warm salty air moving against my face and arms. The trees were moving past much faster than when we went for a walk.

After a few times down the road, I was going too fast for him to keep up. He let go and I found that I could stay up without his holding me. But I didn't feel safe going much further than where he could see me. He kept encouraging me to keep trying when I stopped. "You can keep going, Kathy. But don't go past the turn off to Uncle Joe's."

Finally, I did go as far as the turn off. It was a sandy triangle and when I got there and tried to turn around, the bike slipped and I fell down. "Ouch." My knees and elbows were scraped and stinging. I hurt. The tears started flowing. But dad was far back on the road and I had to get back to him.

I decided to walk the bike back to where he was standing waiting for me. He saw me coming and heard my cries. He came running toward me, taking out his handkerchief to wipe my eyes. He said, "Sometimes you will fall off, but you must always get back up and try again." So I did.

The next time I rode as far as the triangle, I was prepared and got off my bike before I hit the sand. I turned the bike around and rode back without incident. My father said, "See you are learning already how to take care of yourself on a bike. Soon we will be able to ride together all the way to Uncle Joe's house."

I loved that little red bicycle and continued to ride it even after dad went back to Chevy Chase to his job at the Department of Agriculture. He only had two week's vacation in the summer, but Mom and I stayed out at the beach for the whole two months. We went to the beach and to the town park and visited with friends. That same summer was the summer my brother was born and my life changed dramatically. It wasn't his birth so much as the events that occurred concurrently that caused the changes in our lives.

On August 27, 1951 we went to the park in East Hampton as usual. My father was back at his job. My cousin Judy was visiting and she and Mom played tennis, while I pumped myself higher and higher on the swing. Before coming home, we stopped at the fish store and bought some just caught blue fish for dinner. We also stopped at Pat Struck's farm stand in Amagansett to get fresh corn. My favorite meal. When we arrived back at the house, the phone rang.

My mother still in her white tennis clothes and sweaty from tennis picked up the phone. "Hello." I was standing nearby on the screened in porch listening with interest.

My Uncle Harold on the other end said, "You now are the proud parent of one son, born today in our hospital."

Mother was ecstatic! As soon as she hung up with Uncle Harold, she called dad at work in Washington. "We have a son!" He was as pleased as she was. They had been waiting with anticipation for this moment ever since a young interpreter from the United Nations just downtown from my uncles' Park East Hospital had come to the hospital looking for a way to have the child she had conceived with a Indonesian diplomat and not have to keep this telltale sign of her indiscretion.

The next day, we didn't pack a picnic lunch and go to Gardiner's Bay as usual. Instead, we drove into New York City to pick up my new brother. Mom dropped Judy off with mother's sister, Sylvia and went to their brothers' hospital to pick up the baby. Little did we know how this new addition to our family was going to change our lives! It was that night that my father went out for a drink with his best friend, Ben, and went to work the next day to see the note saying, "Resign or be investigated." As a result both me and my mother always saw those two events as inextricably interlinked.

Rick's arrival didn't immediately change our behavior. Mother still brought me to the beach to hang out with her friends under an umbrella while I played with the other children in the calm waters of the bay. Now she had a baby to protect from the sun, but I still needed to be entertained. The mothers brought along sandwiches and soft drinks for the children and thermoses filled with alcoholic drinks for themselves. The children were all good swimmers as we had always played in these shallow waters. I loved the gentle waves and spent hours floating on an inflatable raft or splashing in the shallows with the other children. We built sand castles and dug trenches to move the water as we designed. Mom chatted with the other mothers and watched over her new baby.

However, her call to my father the day she brought Rick home triggered the series of events which eventually led to my father losing his job and our permanent move to Amagansett.

We moved because my father bought the Elm Tree Inn, which opened in April of 1954. That first summer we spent in Amagansett instead of Jack Conklin's we lived on Cross Highway in a "summer house" across from a fish shop. The house was set back in the woods and like so many other houses in that area, shingled with sea salt weathered wood, built to withstand all kinds of storms. It proved its resilience that summer because we had the worst hurricane I ever experienced. Uncle Joe's house on the bay side was completely inundated, drowning all his furniture. The rental house was untouched. Our family, however, was touched by the changes of leaving Chevy Chase.

I didn't realize that this was a semi-permanent move until I started the third grade in the elementary school that fall. The first day of school, I walked into the classroom with the other thirteen children who had been together since they started school. Where should I sit? Who would talk to me? Thirteen faces turned toward me with curiosity and immediately judged me as an outsider. The teacher told me to sit at the back of the room and the children turned to face her. She did nothing to ease my entrance. Staying there for only part of the school year, leaving and then returning toward the end of the year solidified my "outsider" status.

≈≈

When we moved to Amagansett, in the spring of 1955, we first stayed in an apartment over the Inn. I came from school to the motel and found my mother working to get the place ready for customers.

"I don't know about your father," she told me, angrily. She was standing in one of the cottages behind the Elm Tree Inn with a paint brush in her hand, trying to get it ready for guests. "He can't even paint an interior wall! I don't want to be doing all this labor. What's wrong with him?"

I hated hearing her say these things. I didn't know what to do. I stood in the doorway and shifted from foot to foot. "Do you need me to help out, mom?"

"Yes," she said. "Please go up to the main building and let dad know that we need more of this paint. I'll be up there soon to get dinner started." The only place for us to cook was the commercial kitchen in the main building.

Even then, at almost nine years old, I knew my father wasn't doing what he loved, researching the conditions of agricultural workers and publishing his ideas for a better way of supporting migratory labor. Now he was expected to run a bar, restaurant, and motel. He had no maintenance skills, no interest in managing people or even in making money. Making decisions about how much liquor to buy or repairing a leaky toilet were not his strengths.

Later that evening after eating in the commercial kitchen for the Inn, mom, Rick and I retired to the small, crowded apartment above the Inn where we were staying while my parents sought a more permanent home. Dad was downstairs in the bar with Morley serving the few local Bonikers who were slowly getting used to the fact that the business was open. Later, when the "season" began, there would be music by the Atkinson band.

The local newspaper along with advertisements for the business, carried a history of the building. It said, the main building was originally "built on the north side of Amagansett's Main Street by Nathaniel and Betsey Baker Hand who moved into the house the day their fifth and last child, Marcus Bolivar Hand, was born—August 19, 1825. It was a family home when the land around was all farm land. It became a tavern in 1933 and then cottages were built behind it." It was an early version of a motel which was yet to come. "It was bought in December, 1953 by Sam and Terry Liss, who have made many improvements on the original tavern. The old farmhouse now contains a cocktail room, and restaurant facilities; the farmland and cow pasture at the rear now have twenty-four guest cottages. During the summer there is dancing and entertainments and an outdoor sitting terrace has been added in front, this year. Dante Radici of Washington, DC and Robert Yampolsky of New York City have decorated the inn and cottages."

One particular evening before the redecoration, we were upstairs in the apartment we stayed in before moving to permanent housing. The walls were a dull gray and there was a brown rug on the floor in the living room. There were two bedrooms with an assortment of miscellaneous furniture. It was late and I heard my father come up the stairs from working in the bar, not with his usual firm stride. My mother greeted him, tired and stressed from living in these cramped quarters and working to get the place ready for summer visitors.

"This will not do," she said. "I cannot live like this!"

Dad's shoulders slumped. His baggy sweater hung on his lean body. His breath smelled of the alcohol he had drunk along with the customers. Sitting down heavily in one of the ugly upholstered chairs, he sank into himself.

Mother stood over him, still outraged. She is ready for bed, but first she is ready to let him know how disappointed and frustrated she is. "How can you expect me to live like this? This place is too small and dirty. I am tired of doing all the work to get the cottages ready for renters."

"I'm doing the best I can. I'm still trying to find more help. There isn't a lot of money for staff and I have a lot to learn about running a bar." Still sitting on the chair, he slumps down further as he mumbles, "What are you doing to make this work? It's your fault anyhow that I lost my job. Now we are stuck in this situation, which isn't any more comfortable for me than for you."

"I expect you to provide for the family." Mother straightens even in her nightgown. "It's your good luck that I inherited enough money from my father to buy this place. Now it's up to you to make this work financially."

Dad responded, "All I have ever wanted was to be able to provide for my family. I just never imagined I'd have to run a bar and restaurant. You were so proud of being investigated by the Dies Committee. Now where has that left us?"

They were off to a litany of resentments. I was scared. I wasn't happy about the move either. What would happen to us in this new place? I had never heard my parents argue before, but in this cramped space there was no privacy for them or for me. All I could do was hide under the covers and pretend I wasn't hearing these things I didn't want to know.

Then mother started in on us children. It seemed that she resented having adopted Rick and all the subsequent hurts the family had endured. I could hear her loud voice even as I tried not to.

"Kathy is the only child of my body I will ever have. She is mine. Don't try to interfere in my relationship with her." From my present perspective, I believe that mother was trying to punish my father for losing his job by interrupting the close relationship he had with me. She succeeded.

From there on, my father, for whom I had been his adored, fair-haired delightful Chip (off the old block), disappeared from my emotional world.

He still showed up at the dinner table, for which he was often late. But our nights where he rubbed my back to help me go to sleep were gone. He was no longer helping me learn new skills, either, like riding a bike. I was hurt, feeling abandoned by my supporter and retreated into a private world of my own.

Our family became the women against the men. It was exemplified by our tennis games where we teamed that way. Although my father was the best tennis player of us all and Rick was much more of an athlete than I, my mother and I always won. Dad refused to hit the ball anywhere except the back court and Rick lost his temper and hit the ball over the fence. In the end, the women scored higher.

The Elm Tree Inn: a bucolic refuge where cosmopolitan New Yorkers could retreat from the pressures of the city. Amagansett: a hamlet where fishermen and farmers represented America's view of the hardworking, honest, salt of the earth. Oil and water don't mix. The Elm Tree Inn was a safe haven for people who were outcast by society, like my mother and father who lost their roles due to the toxic environment created by anti-communism in Washington, DC. Eastern Long Island, as far from the center of political activism as my parents could go. It also turned out to be a safe haven for many of the gay men who worked on the Broadway stage and in television and movies during those dark times in America.

Driving east on the Montauk Highway from New York City, this little hamlet with a post office and a couple of storefronts wouldn't attract the negative attention my parents were escaping. It seemed they could build a life where the past wouldn't haunt them. The large white building with green trim was shaded by the mature elm trees in the front. The Elm Tree Inn was a former farm house now with twenty four cottages in the back to provide short term housing for tourists. Although my father at first considered it because he thought he would run a summer camp for children of his progressive friends, he quickly accepted this opportunity to own a business that couldn't be taken away from him like his job had been. However, the family story was that when he first got his liquor license there was a letter to the editor in the *East Hampton Star* that asked how a license could be issued to a "known Communist." When I researched the *Star* for that year, I could find nothing related to the business but the ads. Nonetheless, the children called me names and one of them was "communist." Whose truth?

As reported in the *East Hampton Star,* August 1, 1957, "The July 29, 1957 issue of *Sports Illustrated* contains an article by Horace Sutton entitled *The Fabulous Hamptons*, which is quoted as describing Amagansett as 'a sort of hive for bohemians who cluster, come the weekend, in a Bauhaus called the Elm Tree Inn...but, according to this article, they live quietly and paint serious avant-garde impressionist (sic) in their homes in Springs...[but they]'have made no Bacchic beach of the Hamptons.'" In the August 7, 1958 edition of the *East Hampton Star* there is a discussion of a *Harper's Bazaar* August 1958 article on East Hampton which mentions the Elm Tree Inn as "a gay late-night spot."

There was never any intention of making the Elm Tree Inn a gay bar and restaurant. It just happened that way. Those were the people who came to patronize the place and my parents' progressive values were such that being inclusive came naturally to them. It never occurred to them that this would be the downfall of the business.

My parents were very proud that in the early years they had famous people playing music in the evenings on the weekend. In the *East Hampton Star* I found ads for the Eliot Atkinson band with Larry Rivers on sax, Wes Rowland on bass, Jim Reutershan on clarinet and Howard Kanowitz on trombone. They felt as if this was something to draw people in and represented the same kind of "attraction" as the theater posters on the wall which advertised only plays which included people who were regulars at the Inn.

The Purple Room which was used for private parties was where the theater posters hung. It was closed off annually in order to hold my birthday party. Celebrating my birthday on July 4 might seem anomalous given the negative experience my parents had had with the government but they continued to see themselves as patriotic; subscribing to the values the government claimed, not what it did. Beside, it was my birthday and we had a big party, mostly for my parents' friends. We stood on the back deck of the Inn and watched my dad light the fireworks on the lawn below. Everyone oohed and ahed at the bursting lights and the few children ran around with sparklers. There were always more adults than children at those parties.

❧ॐ

Soon after the Inn opened we moved into the Gansett Green. We ran a motel and we lived in the front house of a competing motel just down the street. There was a big hedge between the front yard and the street, screening us from passers-by. It didn't screen us from the judging eyes driving down the street. Behind the house and attached there was an apartment for the manager of the motel but we had little contact. We weren't supposed to notice the motel behind us.

There was a lot we were not noticing during those years. We pretended that there was no prejudice against our family. We didn't notice that the majority of the clientele at the business were people who would be prosecuted for their sexual orientation if they were found out. My brother got an article written in a current local paper, *The Independent* in East Hampton in 2016 that was headlined, "The Hamptons First Gay Bar." It was our Elm Tree Inn. In a sidebar headlined "You Can Come Home Again" Rick talks about how happy he is to be living out there now year round again.

I, however, felt differently. It took me till recently to be able to visit back there even though it is now "the Hamptons" and one of the most desirable places to vacation at the beach, especially if you live in New York City.

Reading these articles, I find myself reliving my years in Amagansett. I see myself being miserable, hiding out eating chocolate. I have a pink plastic box with a black poodle embossed on top locked under my bed which held the fifty cent Hershey bars I love to suck on while reading a book. My chocolate addiction creates my overweight. This leads to the daily litany of, "Kathy stop eating; Ricky eat more," which is heard often at the dinner table. We each have our place. I sit with my back to the kitchen door, my father on my left and my mother on my right, Ricky across the table facing the kitchen. When we come to the table, there is a small bowl on the larger dinner plate. In the bowl is an appetizer; soup or fruit. The main course is served by Ginny on a silver tray with three parts; the meat in the center and a vegetable on one side and starch on the other. At the end of the meal there are individual servings of dessert brought in by Ginny.

One evening after dinner I am getting ready for my first school dance. I put on my favorite full skirt. I come downstairs and twirl around feeling the skirt billow out around me. I feel pretty.

My mother looks at me and says, "You can't wear that. You look too fat." I am crushed. I want to cry, but I remember that I had been told that no one wants to see someone's tears.

My father in his detached way says, "I don't understand why you women can't maintain the weight you want. I have always weighed 165 pounds."

Again, I am seen as an extension of my mother as my father distances himself from us. I go back upstairs saving my tears for the privacy of my room and put on an A-line skirt with no pleats or ruffles.

Then mother is willing to take me to the dance where I sit on the sidelines waiting for someone to ask me to dance. A wallflower in a skirt that doesn't make me look "too fat."

Living in the Gansett Green, I adjust to the new house and neighborhood. The front door of this house opens into a vestibule where we hang coats on hangers on the right. Above the bar is a shelf where my mother puts her purse (making it easy for me to steal change to buy chocolate). Entering the living room, there is an arrangement of chairs and a couch in a small square. To the right, a staircase leads to the upstairs. It is the kind of T shaped staircase that comes down most of the way and then turns both right and left at a landing with a few more stairs either into the living room or the kitchen. This allows us children to run round and round the downstairs as long as we are willing to climb up the small hill of stairs and down the other side. Running around and around is one of the few activities my brother and I share.

There are four bedrooms upstairs: one for my parents, one for me, one for my brother and one for Ginny. I no longer go to my father when I can't sleep at night looking for him to rub my back so I don't know how the beds were placed in their room. Ginny's room next door has the television. Her bed is across the room from the table that holds the television. Ricky and I sit on her bed and watch the *Lone Ranger* or *Howdy Doody* as we had in my father's attic study in Chevy Chase.

My room is under the eaves with a gabled window looking out toward the street. I have a twin bed under each side of the window where the roof slopes. I am sitting on the floor between the beds surrounded by plastic horses which are disproportionately large compared to the farm buildings and fences they are sharing the rug with. I move them around imagining they are real and I can one day get close to this powerful animal which will fly me down the road atop its muscular back.

I am twelve years old and tired of being picked on for being fat, being shunned at dances because I don't fit the stereotype of beauty. I am sad and lonely and scared that my life will continue forever to be as bleak as it seems on this overcast day.

I'm bored with these stupid plastic horses. I have no book to read and can't go to the library until mom gets home to take me. The library is in East Hampton, three miles away and once having tried riding my bike on the roads without sidewalks, I won't do that again. Even if my dad has turned into a zombie and my mother has sunk into her resentment, I still have my bicycle that dad taught me to ride and I can go to the ocean mom has led me to love.

I hop on the bike and ride along the sidewalk thinking, "Thirty years from now I will still remember every crack; I have ridden this way so often." It is the route to school and past that to Pat Struck's vegetable stand and then the Elm Tree Inn. At that point I have to cross the Montauk Highway, but on a winter's day that four lane road is pretty much empty. Peddling down Atlantic Avenue I pass Norma's house. She is the prettiest girl in my class. Blue eyes and blond hair in a page boy cut; her well proportioned figure brings the male attention I crave. There are also some of the summer homes of famous people like Doc Simon, friends through the Inn.

At the top of the hill where Atlantic crosses Bluff Road, I pause wondering if I should ride down knowing I will have to ride (probably walk) back up later. My pudgy body only gets regular exercise in my mind and visualization doesn't build muscle mass. I decide the benefits outweigh the strain and descend the short distance remaining in a fast coast to the white sandy beach.

The reward is the empty vista retreating across to Europe; the sound of the grey sea lapping its steady rhythm against the shore. I see the coast guard house that is pictured in the pen and ink drawing by Tommy Morrow who rented a house across the street from it one summer. His life partner, AT and he met in college and stayed a happily unmarried couple together for a lifetime, even having a joint business. Tommy gave me that picture as a wedding present for my first marriage and I gave it to the Historical Society when I moved into my last house.

I walk along the beach and dream that someday I will come here with some man who looks as good as Tommy or their friend Farley Granger, but likes women. Not just women, but ME. When all those mean children who teased me in school see us together, they will regret the names they called me. They will see that my brilliance has brought me beauty. I didn't know the phrase then, but I was seeking arm candy. I would be the brains and he would be the beauty. Mother might console me about not being beautiful by telling me that brains would outlast beauty, but I still wanted to be beautiful and believed I could not be.

The day dream plays out as I lie in the cool sand. Roiling ocean waves pushed by the wind stir up white foam caps racing one another to the shore; but further out, deep down the fish swim in still water, undisturbed by the surface turbulence. This is the opposite of my experience. I appear calm on the surface, not sharing with anyone how much tumult, pain, and longing I feel deep in my soul.

Eventually, I think it must be time for dinner soon. I'll never miss a meal. What has Ginny prepared for tonight? That, too, can appease my anxious thoughts. Food is always a safe "go to" place for my mind to explore. It will be a slower ride home, starting uphill and already tired from the exertion so far.

Urging the bike along, I remember the day my father taught me to ride. I am sad thinking how unavailable he is now. Will he be home in time for dinner or again make excuses (that infuriate mom) about the obligations at the Inn that keep him away? Did he ride his bike to work today? Maybe I'll see him and he will join me as I ride back home past the Inn.

Besides playing with the horses and riding my bike, I spend my time alone reading books and eating chocolate. I hide the large Hershey's bars under the bed. My room smells strongly of chocolate. Each piece when broken off is about the size of a thumb. I suck on this while I lie in bed for hours reading a book. This chocolate addiction follows me throughout my life. My need to read while I eat and eat while I read, also persists.

My mother and I are major patrons of the East Hampton library. At one point we figured we were about ten percent of the circulation of that small library. Riding in the car to the library in East Hampton one day, I think how much I enjoyed reading and learning. I say to my mother, "It's wonderful that I am going to know everything you know and then I will learn more."

Not looking at me she replies, "You will never grow past me."

I am shocked into silence. She did her best to reinforce that throughout her life, always showing me a better way to do anything.

The one person I feel I can depend on to accept me unconditionally is Ginny. She never speaks much. I can't remember a thing she said. But from the time Ricky was born till I was fourteen, she lived with us. Her warm mahogany skin and liquid brown eyes are the first thing I see in the morning as she wakes me up to get dressed and come to the breakfast she made. She is there at lunch time when we walk home from school for a sandwich and glass of milk. She is there for me at the end of the day when school is over. Ginny makes the bed under which I hide my stolen chocolate and she empties the trash where I hide the wrappers. Nothing is ever said.

Ginny has a daughter, Chris, who lives with Ginny's mother in Culpeper, VA. I don't know if she saw her daughter as much as once a year. I guess she chose to move with us from Chevy Chase (only an hour away from Culpepper) to Long Island—a very long way from Chris. I know black women my age now who feel enormous resentment toward white women (like me) who had the attention and care of their black mothers. I think I felt bad even then that Ginny never saw Chris and had to take care of me, instead of being in her daughter's life. I can only guess at how it must have felt to Ginny.

There must be some benefits Ginny sees to working for us, but I don't know what they might be. In Amagansett she has a bedroom but Ricky and I invade it often to watch television. Mom would not have the television in the living room. She never eats with us. She eats at the kitchen table where Ricky and I have breakfast in the morning.

Mother gives Ginny her hand-me-down clothes. Does Ginny ever wear any of those clothes? I only remember her in the grey dress and white apron, just like the movie *The Help*. Ginny never says anything to indicate she is unhappy, but Amagansett has to be at least as hard on her as it is on me. She is the only black person for miles around. She has no car and nowhere to go. I at least have a bicycle and can bike to the beach.

I think there may be a period where Ginny dated a man from East Hampton who picked her up in a car. I don't know how she could have met him since she never went anywhere. Mom does all the shopping and marketing. Ginny doesn't have a car and probably not a driver's license.

One day I come home crying. I stop in the candy store across the street from the elementary school to buy some candy on my way home. I bend over to pick up a coin on the floor. I am shocked by the electric charge that the owner set up for children like me to be hurt. The owner laughs and I run out of the store and home to Ginny.

I have so many questions about her life. Was she happy? Did she read? Was she offended by the way she was treated? After crying away my guilt for being in this situation, I believe that my feelings about Ginny set up the commitment I have now to the eliminating of racism. My earliest memory of race was getting on a bus in Florida over Christmas vacation in 1953 with Ginny and hearing the driver tell her she had to go to the back. I thought, "Where am I to sit?"

I tried to see her when I was an adult. After she left us, she went to work in Washington DC for a government agency. At retirement, she had a stroke and although she agreed to see me when I was passing through DC, she reneged at the last minute. I spoke to her daughter once, trying to find her, which was how I learned of her stroke. After that I no longer got the annual birthday card, signed Jenny. All that time I thought of her as Ginny, she was really Jenny. Whose truth? ❧

Home is difficult, but school isn't easy. The school is just a couple of blocks away and across the highway. I walk home for lunch and to and from school by myself. Every day begins with everyone in the auditorium. First we stand and say the Pledge of Allegiance. Then we say the Lord's Prayer. I never even knew it was a Christian prayer until I was an adult and asked a rabbi to say it at a meeting and she told me it wasn't something Jews did.

In the fourth grade, Miss Francis is the teacher. She is rather strict and often gave negative feedback, but she doesn't give a lot of attention to what is happening on the playground. Every day we have time outside for recess. Most children love recess. I hate it. The class walks out onto the playground single file and I see the swing set with three swings, a slide and monkey bars/jungle gym. The sky is grey, not individual clouds, just generally overcast. I wish it would rain, but it probably won't. Leaving the building, I look around. Where is a safe place for me to spend these twenty minutes outside? It isn't like Chevy Chase where I could run through the woods. It is all open ground. There is a baseball field where the boys play after school, but with only 6 of them in the class, there aren't enough for two teams so they will be with the girls for this period. After school when there are different age groups, they can have a game.

I, too, like it after school when everyone has gone home and I can play on the swings. I love the feeling of freedom that comes with pushing myself higher and higher. But when the class is there too many other children want to swing and I don't want to compete for a swing. The slide can be fun when it is warm and everyone takes turns. Today is warm enough and we won't need to have mittens on to protect our hands as they hold the cold metal of winter. I decide on the jungle gym.

I like to climb up high and feel separate from those below. I can still hear them, but I can scramble across the bars pretty fast and am rarely bothered when I am up there. I can climb today because I am wearing pants. I don't want boys looking up my skirt. It's cool enough that I am wearing a blue sweater buttoned up to my chin along with my jeans and tennis shoes. I can see across the playing fields to where the baseball diamond is at the furthest end away from Main Street. The trees in the distance are starting to change from green to red and yellow. I know that cold weather will be coming soon. The air is crisp and smells of salt from the ocean just a few blocks away crashing against the white sand beach. I wish I could be there peacefully watching it. It will be many months before I can swim there again.

I see Susie walking toward the jungle gym and think she might join me. But her twin brother, Peter, doesn't like me. He sees her coming toward me and walks over saying "What are you doing up there, Fatso? Don't you know that these bars aren't strong enough for someone so fat?"

I wish Susie would stand up for me and tell him to leave me alone, but she runs off to play with Karen. Now I feel trapped up here. If I come down, he may hurt me with more than words. They say, "Sticks and stones will break your bones but words will never hurt you." But his words do hurt me. Said over and over for years, they break my heart. I wonder what I can say or do that will make him leave me alone. All I want is to escape and be alone, back in my room in the Gansett Green with my plastic horses or reading a book. Maybe Ms. Francis will come over and tell us it's time to go back inside. At least in the classroom I can give the right answers. I am eager for recess to be over. At lunch I can walk the long block home to have my sandwich with Ginny and Ricky, where I feel safe. Will I tell them what Peter said? Probably not.

In the fifth grade, Miss Ward is my teacher. She is my favorite. I think she likes me, too. She held back Danny and Jonathan because they weren't meeting the standards she set for being in the sixth grade. Now there are sixteen of us in the grade, eight boys and eight girls, including me.

Miss Ward gives me a bag of Hershey Kisses for learning the state capitals first. Even though mother had practiced with me for hours, I don't remember all the names of the states. I cheat. When I can't remember which states I am missing, I go to the bathroom and look up the list of states I wrote on a piece of paper in my pocket. Given the state names I can say every capital. I bring the bag of candy home and mother takes it from me and won't let me eat it because she says I am too fat. Instead, I go in her purse and steal money to buy chocolate for myself.

On Valentine's Day I am excited to give Miss Ward my valentine. We all put our valentines for each other into a cardboard box which is covered with pretty paper and big red hearts. I don't know if anyone in the class will give me a valentine, but I feel certain that Miss Ward will like the one I made for her.

But that day, she doesn't show up for school. We all wonder where she is. I am disappointed. At lunch time, someone from the school goes to her house to look for her. We learn later that she was found in the garage in her car with the motor turned on and the doors closed. I also learn later that she and Ms. Francis were partners who had come from a private girls' preparatory school to live in Amagansett where their relationship would cause less concern. Ms. Francis goes on to marry a man.

Handing out valentines that day was cheerless. Ms. Ward's were left in the box.

Mr. Snyder is the principal. He dresses in a suit and tie while most teachers are women in dresses. No one else in town wears suits. Because the school has only one hundred students in first through eighth grades, he is a teacher as well and teaches social studies to the sixth through eighth graders.

Mr. Snyder is the disciplinarian the day I quit the band. I don't just quit, I lead a rebellion. As an all "A" student, I am not willing to get an "F" in music, but I also am unwilling to spend the hour a day subjecting myself and others to the dreadful squawks and squeaks of the clarinet I somehow have ended up playing. Nor am I willing to lie about how many hours I spent practicing.

The day our report cards came out with the "F" I inevitably have earned, I talk the entire clarinet section of five students into turning in our instruments and refusing to go on. The music room is in the basement of the school and I am the one who goes down there to leave the note saying "we quit."

One by one my classmates who had followed me into this rebellion are called to the principal's office. One by one they return silent and sullen. I go on with my work.

Eventually I am called out. I walk down the stairs, alone, with trepidation. I enter the office, alone with the principal. He asks, "Did you write this note?"

Nod.

"Are you willing to take it back and apologize and rejoin the band?"

Shake of the head.

"All the others have rejoined the band."

Shrug.

"I'll call your parents."

Shrug.

He calls my mother. She tells him, "Kathy can do whatever she wants with regard to playing the clarinet." And I never touch the instrument again.

Nonetheless, I have to return to my classroom. Mr. Oliva takes one look at me and suggests I retire to the restroom. There I am free to let loose the tears of fear and frustration I have been holding back, afraid they would tip out of my eyes if I opened my mouth. Eventually, I return to the classroom, red eyed and deflated but not conquered. I retake my chair and go on with my work. No one ever mentions it again.

What did Mr. Snyder think? Did he accept my mother's judgment because my father was on the school board? Was he glad to no longer have to deal with me? Did he feel victorious because the other children had given in and rejoined the band? I will never know. I know that I saw this as my earliest victory over oppression, as my first successful rebellion. Although no one stood with me in the end, I had organized a group of people who followed my lead and I had not given in myself.

Mr. Oliva also taught the 6th through 8th graders. He taught math and health. He helped me to get through that day with my pride intact. Was I being revengeful? Or was it my first try at organizing? I know I felt proud of what I had done, even though I was scared when I did it. It was only one of many occasions when I was able to carry through on something even though I was in terror.

Thank God for Mr. Oliva. He recognized me and challenged me so that I was doing high school algebra in his class when I was in the 7th grade. Math class was the one class where I felt recognized for my intelligence and challenged to stretch myself to really learn something. Mr. Oliva was the one teacher who asked more of me than came easily. This was where I felt best. Learning new information and skills has always been a great pleasure for me.

He also taught health. The closest we ever came to writing a paper was to synthesize an article from the World Book encyclopedia in Mr. Oliva's health class. Most students just copied out the words in the encyclopedia. I at least paraphrased and wrote it myself. We certainly didn't learn research skills. Later, when we moved to New York City, this deficit in research and writing turned into a real challenge for me even when my math skills proved very helpful.

Not everything was about school. When it got too cold to ride my bike sometimes we could go ice skating. At least once a year the pond in East Hampton iced over. Mom took Susie, Karen, Martha and me to go ice skating. It was a cold brisk day and we each had on a warm jacket, mittens, long pants and several layers of socks under our ice skates. Martha's skates were hand me downs from her older sister, Joyce, but Susie, Karen and I had gotten new skates for Christmas. Martha was a Boniker, a local whose family had lived there for generations and made their living fishing. Karen's dad worked for the Coast Guard and she had moved there about the same time we had. I never really understood how Susie and her twin brother, Peter, had ended up there or how her father made a living.

First, we had to establish whether the ice was hard enough to hold everyone. The pond was small and shallow so it didn't take that long for it to freeze over, but it would be terrible if we broke through and got our feet frozen. A couple of days of below freezing weather and it would hold us for skating. There were other children on the pond, but I didn't know them. It felt like a time I could enjoy my friends without being teased. Beside, my mother was there and no one dared to make fun of me in front of her. As far as I know, she was unaware of how I got bullied.

We skated round and round that small space for an hour or so, laughing and throwing snow balls at each other. None of us could do much more than skate forward and backward, but we could stay upright and keep moving. Eventually, it go so cold, we had to go home. Mother served us all hot chocolate at our house and then Karen's mother came and picked her up. We brought Martha home to her shack with the drive paved in broken sea shells. Susie spent the night as she often did.

Early in my time in Amagansett, I remember visiting at Elena's house. She lived across the street. We hid in the attic to read the insert in a box of sanitary napkins. We didn't really understand the insert's message of what we would soon experience as our menses came on. I certainly didn't relate what we shared in Elena's attic room with what I experienced later when suddenly there was blood flowing between my legs.

Elena's dad was an artist. One day he asked, "Would you come to my house and let me draw you? I really like the way your pony tail rests on the back of your neck." I spent some time posing for him as he drew the shape of my head and the way the pony tail hung down my back caught up in a rubber band at the top and curling along my back down to my shoulder blades. But Elena's brother, Tony, disliked me. He had a horse, which I greatly envied, that was kept pastured behind the house. He teased me and made fun of me, calling me "fatso Lisso" and other mean names. So even though the father approved of my appearance, the brother used it as a weapon to hurt my feelings.

One day, I noticed that there was a party happening at Elena's house. Many people, some our classmates, were gathering there and seemed to be having a good time. Why wasn't I invited? I was very hurt and never made any effort to connect with her again.

✒✒

In the spring mom went to the Virgin Islands. One of those days, Ricky and I were playing in the living room and made a fort out of blankets draped over chairs. Dad came home for dinner.

He said, "Dinner's ready. Come to the table."

I said, "No, I want to go out for Chinese food."

"If you don't want to eat, go to your room."

I refused. I sat in the big chair and wouldn't move. He pulled on my arms, but could not dislodge me. We went to East Hampton to the Chinese restaurant for dinner.

Something broke in me then. I knew for sure he could not take care of me, protect me. I was on my own with no expectation of any help from my dad.

Often dad was home at dinnertime. Ginny had everything ready. Then dad remembered something he had left undone at the Elm Tree Inn and went pedaling off on his bicycle. He would stay gone until the food was cold and Mom was hot. At the dinner table, dad distracted me by pinching my knee, which I hated, and then stole my dessert which I hated even more. Was he trying to connect by teasing me since we had lost the tender closeness of earlier years?

My relationship with mom was very different. We played cards, rehearsed the times tables, worked together to address and send out Christmas mailings to the people who rented the cabins, her "boys." I was shocked when I read a letter she sent me in college where she referred to them as "fags."

We spent hours together at the table by the front window. I learned to play Russian bank which is a rather complicated card game with two decks of cards. She was reluctant to play Scrabble, her favorite game with her friends, with me because I didn't play well enough to challenge her. When we did play, she played my hand for me because I was too slow for her.

I tried to get attention from my mother's friends by showing off. When guests arrived, I said, "Can I show you what I can do?" Then I balanced on my bongo board (a flat board resting on a roller) spinning the hula hoop around my hips and reciting a poem in French all at the same time. When the performance was done, mother said, "Go upstairs and play now." Sometimes I sat at the top of the stairs and eavesdropped. Oh, this is how women are friends with each other! I learned that women's friendships were often based on complaining about their men.

One day I was walking down the street and a large Rolls Royce pulled over. It was Robert Q. Lewis, a friend through the Elm Tree Inn. The children who saw us came running over and said, "Get me his autograph." Perhaps they were impressed by his Rolls Royce. I asked him if he would sign his name for them and he did. When he drove off, they looked at his name and said, "Robert Queer Lewis."

Did his gender identity make him less worthy? Whose truth?

Although many of the people who patronized the Inn were famous, I found that if I dropped their names my peers didn't like me better for it. There are a few people I remember from our years in Amagansett beside Farley. Marilyn Monroe came out with Arthur Miller (who was a good friend of my uncle Joe as they worked in the Works Projects Administration where they used their playwriting skills together). I was also good summer friends with Ellen Shaw whose uncle was Irwin Shaw and whose father, David, wrote for television. Johnnie Arthur and his siblings, Timmie and Gretchen, whose father was Robert Alan Arthur, the movie script writer, also spent time with us on the beach. Bob's wife Ginnie was one of mother's best friends and Timmie and Ricky played together. Timmie being albino and Ricky being dark they made quite a picture. Eli and Annie Wallach were people my parents socialized with. Zero Mostel suffered from the blacklist. His family visited and he gave us courtesy tickets to all his shows in New York when he became employable again. I remember walking on the beach with his son, Josh, who later went into movies also.

The adults went skinny dipping in the ocean late at night after having barbeques on the beach. My mother was very progressive in her personal life as well as her political life and she continued to go skinny dipping with her women friends (always including Cora Zelinka, wife of Sid who wrote comedy for television) at 8 a.m. until she died at seventy-five. They called it, "mikva at 8." (The ritual Jewish cleansing bath for women is called a "mikva.") They had t-shirts printed up that said that. The local garbage men scheduled their arrival to pick up the beach trash receptacles to coincide with the morning swim.

I only got to go skinny dipping in the bay at night after we moved to New York City and became summer people ourselves. I loved the green phosphorescence sliding through my fingers as I moved my hand through the warm, soft water. Growing up by the ocean, being near water is very soothing to me. But I was glad when I no longer spent my winters in that narrow place.

One of the things I disliked the most about living in Amagansett as that there were only two possible directions to drive —east or west. To the east there was one more town before land's end, Montauk. The drive takes you across a narrow spit of land between the ocean and the bay. In hurricanes, that empty stretch of road is swallowed by the sea. In the 1950s, Montauk was a smelly fishing town with a couple of strange attempts at tourism, like the Montauk Manor. The only times we went there were to find lobsters from Gosman's dock, the simple seafood stand.

It is so strange to see how the area has changed now. I even met a black woman in Baltimore who said she had moved from Montauk. My first thought was, "There are no black people who live in Montauk." I didn't even think there were any people I would want to know there. But then look at Gosman's Dock today. It is now several buildings, gift shops with different merchandise, a huge restaurant with several styles of food on different floors. Lobster is still the core of it and you can still go to the tanks and pick out your own lobster, take it home alive to be thrown into the pot of boiling water. Back then, we ate it with a fresh ear of corn picked from Sandra's vegetable stand which was later owned by Zabars! Sandra is no longer running the vegetable stand, nor does the field she used to rent from my Uncle Harold grow corn. Like me, Amagansett has changed over the last sixty years. The changes in Amagansett are no more or less than those I have experienced over these years. But some of the feelings have continued to affect the choices I have made and behaviors I exhibit.

The main reason I disliked Amagansett was that we were outsiders and would always be. We were Jews where there were no Jews. My father's reputation as a Communist had followed him here. My brother was half Asian; we had black live-in help; the business catered mainly to gay men so the children taunted us by calling our father "faggot."

⤬

In 1959, an article in the *East Hampton Star* says four boys were served alcohol at the Elm Tree Inn. They went on to have an auto accident. One was a minor who was driving without a license. He was then charged with "concealing an accident." The other boys signed a complaint against Mo, the bartender, for serving them. Eventually, the charges were dropped, but at that point, we moved to New York City. How are these events connected? The family story was that we moved because we lost the liquor license because of soliciting, but the license wasn't lost until a year later in December of 1960.

The Elm Tree Tavern was first issued a liquor license on November 15, 1936 when Frank J. Eck, was the proprietor. During my parents' ownership Mo put a beer bottle in a certain location so the men would know there was an undercover cop in the place. One night he hadn't noticed the cop. The *East Hampton Star* August 4, 1960 said, "Three men were arrested early Monday morning in Amagansett by plainclothesmen of the County detective force on charges of soliciting males for immoral purposes. They were arrested in autos outside the Elm Tree Inn." This was a decade before the Stonewall riots (June 28, 1969), which started the change in attitudes toward gays.

In 1960, homosexuality was a crime. The bar never reopened. My father got his real estate broker's license and there was (according to a family story) another letter to the editor in the local paper asking how a license could be issued to a "known communist." I haven't been able to establish the truth of this despite researching the back issues of the *Star*. How could people still notice his political history and still care? How could he, as a socialist, choose to make money from real estate where there was no value added? I was confused and still am. Why did we move to New York City in 1959? Where is truth?

All I know is that my mother insisted we move to NYC where her siblings lived. She still wanted access to the beautiful beaches in summer and had a house built on an acre of the land belonging to the Inn. The house was a 24-foot by 24-foot Cape Cod cottage where we spent our summers from then on.

My first memory of the house was when it was under construction. There was a second floor loft where Ricky and I had our bedrooms and a shared bathroom. Before the stairs were built, there was a ladder from the downstairs to the upstairs. The tile floor was put in before the stairs and one day I climbed the ladder. As I stepped from the top rung to the floor of the loft, the ladder slipped out from under me and I fell to the lower floor. Now I can only climb a ladder if someone is holding it on the bottom.

In spite of the fact that it was in Amagansett, I came to love that house enough to use the basic outline for the two houses I eventually built. In 1959, I was very glad to leave Amagansett as a year round place to live. Those were five years of living in hell as far as I was concerned and the scars from the burns I experienced have stayed with me for a lifetime just like my fear of stepping off a ladder and my addictions to chocolate and reading, my feelings of being fat and unloveable. So many subtle decisions were made during those difficult years. It has taken me years to take apart these patterns layer by layer. I believe it shaped my fierce commitment that no one else around me should ever feel marginalized like I did.

During the years I lived in Amagansett, my only connection to Chevy Chase was spending the summers at Camp Lakeside, in Connecticut. During the fifties several summer camps were established for the children of progressives to get them out of the cities and into an environment which supported the values of their parents. Lakeside was one of them. The camp was run by the Alphers.

To save time, my mother and I flew over the Long Island Sound in a very small plane to deliver me to camp. Camp was an opportunity for me to be with other young people whose parents shared the views of my parents. Most of them lived in the DC area and had year round relationships with one another. So, even in this different environment, I felt different and disconnected. They had no idea what my school years were like, what it was like to be in a class with only 15 other children, to be teased and picked on all year long.

A few years ago we had a reunion of the campers. Jessie said to me, "You made yourself separate from everyone. You thought you were so different. You created that yourself." I don't think so.

Jessie was Ben's daughter, the man my father was seen walking with which started the whole blacklisting process. She grew up in an apartment community that was known for housing progressives. Ben owned a pottery business that wasn't affected by the blacklist. Although he was a "known communist" his family didn't experience the impact that McCarthy had on my family. Years later, Ben came to visit my parents. He had an argument with my parents that I overheard in which he supported the government in maintaining a list of everyone who belonged to the Communist Party. My parents were furious and I was devastated and confused.

I certainly had patterns of feeling left out. However, Jessie did not help. She didn't understand the situation of our family. She couldn't understand why when she was visiting in Amagansett and her aunt called our house, her aunt was told we didn't know any person named "Benjamin." Her family never experienced the persecution that mine did.

I have many good memories of camp. I was especially connected to Wylie, the waterfront counselor. His dark skin glistened in the sunlight as he stood on the floating pier in the middle of the lake chanting "stroke, recover, glide" as a way to teach us the breast stroke. He was strong and beautiful. Did I notice that he was black? I remember him as brave and solid. I was scared that I couldn't dive down deep enough or be strong enough to pull him from the bottom of the lake when he was testing us for the Red Cross Lifesaver test. It was fun to be one of the better swimmers when we went to the beach so I could play in the waves and show off for this handsome delightful man whose attention I sought. I loved learning water ballet, swimming in synchronicity with others to music. I used his words as a mantra to make my strokes even and in time with everyone else's.

At least once each summer we had a Jell-O fight. Going to the field and throwing Jell-O at each other until we were all multicolored, including our bathing suits and then running down the hill past the cabins to jump in the lake and wash off. We made lanyards from gymp, plastic string to weave together into a shape which held a key or some other object one didn't want to lose. Sitting under the tree with others, the counselor playing the guitar told me that I was tone deaf and I shouldn't sing. Even Rickety Tickety Tin, to which I knew all the words because I listened to Tom Leherer at home. We sang a lot of union songs and I remember them with great tenderness. I loved, "Union Maid" and always sing it to myself when I hear the traditional tune played at a contra dance. The thought that I can't sing was reinforced by the music teacher in school telling me to, "Just move my mouth" when we had a choral presentation for the community. One more deficiency.

As fun as it was, I never got over feeling isolated. I lost a lot during those years. I lost the self-confidence I had as a child, believing that everyone was there to be my close, warm and dependable ally. I became unsure of myself and began expecting people not to like me, not to want me to be part of their group.

The years in Amagansett both summer and winter have left me with deep scars. All the learned conflict resolution skills cannot overcome my angry reaction to having the feelings from those years triggered. Even though the knife has been withdrawn and the skin has healed over, there is still a weakness in my soul which responds when the ancient hurt place is touched upon. I yearn to feel that I belong and that people accept and welcome me. People often don't understand this as I appear to be whole on the surface, even powerful and domineering at times, certainly competent when I am teaching or leading a group. Nonetheless, with the right provocation, I can behave in ways that later I wish I hadn't.

"I believe that everything happens for a reason.
People change so that you can learn to let go,
things go wrong so that you appreciate them
when they're right, you believe lies so you
eventually learn to trust no one but yourself,
and sometimes good things fall apart
so better things can fall together."

- Marilyn Monroe

CHAPTER THREE

LIFE CHANGED DRAMATICALLY WHEN WE MOVED TO NEW York City. My father didn't come with us. That first winter he stayed in East Hampton, renting a room from the woman who had been the housekeeper for the cottages at the Inn. Mother was deciding whether or not to get a divorce and wanted time living without him to make her decision.

Unpacking our boxes as we moved into the apartment, mother turned to me and said, "Don't you think that your father could have helped more with this? Where is he when I need him? My father was always there for the family." Of course, she had made dad feel unwelcome, telling him that she needed some time alone to get clear about their relationship.

Her biggest resentment was that he was not providing financially for the family. She had to depend on the income from her inheritance. Her father had been an outstanding provider who had lost everything in the Depression and gained it all back and more before he died in 1950. Living in that small town with so little stimulation for five years had worn away at their relationship. She devoted a lot of time to managing my life. All this brought me closer to my mother and further from my father, whom I saw as weak and inconsequential.

Mother shared her disappointments with me. In a letter she wrote after my dad sent me $150 when I was in college, she wrote, "In sending you the $150, he is saying 'I want you to love me,' and I will give you gifts for it...Dad likes 'largesse.' Giving you $150 makes him feel like a big shot and a most generous person...Which is why

I want him to give me a weekly stipend—he now says he is going to give me $100 a week. He, however, gave me $500 two weeks ago, which is exactly what I don't want. He feels that he is giving me a present instead of money to support him and his family." Of course, selling real estate, his income was erratic, sometimes having a big commission and then going for long periods without any income.

Mother was 5'4" 165 pounds; short dark brown wavy hair, brown eyes, skin that darkened in the summer sun so that she could be mistaken for a person of color. Her voice, inherited from her parents, was so deep she was often taken for a man on the telephone. For the many years she smoked cigarettes, there were often holes in her clothes where they had been burned. Even after she gave up smoking there were stains on her blouse where the shelf of her large breasts caught the food that didn't make it into her mouth.

She, Ricky. and I were glad to move to New York City where we started spending all our holidays together with mother's extended family. At Thanksgiving we watched the Macy's parade from my uncle's apartment which overlooked Central Park West. Passover was at my aunt's on the Upper East Side. And Christmas everyone came to our house because we always had a tree and decorations. My mother's siblings were very important to her and the early death of her younger brother, Sidney, from cancer, was tragic. I don't remember Sidney and his wife, Yvonne, ever being at our Christmas dinner. That may have been because mother didn't like Yvonne and called her "the French whore." It was only during the time that Sidney was dying of cancer that I remember visiting at his apartment.

At Christmas there were a dozen people but we all fit around the cherry table in the dining room and the food was served buffet style from the side board mother had commissioned to match. I have the diagram of the original design. She bought it through her brothers' hospital probably to get a better price. I also have the bill of sale. It came with six matching chairs which for some reason she painted black. She must have rented or borrowed extra folding chairs for the other six people.

I enjoyed setting the table with the set of twelve place settings of monogrammed silver plate eating utensils which were kept stored in soft burgundy cloth in a drawer in the sideboard. All the similar utensils were kept together in one wrapper with slots for each item. I unwrapped the large forks, the small dessert forks, the teaspoons, the knives. I placed them in their appropriate location next to the plate: the proper order for the forks; the place for the various glasses. This was my favorite part of getting ready for company.

The plates sat on the sideboard waiting for the diners to pick one up and fill it with pot roast, kasha (a bulgur wheat commonly eaten in Russia), salad and a hot vegetable. It was always the same menu. I don't remember what we had for dessert, as that could vary depending on mother's mood. There was a Jewish bakery (named Babka) on the ground floor of the apartment building and she bought something there or at Zabar's (the world famous delicatessen) a couple of blocks further north on Broadway. After the first year we no longer had live in help, so mother did the cooking. We children cleared the table after and left the dishes on the kitchen table to be washed by hand, dried and put away in the glass fronted cabinets.

After eating, we would gather around the Christmas tree decorated with lights, tinsel and the bulbs my brother and I had painted. Ricky and I enjoyed getting out the paints and each making our own design on a bulb. I painted an abstract using colors I liked and words that pleased me. Ricky is an artist and painted intricate designs.

My favorite part of the Christmas gathering at mother's house was when mother said, "OK, it's time for charades." Everybody clustered in their groups: the older generation played against the younger generation. Each group came up with titles of books, plays, movies or songs for the other group to act out and guess.

One title was *Some Like it Hot*. Cousin Judy started with

winding one hand while pointing the other: movie! First she indicated how many words were in the title by raising four fingers. Then she indicated it was the fourth word by reiterating the four fingers. Next, she pulled on an earlobe, which meant that the words "sounded like" in this case "pot." She pointed to a pot, or rounded her hands to indicate a bowl. If they said, "bowl" she gestured to indicate they were on the right track, but encouraging them to give a synonym. Once we got "hot" there was wild guessing of titles with the word "hot" in them and pretty soon the title was identified.

A Streetcar Named Desire required demonstrating a multisyllabic word. Cousin Victor tapped his wrist with two fingers indicating the number of syllables in the word and that he was going to play it out one syllable at a time. The first syllable was indicated by the finger held up next. Pointing out the window and then showing a long stretch with a hand holding thumb and forefinger down helped the guessers to choose the first syllable as "street." Then he got down on all fours and said, "Vroom, vroom." Okay, that's a car. Aha! "Streetcar."

We younger ones thought *Brecht on Brecht* would be the hardest. Little did we know that it meant vomit in Yiddish. Uncle Harold got up and indicated "play" by using both hands to indicate a curtain. Then he pantomimed vomiting and it was all over in seconds!

Who were the guests at this event? My uncle Harold is the eldest and the patriarch. Harold and his son, Victor, also had the deep resonant voice. Harold settled his large body in the brown corduroy "man chair" in the furthest corner of the room and held forth. He told stupid scatological jokes and asked me questions about my love life that made me blush and stumble over my words. Victor's mother had died. I don't know if Harold ever married Rose who always accompanied him to these gatherings. She was in theater production and he supported her projects financially. She nagged him about his eating as he had gall bladder problems and probably was diabetic. Mother scowled when she heard Rose say, "Don't eat that," as she took some treat away from Harold.

Amy, Harold's second child with his second wife, is the closest to me in age, but we were not close growing up. She has always been into horses and most of the time had one stabled outside the city. I never saw her horses, but I was very jealous of her having one. It has always been a dream of mine. Now she lives on a farm near Albany. Her second husband, a stock broker, has died. Her daughters and stepchild have grown and gone away and when we visited her, a couple of years ago, she was rattling around in her overlarge country house, writing poetry and trying to decide what to do next with her life.

Her elder brother, Victor, was my mother's political heir. He became the leader of the upper west side Reform Democratic Committee and married Sarah, the leader of the Village Reform Democratic Committee. Victor is tall and solid like his dad and Sarah is a petite woman. However, they are equal in power in the world. Victor trained as a lawyer and practiced throughout his life. He never gave up his political involvement and one of his partners became mayor of New York, Ed Koch. They inherited the hosting of holiday parties for the family and had traditional Thanksgiving and Passover gatherings. Christmas disappeared when my mother was no longer available to host.

The other family that joined us was my Aunt Sylvia's. She was a psychotherapist and her husband, Sandy, was a lawyer. They had two daughters, Anne and Judy. My grandmother died when my mother was only seventeen and my mother went to live with Sylvia and Sandy. My mother had been the last child at home and had cared for her mother as she died of cancer. I found Sylvia aloof and not at all compassionate. As each person entered the apartment, we hugged, but her hugs were not comforting or affectionate. I couldn't imagine her helping anyone with their psychological problems.

My cousin, Anne, married an Israeli, but when her younger sister, Judy, married the head of the history department in her graduate program, Anne divorced and married the head of her art history department. Now both sisters are professors and for many years taught in the same universities as their husbands, not an easy thing to do.

Competition was a natural part of the family norms. My grandfather created a pattern of dividing his estate unequally. He gave his elder daughter, Sylvia, a twenty percent share and his younger daughter (my mother) half that much of the shared ownership of a building on Sixth Avenue in New York. Sylvia continued the pattern by giving Anne a fifteen percent share and she gave Judy the same five percent share that Ricky and I each got. This required all four of us to work out financial agreements (along with the other descendants of grandfather's partners). The fact that Anne held a portion equal to the collected portion of the other three of us made it necessary for me to mediate between the two sisters who do not talk with each other without rancor. My mother broke the pattern by her equal division of her estate between my brother and me. She was always the different one in the family, not ascribing to the norms of inequality.

My mother's brother was Sidney who met and married his second wife, Yvonne, in France. She was considerably younger than he and very pretty. Mother deeply resented her. I don't remember them at the Christmas party. I don't see them in any of the photographs. However, mother was very close to Sidney's eldest son, Tony, and saved letters from him which I found in her files when she died. His younger brother, Joel, moved to California and died young.

Tony was actually the eldest of the cousins. Since his father and uncle owned the hospitals they had inherited from our grandfather, Tony studied hospital administration in college expecting to be a hospital administrator. He eventually got a PhD in it. However, when Sidney died, whatever the disposition of his estate was, Tony was not in a position to run those hospitals and ended up teaching hospital administration.

Yvonne and Sidney had a daughter, Kiki, who was actually

the youngest cousin. My brother was next and I was after that. All the other cousins are older than I. I saw Kiki once not too many years ago at Victor's last Thanksgiving party. I would never have recognized her on the street as I never before had seen her as an adult. At that party, I also saw Yvonne and reconnected with her. She invited me to her house for dinner. She still has an apartment in the building where she lived with Sidney, but can't afford it alone and has a housemate. She looked at me and laughed with delight saying, "You look just like your father. That would disappoint your mother." Animosity lasts a long time!

Moving to New York City was a big improvement for me. The first year in New York, I was in junior high school. The school was in a neighborhood with 40% black, 40% Puerto Rican and 20% other children. Luckily for me, most of the "others" were Jewish. Because they had given me the exact same IQ test every six months for three years in Amagansett, I had scored 161 on it and the school in New York decided to put me in the 9SP class. The SP "special progress" program meant that students completed the three years of junior high school in two. This allowed them to segregate the students and keep most of the students of color in the regular progress classes. Since I had not been in eighth grade anywhere, I was put in the lowest of the SP classes, 9SP3, with the majority of SP students of color in SP, but still a majority of white Jewish kids. There was and is just as much racism in the north as in the south; it is just more subtle.

The expectations in this school were much more demanding than those in Amagansett. The most challenging assignment was in science class where we were to write a paper on where some natural resource came from. I wrote a paper based on geography when it was supposed to be about geology. My mother taught me how to do research as I had learned no skills in Amagansett. She also rewrote every paper I wrote until I was a senior in college. Luckily, the math skills that Mr. Oliva had taught me got me through the math classes and my reading skills were good enough to manage the English classes.

In English, we were taught to parse sentences and required to learn and recite a poem. I think the one I chose, *Lone Dog* by Irene Rutherford Mcleod, is indicative of how I saw myself.

I'm a lean dog, a keen dog, a wild dog and lone
I'm a rough dog, a tough dog, hunting on my own
I'm a bad dog, a mad dog, teasing silly sheep
I love to sit and bay the moon to keep fat souls from sleep
I'm not a lap dog licking dirty feet
A sleek dog, a meek dog, cringing for my meat
Not for me the fireside, the well filled plate,
But shut door, sharp stone, and cuff and kick, and hate
Not for me the other dogs running by my side
Some have run a short while but none of them would bide
O, mine is still the lone trail, the hard trail, the best
Wide wind and wild stars and hunger of the quest

Despite the isolation this poem expresses, I did feel as if I had a social life for the first time since I left Chevy Chase. I had a boyfriend, Peter, who had his bar mitzvah (where he kissed me for the first and last time) on the top of a building overlooking Central Park on 59th Street. We also played tennis together. This felt like a contradiction to the previous five years when I had felt that no boy would even look at me without thinking I was unattractive. I had two girlfriends, Alice and Hedy. Alice lived next door to the Park East Hospital owned by my uncles and her family kept Kosher. Hedy was an immigrant from Egypt, also Jewish.

One day I asked a classmate, Brenda, to come over after school. Her father was the minister of a Baptist Church on 79th St. When she left, mother remarked to someone "Isn't it wonderful that Kathy brought home a Negro and never even mentioned that she was Negro!" Overhearing this was very confusing to me. I wonder what Ginny thought when she heard it. Even though mother had black friends, particularly Oscar who had fought in the Lincoln Brigade in

Spain, she still had strong race consciousness.

When I started high school, dad moved back in with us in the New York City apartment and Ginny went back to Washington. Mom decided she was better off with him than alone with two children. I was busy being a teenager in high school and hardly noticed the changes, except now dad was making breakfast before I left for school instead of Ginny. In the morning he came and knocked on my door and told me it was time to get up and get ready for school.

When I entered the kitchen, I found dad sitting waiting for me at the kitchen table. I was still resentful of him for having "abandoned" me for those years in Amagansett. Conversation looked like this:

Dad, cheerful, "What do you want for breakfast?"

I still sleepy and just wishing he would leave me alone, mumbled, "I don't know. Why don't you give me some cereal?"

Dad eager to make contact, asked, "Okay, what kind?"

Still disgruntled, I replied, "*Rice Krispies.*"

Dad hoping to say the right thing, "Do you want a banana with that?"

"No."

Dad still trying to engage me. "What will you do today in school?"

"I don't know."

Dad tried another opening, I deflected, and so it went. He tried buying me gifts, like earrings I never wore. He tried talking to me about friends, but I felt he didn't know my friends. He tried to discipline me by setting times for me to get home at night. I never paid any attention to his attempts. All three years of high school we rehearsed this pattern.

High school in New York is divided between what we would now call "magnet" schools and "neighborhood" schools. None of the neighborhood schools were very good because the best students either went to private schools or the specialized magnet schools which required an exam to get in. I was encouraged to apply to Bronx High School of Science. There were 6 sections on the test and I didn't answer any of the questions on one section because it was all about "this is to that as something else is to something else." I didn't realize that these were meant to be algebraic equations and pretty much left it blank. Nonetheless, I was accepted to the school and my parents chose for me to ride the subway forty-five minutes each way each day to and from school.

Bronx High School of Science was one of the top ten high schools in the country. It had been upgraded in response to the Russian challenge that Sputnik posed. The school had a dome that was a planetarium. There was also one of the first computers. It took up a whole classroom. Several students in that school got 800 on both parts of the SATs. I was only in the top quarter of my graduating class with 717 on the English and 696 on the math. I struggled with calculus. We were expected to learn trigonometry on our own over the summer between junior and senior years in order to prepare for the calculus class. I passed the trig test, but struggled with the calculus.

One time I had an assignment by my social studies teacher to write a paper over spring break. I thought that was most unacceptable —breaks are supposed to be breaks and not times to do long assignments. I complained to Mom and she said I should ask dad. In the end, he wrote the paper and even footnoted his own work from the time he worked at the Department of Agriculture. The teacher was very impressed and never even doubted I had written it!

That same teacher wanted us to write about the differences

between economic systems. Mom again sent me to dad to get his views. He told me that all economic systems have the same goal: to increase the wealth of the nation. The difference is how they understand the nation to be wealthy. For capitalists, it is the total GNP regardless of how it is distributed. For socialists, it is that everyone has enough to live a decent life. I don't remember how he distinguished between socialists and communists although I think he would have said that Russia had not achieved communism even if they called themselves a "communist country." This has stayed with me all my life. Having parents who were both economists has shaped my commitment to overcoming the increasing inequality as time has gone on in America.

To graduate with honors from Bronx Science you had to have a certain number of service credits. I earned my service credits by being on "hall squad" and guarding the elevator so no one could use it without a pass. I shared this task with three boys who were a year behind me. One was Sande. He became my boyfriend. We spent a lot of time together, especially going to movies, lots of grade B French movies. He wanted to major in French literature, though he eventually became a professor of sociology. He was my first lover and it was a sweet and tender way to lose my virginity. We spent lots of time walking in parks and making out in any corner we could find. One day when we were necking on a park bench, someone came and took a photograph, an image of "sweet young lovers in NYC."

In the summer, and on weekends in spring and fall, my family went to the house in Amagansett. It was a three hour car ride. I never looked forward to it. I told my mother either I had to have a horse or a boyfriend. She let me bring Sande out there. We had many sweet nights quietly making love in my bed above my mother's bedroom with her being as oblivious as she had been to the chocolate under my bed when we lived at the Gansett Green. It wasn't until she found my journal from my first trip to Europe that she realized Sande and I had an active sex life. It astounded me that for someone so tuned in to what was happening in the world, she was so unaware of what was happening in her own home.

Despite having better relationships in New York than I had in Amagansett, I wrote in my journal in high school, "I always felt that the reason no one liked me was that they felt I was a cast-off. I felt that if one person liked me, no matter what he looked like or what I thought of him, I could make others feel 'see, someone likes me, maybe you are the one who is mistaken.'" This thinking was the next stage after wanting to walk on the beach in Amagansett and be seen with a handsome man. I notice now that I thought "no one liked me." It has taken me a lifetime to recognize that there were people in Amagansett who liked me, but the overwhelming feeling was of isolation. And I thought the solution lay with having a man who valued me. Somehow that man would prove my worth. Where was the truth?

Back in New York City, I could now get around by myself, go to a movie, walk down to the pizza place where I could get a slice for 15 cents, the same as the cost of a bus ride. I could go shopping by myself and had lots of interesting places within walking distance: Central Park, Riverside Park, the Museum of Natural History. I could take the subway down to the south end of the island and ride the ferry across to Staten Island. Indicative of my future choices, the places which called me the most were those that were most natural, parks and rivers.

My high school years seemed like the upward trend. There was so much more freedom and stimulation. I was with young people more or less like me. My rebellion was to wear all black clothes and refuse to say the pledge of allegiance or participate in bomb shelter drills. We would never survive a nuclear attack by crouching in the corridors. Instead I was required to walk through the halls to the principal's office each time there was a drill. This allowed me to parade my resistance through the building although I suspect the authorities thought it would embarrass me. It didn't.

I had friends. Sande and I shared hall duty with two other

boys, David and Mark, and we were all friends. I was still friends with Hedy and Alice who lived in our neighborhood and also went to Bronx Science. My circle was small, but I felt included and no one made fun of me.

I also had some teachers who cared about me. Mrs. Tropp taught French and took time to tutor me when Mr. Furman had decided I was hopeless (even while he spoke French with a Yiddish accent). We fooled him. I got over 90% on the required state Regents French exam. He was astonished. Mr. Shaw taught English and really inspired me, even though I couldn't get through *Moby Dick*. I still have a postcard he wrote me thanking me for writing him to ask why he wasn't in school in my senior year. I still don't know why he wasn't there.

I became aware of politics during this time. John Kennedy was elected president. My parents weren't very excited. They supported Stevenson, but felt compelled to vote for Kennedy against Nixon in the election. My parents were never great John Kennedy supporters. He was liberal, not a radical or progressive, like my parents. Also his brother, Robert, had worked as assistant counsel with the McCarthy Senate Committee. John Kennedy allowed us to get into the position with the Russians over the Cuban missiles and supported the Bay of Pigs invasion. When the Cuban Missile Crisis happened, I thought that I rather be at home and not in school if we were going to be bombed into oblivion. I didn't trust Kennedy to forestall an attack. But most importantly, he appointed his brother, Robert, as Attorney General. My parents remembered Robert Kennedy vividly from his role during the McCarthy hearings. It is interesting to me that progressives in the 1960s somehow forgot how awful things had been just a decade before. My mother never forgot a hurt. She was sure the Kennedys were not her allies.

❧ ❧

Often, coming home from high school, I found mother on the couch in the large living room reading a mystery novel she got from the membership library she accessed via the cross-town bus. There was a public library three blocks from our apartment building but she couldn't get the newest books there. I went to the public library for my reading material. I only went into the fancy east side brownstone that housed her library once in all the years we lived in New York.

Our apartment was larger than any house I had lived in up to that point. It had seven rooms and each one was larger than any I had experienced before. I walked into the apartment and saw a wall of bookshelves filled with books to my left, the matching small and large yellow, white and brown patterned rugs; the smaller defining the foyer and the larger the space around which chairs and the couch were arranged, the same ones that were in the house in Chevy Chase and Amagansett, but with new covers; two chairs of which I still have—with different covers. They were made to last.

Seeing me come in, mother lifted her eyes from the book and put down the carrot stick she just took from a jar filled with water so they wouldn't dry out. She has passed on to me the difficulty in reading without eating something. She was always trying to manage her weight, as well as mine.

"How was your day?" she asked, cheerfully.

"Fine."

"Did Sande come home on the train with you?"

"Yes." (He would come with me and then take the cross town bus to get to his home on the upper East Side.)

"How is Hedy doing?"

"She hopes her mom will be home soon." (I later learned that mother had helped Hedy's mother get into a mental institution to deal with her disorientation coming from Egypt into a very different life in New York City.)

Mother went on to ask more detail about my friends which seemed to me at the time to indicate her caring and concern for me.

Many years later, I was asked in a personal growth training, "Who did you take care of as a child?" I answered, "My mother." Surprising myself. Since then, I have shifted my thinking and imagine that her days didn't have enough in them and her involvement in my life was intrusive and part of how she kept herself engaged. The pattern started when we lived in Amagansett and she had nothing to do and spent hours working with me to memorize facts. When I was in high school, she rewrote my papers because what I wrote was never as good as she could make it. Whose truth?

During those high school years there were also times when I arrived home to find her with a group of women in the dining room, putting together a mailing for Women's Strike for Peace. She was working with Bella Abzug (eventually a Congressperson and known for her outspoken commitment to peace and wearing large hats). Peace had always been mother's most important issue. I think she recognized that there can be no peace without justice, but peace was always foremost. She did travel down to Mississippi with clothes to donate to the freedom marchers. Segregation was her impression of the South so that when I moved to Georgia after graduate school, she was appalled.

Perhaps my aversion to marches and demonstrations is not just that I think it foolish to walk around with signs that say that someone is misguided. The first demonstration I went to with my mother was when I was thirteen. I don't remember the issue but at the time she was mostly concerned with ending the testing of nuclear weapons. Masses of people filled the open space and police on horseback controlled the crowd. I love horses, but when I was on the ground and the horse was being used to push the crowd back it was very scary. I imagine that scene whenever I consider going to a demonstration. It doesn't mean I never go, but I notice that I do it much less often than others with my political interests.

I stood in front of the Beacon movie theater down Broadway from our apartment when they were showing the movie *The Day the Earth Stood Still*. We handed out flyers explaining how the testing of nuclear weapons was changing the environment in ways that might have negative unintended consequences. This was a time when women were beginning to make their voices heard in ways that have matured today.

My mother continued her social activism throughout her life. Although she became active in the Democratic Party, her heart was really in more radical politics. During my high school years, she was still trying to be a mother. Ginny only stayed with us the first year we were in New York. Mother had to do daily chores like cooking, but she still had someone come in to clean weekly. Ginny's room became dad's office. I have some stationary with his name on it identifying him as a professional in real estate. On it he claimed to have an office on Murray Hill. Whose truth?

Dad worked in that study, making phone calls to try to sell property and writing. I have no idea what he wrote. He occasionally succeeded in selling some property but he was not able to contribute steadily to the costs of running the house. What I remember most was his having to schedule his day around what time he could move his car from one side of the street to the other to avoid an expensive parking ticket.

As far as I could tell, my father never really made any money as a realtor. Mother seemed to be covering our living expenses with income from the investments she'd inherited from her father as well as the money which came from the sale of the Elm Tree Inn. I never really understood how this sale was handled. My brother says that he overheard a conversation on the Long Island Railroad that implied that the building was burned down for the insurance money and for the man who bought to avoid paying all that was due to our family. Whose truth?

The cottages were sold off separately and moved away. One

ended up next to the summer house we built. My mother was able to rely on the income from her inheritance and eventually she went back to work for social justice causes. She always grumbled about how dad handled money.

৵৽

The summer after 9th grade, I spent in a "red diaper" camp in New Mexico, called Cibola, where I was one of the youngest campers and felt rather overwhelmed. There is a good deal of literature written by and about red diaper babies and these camps are often mentioned. Reading others' experiences has informed my understanding of how so many of us developed, although we have each had different responses to growing up in families with radical politics. I have sought out others who shared this experience and learned a great deal from them about our similarities and differences.

In the 1980s there was a conference of red diaper babies in New York City. Some of the discussion from that conference was gathered into a document which I had the opportunity to read. I copied a number of statements which I felt reflected my own experience:

"My father quit so he wouldn't be fired; he found himself alone."

"There was a group of people who had similar vision or at least you felt they had similar vision. I don't find that I have a community. I often feel like I'm looked at as some sort of a nut."

"We are plagued with social responsibility and think we're selfish if we don't somehow involve ourselves in that. We can't see just taking care of ourselves as being sufficient."

"These values make me happy. I'm not sure that this is true. Perhaps these values make me unhappy. I am unhappy with how the world is. I am unhappy with myself for not making more of a difference."

"But you grew up with a mission and a focus, just by talking about the worth of other human beings, by feeling empathy toward people, and realizing that the world can be changed and that it's humans who do it."

"We are struggling to find ways of living out our values. If I lost that part of me, I would feel empty. That would be a terrible thing, because that is the core of who I am and what I am very proud of."

"We look at the broader picture and become immobilized because we're not doing enough."

I see something of myself in each of these statements. Certainly my father found himself alone after he lost his job. This left me with a lot of uncertainty about whether or not I could trust that people would be there for me when I got into a difficult situation. I have also easily felt that I am being attacked when others don't think that is what is happening.

I also often feel separate from other people. Most people I know came to progressive politics on their own; I was born into it, which left me feeling that I can't "not" have these values. "They are the core of who I am and what I am very proud of," though it wasn't until my forties that I felt bold enough to tell someone I was the child of a man who had been blacklisted.

And I feel a very strong sense of obligation to make a difference in the world. I feel guilty when I am not engaged in social change work. I feel as if I am not making a contribution and this is unacceptable to myself.

Camp Cibola was run by the Orrs. They were friends of my parents in Washington, DC. The campers and counselors travelled out to New Mexico in rickety second hand busses, camping along the way. Often at the permanent camp, we were awakened in the middle of the night for some adventure. One night, I was shaken awake. I reached out and put my hand in a furry coat. I turned over, saying "leave me alone," and went back to sleep. In the morning, I learned that the nearby Pueblo Indians had come dressed in bear skins, drunk, and woken up the whole camp, except me. Everyone else was in a tizzy about the bear (or the Indians, equally scary) that had come prowling around during the night.

Some nights we gathered in a loft space and listened to one of the counselors play the guitar and sing or share stories. We sat up listening to the Democratic Convention on the radio where we were all rooting for Adlai Stevenson. Not everyone was the child of someone who had been mistreated during the purges, but everyone was left-leaning. We also did ordinary camp things, too. We played Capture the Flag and rode the camp's horses up into the mountains and camped out overnight. We visited the Pueblo Indians on their own territory and went into Taos which was the nearest town.

The next two summers, I went on trips with the American Youth Hostel Association (AYH). The first summer, I travelled with a group of nine young men and three other young women by bicycle through the Canadian Rockies. We took a train from New York City to Montreal. We had a private car with bunks and a kitchen. Each day the train car stopped at a siding in a city and unhitched from the train. We took our bikes off and rode around the city. In the evening, we came back to the car and it was reattached to a westbound train that moved us through the night to a new city. The city I remember best was Calgary because the Stampede, a combination of rodeo and fair, was on. The newsboys hawked papers screaming, "Calgary Herald, late city edition." It had a singsong rhythm that has stuck with me like an effective commercial.

When we got to Lake Louise, our leader, Gordon Gilbert, fell off his bike and broke his collarbone. Gordon drove a car with our packs and food and we met him at the hostels which were about fifteen miles apart. We rode from Banff to Jasper over about a week. On that trip I learned that not everything that goes up comes down. I was the only one on a three speed bike while all the others had ten speeds. I plugged along and kept up reasonably well. At night, we cooked our food over a wood burning stove and washed up in the water melting off the glaciers we walked on during the day. The water was seriously cold. I had waist length hair and the one time I tried to wash it in the stream, I thought my head would freeze before I could get the soap out. I learned to play Hearts on that trip. I also learned to take my Schwinn bike apart and put it back together again.

The next summer, I took a bike trip to Massachusetts. Mother talked AYH into taking me even though it made our numbers uneven. We had nine girls and seven boys along with our leader. One day on Cape Cod which is fairly flat, we rode 100 miles. I was very proud of that. We slept in hostels, but they were much more comfortable than the ones in Canada. I rode more slowly than the boys but faster than the girls and that meant I was isolated again on the road. That summer, with dogs running out to bark at us, I decided it didn't matter if you used curse words or just made up sounds, they equally expressed the frustration of unexpected and unwanted events.

Travel and interaction with people from different cultures has been one of the greatest influences on me. Getting to know and experience different cultures opened my mind to the possibilities beyond the either/or world view my mother espoused.

My first trip away from North America was to Europe, after those hostelling trips in high school I had a yearning for more adventure. I asked my parents to send me overseas as a gift for my graduation from high school. They arranged for me to stay in Paris with Dr. Madeleine Kieger, my cousin Tony's mother-in-law.

I travelled from New York to Rotterdam on the *S.S. Waterman*, a Holland American Line ship. Most of the other travelers were college students and since I had yet to go to college, I was a bit young for them. However, the sailors took a shine to me and we had great times together. When they were off duty, I could hang out with them below decks. I learned to love the Dutch and to swear in Dutch. They were delighted to have female companionship.

When we docked in Rotterdam, I found my way to the train station and bought a ticket to Paris where Dr. Kieger met me. After a brief stay in Paris at her apartment, Dr. Kieger arranged for me to stay in Montargis, a small town in the Loire Valley. At first I was with the Szigetis whom I liked a lot. The grandfather was the town's mayor. When I arrived, my French wasn't very good, but I could understand when the eight-year old son, Pierrot, asked his mother, "Will the American put her feet on the dining table?" It was clear that the impression of Americans in France was that we were uncouth. I enjoyed Pierrot's parents, Bernard and Isabelle, but they really didn't have room for me. I was in a closet with a mattress on the floor.

So they arranged for me to move to the Lesages who lived in a large house. It was not easy living with them and I spent a lot of time walking around the town. The day I got the news that Tony's father, my Uncle Sidney, had died I was travelling in the car with the Lesages. I was very upset and remember putting my head out the window to let the wind blow away my tears. I did not feel that I could get any sympathy from them. My letters from that summer were saved.

"Here are these people with two fabulous homes, vacations in Germany, and an Italian car, everything you could want. Living next to them are these people in filthy houses, washing their clothes in the filthy canal, pumping water from the public pump and there is no communication. I doubt the Lesages even consider the others part of the same country or city. It's amazing...She is just like a kid and rather proud of it. The only problem is she wants to keep house like a princess with all the royal graces and it is rather difficult for an innocent."

Another time I said about Mme. Lesage, "I am simply very critical of the kind of character who is always apologizing for things she has no intention of correcting and therefore might as well not mention."

On the other hand, I wrote,

"You know, I love those people—the Szigetis, the whole clan of them. From grandma with her stuffy bitchiness and grandpa the handsomest mayor ever to Marie Rachel with all her warmth and puppy-dog loving and Pierre-Alain, the little boy who may never love girls. I love Bernard, with his giving soul and Isabelle who must learn. I even love Maurice (Bernard's brother, 31 years old) who will never even grow up enough to feed his three kids and poor pregnant wife. I love them all and leaving them will be a very painful experience... When I said goodbye and knew I wouldn't be seeing some of them again, I really was brokenhearted. I know I couldn't have done without them. Why is it one never appreciates things as much as when one knows they are gone forever?"

In France that summer I didn't feel I was getting enough exercise, and I was eating too much rich food. I wrote home, "What I miss most is the opportunity to use my body. To play tennis or run along the beach and roll in the sand. These things would give me such a lift." I can read in my letters how much I struggled with my weight.

The second month, I spent in a camp for French teenagers in an Italian small town called Cavi di Lavagnia on the Mediterranean Sea. The other young people in the camp with me could not speak English so it was necessary for me to speak in French to have friendships. The young people were particularly interested in American music and asked me to translate Elvis Pressley songs like *Jail House Rock* and *You Ain't Nothing but a Hound Dog*. It was quite challenging. We spent the days at the beach and the evenings in night clubs listening to music, dancing, and generally hanging out like teenagers do.

Once I got to Italy, I enjoyed swimming in the sea even though the beaches are not as nice and white as on Long Island, "The sea is such a beautiful color there (Portofino). It is exactly as I pictured it, a real deep blue with a bit of green and a few white ships. The whole coast is visible for quite a distance and one can see the little towns and the mountains rising behind…Swimming at night with a sea of stars above and the sea soft and calm, slipping gently around me."

The housing for the camp was on top of a steep hill above the water. Our only requirements were to show up for the three meals a day and be in by midnight. Each camper seemed to be on a different schedule, so my roommates were ever changing. I mostly hung out with Franca and Catherine. Based on the letters I wrote home, I thought that Franca took too long to get ready to go any place and Catherine was rather boring, but I preferred to go with them rather than risk being alone in an unknown place. A lot of my letters were filled with the various men I met and how I felt about them. Clearly American women were seen as "easy." I was still carrying my self image from Amagansett, so I lived up to their expectations.

Interestingly I was already interested in racism in the U.S. and wrote, "I don't get any world news here, but particularly no information on the racial problem. People often speak of it, but they don't seem to have any particularly interesting views. Everyone says it's terrible. I met one Dutch boy who said he couldn't understand prejudice, but wouldn't want his sister to marry a Negro man. That is the way it is."

Other thoughts from that summer,

"The U.S. and Russia are now in their Middle Ages, dark ages, ages of superstition (science) and prejudice (politics). Now Europe has become more the land of the free and the home of the brave, where one tries to prove that Castro is not helping his people rather than proving he is a Communist. Where the important thing is the result, not the title; that is where there is liberty. Where people dislike people with different ideas, but don't despise them. That is where there is equality.

"I think that these things are more easily found in Europe than in the U.S. and that is why I think Europe is more cultured and more civilized, not because of their table manners or the literature they produce, civilization is man's relation to man in a larger way than that. I think, perhaps, because I can't understand the language instead of getting the little parts of culture, I get the big things that are civilization."

A different letter, "Yesterday I read Fromm's *The Art of Loving* and I had so many thoughts on it...I decided that you [Mom] were a pretty good person and mother by his [Fromm's] standards, but I couldn't judge dad as a person and I found him lacking as a father."

By the time I started college, I had pretty much dismissed my father as an important part of my life. One day we were driving on the road where I had learned to ride a bike. He said, "I love you and miss you when you are not around."

Still resenting his absence during the years we had lived in Amagansett, I said, "I don't understand what you mean by love. When I am home we rarely talk."

Hurt, but not giving up, he replied, "I just like knowing you are around. We don't have to talk for me feel good about your proximity."

I didn't appreciate how hurt he must have been by my dismissal. I don't think he really understood how hurt I had been by his absence. Many years after his death, I came to appreciate how loving and accepting he was. I regret I didn't receive it while he was still alive.

"When I discover who I am, I'll be free."
- *Ralph Ellison, "Invisible Man"*

❦

CHAPTER FOUR

IN MY FRESHMAN YEAR OF COLLEGE, PRESIDENT KENNEDY was shot. I was walking down the street when Susan Hunt told me the news. She was later my roommate and came from Tulsa, OK. My first thought as a New Yorker was, "Oh, she's from that part of the country. She's exaggerating to make her home more interesting."

I entered the dorm which was actually a large lake house that contracted with the university to accommodate students. Instead of going up to the third floor where I shared a very small room with a messy artist from New York, I stayed in the parlor in front of the television. Several of us watched with anxiety to hear if Kennedy died. We were shocked when his death was announced. What would this mean for the country, for us? Having been on campus for only a couple of months, we were mostly interested in what was going to happen to us.

It was just before Thanksgiving vacation and I had reservations to fly home on a charter flight for vacation. I was excited to hear that classes were cancelled but there was confusion about when we would actually leave campus. We had an extra long vacation that year.

Although I did reasonably well in college academically, I spent most of the four years with my extra-curricular activities with the International Club. I often say I majored in International Students. Arriving at the University of Wisconsin, I saw an advertisement for an exhibition of clubs and groups to join. Wandering around the exhibit, I noticed the International Club. Oh, I just came back from two months in Europe; I think this would be interesting!

I had spent the summer in France and Italy. I had learned to have a conversation in French and should be able to do well in that class. However, the teacher who was a graduate student didn't like the colloquial way I used the language and kept trying to change my writing style to one more academic. I quickly decided this was another "Mr. Furman" (my high school teacher who told me I was smart but just couldn't learn languages) whom I could never please. I changed to taking Russian as my second language which was required for graduation.

I could generally be found in the offices upstairs in the student union building from which student activities were organized. Rachel was the International Club advisor and she and I became quite close. Rachel was a soft spoken woman of Mexican-American ancestry who had grown up in Texas. She was lovely and supportive and a great resource for me. Her husband, Tom, was a photographer. I have a number of great photos he took during those years that show me with students from Nigeria, Nepal, Trinidad and Tobago and other exotic places.

I had the privilege of being in a special program called ILS, Integrated Liberal Studies. It meant that for the first two years I was with a cohort of 200 students who went to every lecture together. Each semester we were divided into "discussion sections" of twenty-five. For all the three or four lecture classes that semester we were with the same twenty-five students which allowed us to get to know each other fairly well. This provided a sense of belonging that was not otherwise available on a campus of 50,000 students. Leadership in most of the clubs was generally drawn from the ILS students.

It didn't matter that students called me a, "NewYorkCommieJewBeatnick." It seemed a whole lot better than being called "fatso-Lisso." At least it grouped me with other people instead of isolating me. It is only now that I am coming to realize how much anti-Semitism there was in that phrase. Again, the illusion that we live in a free country where people have tolerance for others who are different. It still amazes me that I keep forgetting that this tolerance is only hypothetical. Today people say this is a, "Christian country." Whose truth?

One time I arranged for some Soviet students to speak at the International Club. The next summer the FBI came around asking Rachel questions about me. She told me about it when I returned to school in the fall. I figured it didn't matter what I did because I was born on a blacklist. The International Club was a place where I belonged.

UW-Madison had the largest number of international students of any university in the U.S. Most of them were graduate students, men from the Indian subcontinent or Africa. Many of them were Muslims. However, by the second semester of my junior year, I was the president of the International Club. It wasn't easy for a young, Jewish, undergraduate female to be elected president. However, since I had done most of the work to keep the club going, from silk screening posters to arranging Friday night discussion programs and being at every Saturday night dance, a leadership group figured out a plan. Shukla from Nepal ran for president and I ran for vice president. He knew he would be leaving at the end of the first semester and I would ipso facto become president. Which I did. One of my highlights was the Octoberfest polka dance in the Rathskeller after we had been elected. Shukla had earned a living as a dance instructor and we danced so many dances together other men complained that he was not sharing.

Shukla's skill on the dance floor was amazing as he was quite a large man around the middle. He had been a high-up official in the Nepalese government and when the control of the government changed he had to leave for his own safety. He was much older than I, married with his family left behind. He had initially immigrated to Canada where he taught dance to earn the money he needed to support himself. He came to Madison to get a degree in economics. I visited in his apartment where he taught me how to cut an onion efficiently. Later my mother saw me cutting an onion this way and disapproved because it wasn't the way she would do it.

At orientation for new students one fall, when there was fighting between Pakistan and India, I looked around at the men in the room watching television news, some from each of those countries, and thought "What is wrong with this world?" Here we were with men from each country feeling scared for their families at home and unable to do anything. They were not hostile toward one another, just jointly scared. Is this the truth about war?

My photo was all over the yearbook in my junior year. I was invited to join Mortar Board, the American national honor society for college seniors, honored for scholarship, leadership and service. I was not seen as a rebel. I was well known to the administration in a very positive way.

This time instead of missing honors because of service credits as I had in high school, I missed because I didn't get a high enough grade on my honors thesis. It was the first paper I ever wrote without my mother's input. The professor I worked with on my thesis didn't think very highly of women and was not very supportive of my work. He was the only professor who taught political philosophy, but he had very little consciousness or analysis of the dynamics of power and oppression as relates to gender.

My paper was about the possibility of representative government being a democracy. I felt strongly that representative democracy could never be true democracy and that there needed to be more discussion among ordinary people and more participation in the decision-making process. That interest has persisted and shapes much of my work today. I believe that the work of facilitating dialogue and deliberation on public issues is key to our future.

By the time I walked across the stage (in a graduating class of several thousand) every professor and administrator I encountered knew me by name, including the Chancellor, in whose home I had been for social activities. I felt known by those in charge. I felt I belonged.

❧

One night in the winter of my sophomore year in college, I went out with Bob Quinn (who turned out to be the son of friends of my parents from Washington) and some friends of his. I rarely drank and had never been drunk. But that night for some reason, I did and was. I staggered back to the dorm. In the middle of the night I woke up and had to pee. I stumbled my way to the common toilet area and peed. Then I was thirsty. So I stopped at the water fountain on my way back to the room.

Arriving at the door, I couldn't seem to open it. I tried twisting one way and then the other. Nothing was happening. I couldn't hold myself up. I fell over and hit my head. In frustration, I sat down in front of the door and cried out for Susan. She opened the door. Seeing me sitting on the floor clearly not able to function, she went for the resident assistant. They decided I should go to the infirmary.

I don't remember how I got to the infirmary, but the medical resident there decided I should stay overnight. I had vomited in the emergency room and they were concerned I had a concussion. I was perfectly happy to sleep wherever I could. When I awoke in the morning, I thought I should go to class. But I was still feeling pretty bad. I must have gotten cleaned up because eventually I was walking down the street on my way back to the dorm. The sky was overcast and I was feeling pretty awful.

Out of nowhere appeared this 6 foot 2, blond haired man wearing a blue jacket (to match his eyes) belted at the waist. He was in my discussion group but I thought he had never even noticed me. Eric strides rather than walks on his long legs. He slowed down to start a conversation with me.

"Kathy, where were you? You missed class today."

Surprised he even knew my name I replied, "I wasn't feeling well and had to go to the infirmary."

"You missed our writing exercise. You will have to make it up."

Suddenly, I wasn't feeling so bad, "Why don't we sit down in the Rathskeller and you can tell me what I missed."

And we did. That was the beginning of a long and complicated relationship.

He wrote me notes and put them in his shirt pocket for me to find. He couldn't really tell me he loved me but wrote something like this,

"Dear Kathy, People without shirt pockets are at a tremendous disadvantage in the line of communication. I think I've perfected a system, which I shall here explain.

"I shall make it a practice to write at least one story nightly. You may read every seventh word, disregarding the second seventh and adding the third fifth, of the first paragraph...[lots more crazy directions]...If by any horrible chance, I am required to write more than that, instructions will be forthcoming in the story. My only question becomes this: how can one fit the word 'love' into a story about the snarly-old stupid Senate? Sounds difficult, eric"

Why do I know this? Because I kept many of his writings and letters to me. And still don't want to throw them away. Every now and then I try reaching out and am told "It would upset my wife if she knew I was in touch with you." However, one time not too long ago I initiated contact again. He responded that his credentials as a "crusading reporter" had been challenged and he had tried to find the first investigative article he had written for the Daily Cardinal and couldn't find a copy. I sent him the original on browning newsprint. He was appreciative, but wouldn't continue the correspondence.

❧❧

When I first met Eric, I was anticipating a visit from my high school sweetheart, Sande. I wrote to my mother about my conflict over whether or not I should let Sande take the long bus ride from Ithaca to Madison only to disappoint him. She wrote back,

"I know that when Sande comes you will not do anything to hurt him. I don't think you can, because he is and most probably will be one of your best friends. And although you are filled with all your feelings about Eric...in terms of Sande, you don't have to exaggerate your honest feelings...My love to you and Sande—Eric will have to wait."

Mother had spoken on the phone with Sande since he had gone to Cornell and was sure that her feelings for him reflected mine.

I didn't tell Sande about Eric before he took the bus to Madison. Eric, who grew up in Madison, found Sande a place to stay while he was visiting. When Sande arrived, Eric called and arranged to meet him in a pool hall to talk. I never did learn the content of that conversation, but when I saw them come into the large biology lecture room together I knew I was in trouble. Sande came and sat with me. I could tell he was upset.

We left after class and went to the Rathskeller where Sande told me how hurt he was and that he was leaving on the bus to go back to New York City that day. My girlfriend, Sybil, helped him get on the bus. I went back to my dorm room. Eric called that evening and asked me to go to a movie with him. I was pleased even though I felt guilty for how I had treated Sande. The next morning, I found a photo in my mail box with a note from Eric. It was of the top of the journalism building with its capstone missing; the note said Eric had taken it down. He often did reckless things and told me about them, like running along the tops of stationery railroad trains. Or sending me a postcard with a photo of, "The ledge I dive off of drunk...The water is about 85-90 feet deep below." This was the summer when I was at camp as a counselor and he was a barker for a show in Wisconsin Dells between our sophomore and junior years.

We had a conversation in a bar before we ever made love, where he said, "But I'll hang over at the ends," referring to the fact that he is a foot taller than I. When he found out he was not my first lover, he climbed through the window of the journalism building (where we used the couch and he didn't hang over at all) and left me alone there for an hour while he strode off his upset. We went to a conference in Chicago together and came back in the middle of the night past curfew for me so we spent the night in the back of his car. He lived at home with his parents, so I couldn't go home with him and I couldn't enter the women's dorm after 11 p.m. That spring was an exciting time for me. I was completely in love.

My mother was so emeshed in my life she began a correspondence with Eric. He was trying to decide whether or not to get an apartment for his junior year so that he could move out of his parents' home. One question was whether I should join him in the apartment or stay in the dorm. We each tried to consult our parents about it. His parents didn't want to discuss it. My mother was only too willing.

This generated a great deal of written communication among Eric, my mother and me. I have several letters which refer to the decision-making process. Apparently, mother was not adverse to my sexual relationship with Eric but she felt that it would be better if we didn't live together. She wrote,

"Eric sounds in a real clutch about next year. I can understand his parents, who really sound very sensible...[even if you do live] in a dorm, you still will have enough time with each other—and to be alone with each other. I am not moralizing—you know that. I rather think there is more bloom when there is not too much being together...Remember, darling, he comes from a different background than you, and that he feels some guilt about you and his relationship with you. No matter what you say, his feelings come out of his background, not yours. And if he is guilty, he will have to have you share the punishment..."

What made her decide that he would feel guilty about living with me? Eric wrote a letter addressed to both my mother and to me, which says,

"Dear Katharine (and potentially Mrs. Liss also)...The second question (or doubt) seems to be that I can't love you fully or be proud of you while living (or semi-living) with you, due to social, parental, and background pressures...Should this break up parental relations, I could not and most emphatically would not blame you. These decisions are strictly my own, and the responsibility for what I do will be strictly my own also. You are merely providing additional possibilities for action, possibilities which I find very exciting indeed, incidentally."

I wrote to my mother,

"He wants a relationship simply separate and apart from ours which is what is should be. Yet you will obviously influence it. You will always influence me unless once you go too far...[My friend] said she felt that it was wrong to make Eric justify himself to you. I said that it was necessary for our relationship because you could make it very uncomfortable for me. She also was amazed that you felt all the problems he and I would face would be due to his background."

This was the first time in my life where I chose some other relationship over my closeness with my mother. We were having a conflict about how much time I would spend at home over spring vacation. I wrote,

"I think now it is you who have to accept the idea of this being my home at least the idea that my home is no longer with you, necessarily. I don't mean to say that I don't feel that I can go home, just that I don't need to go home. That where you are is not the only place for me to feel comfortable and right."

In the same letter, I describe my feelings about Eric,

"I don't know why I like him so much. I am sure it is for really terrible reasons...He is big and tall and strong and handsome. He is brave and daring in an almost reckless way, but he is always aware of his abilities and hasn't gone beyond them since I have known him. ...he knows what he wants and has stronger beliefs than the typical 'liberal.' It is really great to see how different we are and how much we can learn from each other. There are whole areas where we have no common ground but we are learning one. It gives us each a great deal of pleasure. We each bring so much to the relationship. We each amaze the other continually."

In the end, he got an apartment with a friend and I lived in the dorm in a single room in our junior year. It turned out that this was a good decision as our relationship didn't survive the school year. However, from today's perspective, I wonder how much my mother's involvement in our relationship affected the outcome.

I have many memories I treasure of the time I spent with Eric in Madison. We made love wherever we could, whenever we could. We talked and talked about our views of the world and how we each saw ourselves. We shared many intimate times. One of the best was spring break of our sophomore year when I stayed in Madison and we hung out together in a friend's apartment for several days without interruption. I spent the time reading *Absolom, Absolom* about which I remember nothing!

It was a good thing I didn't get that apartment with Eric because at Thanksgiving of our junior year, he went to a conference (while I stayed in Madison expecting us to have time together at his apartment) and came back with a new woman in his life. Standing in the foyer of the dormitory where men weren't allowed past the hallway, he told me that he couldn't console me because he was the cause of my pain. Very astute of him.

This describes the internal conflict he dealt with,

"Katherine, I'm writing to please myself and my standards. Rather than you and yours. A diff.

"I want you physically very badly. And I'm getting less drunk. I fear I want your body more than your person. That is lust.

"But you can make me happier and sadder than I've ever been before. And more tender (your word and my feeling).

"But I'm unsure sober whether it's real – whether I rationalize because I want so much. So I usually can't say I love you, and feel guilty when you can.

"Your love is so much bigger (greater) than mine. I feel a liar. Love is reciprocal, and equally so; never unequally so.

"Between us there is a lack. You know my reservations, as do I. Yet we go beyond them to a point where I must rationalize and say I hope one day to love you enough to return your love.

"You tell me that's the way love is. A lie.

"You point comparisons between Sande and me. He loves you, you love me. I am two points down, because he is two giant steps bigger than I am.

"You've rationalized for me very nicely. But I can't accept that. My standards have to be met or I'll crumble.

"You've tried to substitute your strength for mine (as have I) and it can't be done. I've got to grow until we can meet as equals.

"All that remains is honesty in the pulp. Whether it is an affectation or a humble truth, I cannot tell.

"Here is my flaw: I am very tired. And I want to say I love you and need your security. Oh Jesus, Kathy, Jesus.

"Listen to me now, tired and drunk, rather than tomorrow whining and excusing.

I love you and cannot, Eric"

His reference to Sande loving me more than I him and my loving Eric more than he me is to a belief I held then (and still hold) that most love relationships are unequal. There is always a pursuer and a pursued. I have married those who pursued me as I generally pursued men who are unavailable for one reason or another. Is this a fear of deep commitment or a failure to permanently attract a man whom I find terribly attractive? Does it reflect the conflicts I experienced growing up? Losing my father's loving attention when I was 5 was a deep hurt. Hearing my mother disparage her husband for not providing as she wanted definitely shaped my attitudes toward men which have only been altered through deep personal growth work.

However at this time, mother wrote to me about her relationship with my father,

"I think I have persuaded daddy to come with me on a cruise. I am lending him money, since the first thing he said is that he couldn't afford it. I can...(she talks about all her friends who are divorced or divorcing) I, who have been screaming for ten years about my terrible marriage is (sic) going to end up the only happily married person I know. I am embarrassed. Daddy and I get along so well these days, that when I spoke to him about the cruise I said that I truly would enjoy it with him so much more than alone – I am having such a really pleasant relationship with him. It must be working, my God, I can just see me, working away for the rest of my life, just so I can have a pleasant relationship. Oh, well..."

How much did my relationship with my mother contribute to the impossibility of being with Eric?

By April of my junior year, I was seeing David Hansen. However, Eric and I were still talking to each other as evidenced by a letter I wrote home, "Talked to Eric for an hour and a half yesterday. It was really nice to be able to talk like two people who know each other very well and enjoy each others' company."

In September of '66, when I was a senior and living in an apartment off campus and David was living with me until my roommate came back, I wrote to my mother, "I went out to dinner with Eric the other night. It was very good. For once I could turn him down. He is terribly lonely. Also very unhappy and broken. [His girlfriend, eventual wife] graduated and is back in Pittsburgh. He has no money and he says if he doesn't get a news writing job [after college] he will join the air force. I don't believe him."

David became my steady partner, but I was never really committed to him. I guess I chose him because he reminded me of Eric, tall and blond and grown up in Wisconsin. But they were totally different in personality. The best I could say about him was "There is so little we disagree violently about and even that is mainly because we understand each other so well in understanding ourselves...It's not that I love him in a needing, clinging way. I merely love him and would prefer to be with him."

In our senior year, I got engaged to David, who went into the Peace Corps that winter. Eric's fiancé (the same one he had met that Thanksgiving) had graduated, Eric and I got together again from time to time and he spent the night. I felt redeemed. It wasn't the end of this relationship.

Christmas 1966, there was a conflict between spending December 25th with my family in New York or spending time with David in Madison. My letter said,

"I need some person around whom to focus my existence. His importance to me is not that he limits my existence, but that with him as a focus, I can live a more expanded life. I have in no way cut myself off from you, but I am twenty years old (I know, still a little girl) and it is time for me to find a focus and base for my life outside the family.

"I cannot thank you enough for the home you have provided me. It has given me the basic stability to do all the things I have done and to make the sort of independent plans I now am making. Do not suddenly change your attitudes and put pressures on me that you never did when I was younger. In some very central way, you will always be most important to me. Be glad that the firm base you have given me now permits me to stand on my own two feet. Whether or not David will be central to me for the rest of my life (and I believe it would be a good thing if he were) you have made me the person I am...I can no longer rely on you for all the answers."

I used these men to provide a shoehorn to pry myself free of my mother. Despite my protestations, she was still calling the shots and telling me how to live my life. I may have gained a bit more distance, but the strings were still there.

These were the days of the protests against the war in Vietnam. Eric and I went to a demonstration so that Eric could cover the story for the *Daily Cardinal*. I looked around and didn't see people I knew. International students were not going to participate in demonstrations against the government that was hosting them. I felt I should be on the protest lines myself. People marched around with picket signs deploring the war. I felt both ahead of them – having written about the U.S. sending in "advisors" while I was still in high school – and at the same time guilty that I wasn't participating as my mother thought I should.

The protests only started in 1964, and I had been aware of the U.S. involvement since 1962. Madison was a hot spot for protests, but most of it happened after I was graduated. The draft was a trigger for college students who were afraid they would be forced to fight in a war they didn't believe in.

The strongest opposition to the war actually began the spring

I was graduated, so in my sophomore year (1964-65) there weren't many demonstrations. Still I struggled with the decision to attend. UW was known for their radical students ("Were you there when they blew up the building?" No.) And I had the "right" background to be one of the marchers. But I wasn't.

Mother was deeply involved with the antiwar movement, even organizing college students during the Vietnam Summer where they took the movement off the campuses and into the streets, going door to door to talk to people about the issues.

I never felt that I fit in with the young people who were suddenly aware of the hypocrisy of our government. I had been aware of it since my father's blacklisting. It wasn't something new to me and it didn't seem like something I could change, despite my mother's strong beliefs and efforts. In many ways she still believed in democracy, that if enough people turned their minds to opposing the war, it would end. And perhaps in the end, she was right, because eventually the government did withdraw, albeit pretending we had won.

Yet, I felt guilty. Who was I to assess whether or not this tactic had merit? I only knew that my mother had been protesting in public demonstrations and raising money for lost causes all my life and long before. All I could see was that the conservative viewpoint had the money, position and power to squash the liberals. And I wasn't going to waste my time running around with a bunch of people filled with hot air and busy using it to argue with one another about meaningless tactics. The left at that time was just as self-destructive as ever, insisting that people accept a narrow range of thinking in order to be included.

Even though I wasn't following the path mother wanted for me, she was very much a part of my life during this period, including writing me at one point that she was glad her typewriter had only broken down after she finished typing my paper!

During my senior year, my mother was the development coordinator for the National Conference for New Politics (NCNP). She tried to get me to help find a place for the conference to be held in Madison, but I really wasn't interested. The NCNP nominated Martin Luther King, Jr. for president and Benjamin Spock for vice president in 1967.

The conference was held from August 31st—September 1, 1967, in Chicago while I was travelling in Europe. The co-chairmen for the group were Julian Bond and Simon Casady. Members of the National Council included Stokely Carmichael, William Sloan Coffin, Erich Fromm, and Herbert Marcuse. Their statement was "New Politics is an organized effort to return decision-making to the people by providing a democratic way to take effective political action at a time when the conventional American politics of party labels and personalities has become sterile."

As we know, MLK was killed before he had the opportunity to actually run. The *Chicago Tribune* article about the conference says that 2,000 "revolutionaries" would be meeting at this event. They claimed that the destruction in Detroit shortly before was the kind of action that this group recommended. The article says that many of the participants were members of the Communist Party which was (from my point of view) basically defunct by that time. (*Chicago Tribune*, Sunday, Aug 27, 1967)

Whose truth?

I still hear my mother's voice on my shoulder telling me that I should be creating more significant results. I struggle with how much of my drive to make a difference comes from my own internal need and how much of it comes from demands she made on me to follow in her footsteps, even though she told me as a child that I would never exceed her.

I may have been able to choose men she didn't approve of, but I was not able to get rid of her voice in my head telling me what my political views should be.

"It seems to me the world is getting smaller every day
Or is it that we are nearer to the places far away
A speeding train, a fleeting plane, a radio and phone
Have made the world my neighbor
So my neighborhood has grown
Travelling broadens one
A little English friend of mine said come and play with me
I took a plane one morning and arrived in time for tea
Before I went to bed I said
I'd like to talk to mom
He said pick up the telephone and tell her how you are
Travelling broadens one
I've got a cousin in Brazil
My uncle lives in France
In Ireland and in Mexico
I have two favorite aunts
I know a girl In Russia and a boy in Italy
I think of them as neighbors because they seem so close to me
Travelling broadens one."

Little Songs on Big Subjects

❧❧

CHAPTER FIVE

INITIALLY MY TRIP AFTER COLLEGE WAS TO IMPROVE MY Russian language skills. I went with a group from International Ladies Garment Workers Union (ILGWU) a very progressive union. The tour was arranged through Sputnik, the youth travel organization in the Soviet Union. Our group was hosted by young communist laborers and led by two union leaders. This was 1967 and the Cold War was still very much in place. As Americans, we had very little information about what was really happening in the Soviet Union.

Our group flew to London where we took a ship through the Baltic Sea to Leningrad. It was July and the weather was warm even that far north. The nights stayed light until eleven at night and the sun came back around three in the morning. I was out on the deck waiting for it to get dark when Marina and Juliette came along speaking French. My French was still enough with me that I was able to greet them and start a conversation. Marina quickly shifted to English as she could speak that better than I could speak French. We chatted about how strange it felt to have sunlight so late at night.

The next day, we celebrated my birthday with fireworks and a cake. As I oohed and ahed over the fireworks reflecting in the dark waters, I thought, "What are we doing celebrating American Independence on a Soviet ship in the middle of the Cold War?" That evening I was pleased and surprised to get a telegram from my parents wishing me a happy birthday. Months later, when I landed in Paris, Marina and Juliette were helpful to me. Marina's family even took me for a weekend to their country home in Brittany and we visited the World War II memorial. The war was still alive for many people only twenty years after its end. On this trip, I became aware of the scars still on the people who lived in places the war had devastated.

Arriving in Leningrad, our group met our guide, Anochka. Her hair was bleach blond and bobbed in the contemporary style. She was slender and fashionable and looked more like an American than I did in my peasant blouses and long skirts. I had studied Russian for two years, but still spoke it very hesitantly and I could only say the most basic things. When we met Russians in the places we were touring, they looked to me to translate and wondered why this young woman with blond braids and a zaftig body was not responding as they expected. Anochka would step in and they looked at her puzzled as to why this more modern looking woman was the one with the language skills. She and I got to be friends and often went out together when there weren't group activities.

Standing in a railroad station with other Soviets standing all around, a man in a brown suit, usual for middle managers in the Soviet Union at that time, came up to me and said in English. "You are so lucky to live in the U.S. where you can read anything you want. We have to hide our written materials which disagree with what is written in *Pravda* and *Izvestia*. We copy our writings and pass them from hand to hand. They are called 'samizdat' or self-published."

Surprised that he was brave enough to share this information in public when I understood that there were spies everywhere who reported anyone whose behavior seemed deviant, I replied, "Yes, I get to read *The Nation* and *I.F. Stone's Weekly*, but very few people read the ideas which are not popular. I only wish Americans would read different points of view. We are lazy because we think we live in a democracy and most Americans only read the mainstream media. When you are restricted from reading certain things it increases your desire to get hold of them. When they are freely available, people take them for granted."

The Soviet Union, it turned out was not really the land that

Communists of the thirties and forties thought it was; nor was it the bogeyman that the anti-Communists of the fifties thought it was. When I experienced it in the sixties, I found it to have a class society where some people clearly had much more than others, but I also found that there were no people so poor that they were homeless or begging in the streets. There were make work jobs where one person could have done the work that was being done by several but everyone could work and earn enough to have shelter and food, unlike in the U.S. at that time and this. As we visited one war memorial after another I became aware of the fear of most people there that they might experience the ravages of the Second World War again.

We spent the bulk of our time in the Republic of Georgia which later became a very significant place in my life. We spent a few days in Tbilisi, the capital where we were hosted by the Young Communists (Comsomol). Their leader was a very large man who treated us to the ritual supra (a meal of a dozen toasts) atop Mtatsaminda mountain. We all got very drunk and the Georgian interpreter kept saying, "The leader, she said ..." even though the leader was a very large man. It made us laugh and laugh. In the Georgian language pronouns aren't gendered.

We spent several days at a ski resort which was set up to be a place of rest and relaxation for average workers. It was weird to be there in the summer and there wasn't much to do. One day I walked into town and was tired so I tried to hitchhike back to the resort. I was picked up by a heavy equipment operator in some kind of land moving equipment. We communicated mostly in sign language. I found him very attractive and we found a common ground in sex. We could hardly talk to each other, lacking a common language, neither of us speaking much Russian since Georgian was his first language, but we could figure out sex.

One day our Georgian local guide, Katie, invited us to her family home. She was unusual because unlike most Georgians who had black hair, she was a redhead. She took us to a rather simple wooden house with just three rooms. She shared some bread and jam and tea with us and gave us a picture of a typical home, though I suspect it was her family's dacha, or summer home. This excursion was significant because many years later, I met her again in Tbilisi when I was doing exchanges between Atlanta and Tbilisi. Meeting her again reminded me that I had a long history with this particular country. I remembered her by her red hair and we were able to reconnect.

When the group left the Soviet Union we travelled by land into Poland. I left the group and I visited the site of the Jewish ghetto which had been burned down during WWII. I wanted to see it because I was curious about the experience of Jews in Poland during the war. In general the picture we have been given here was that the Poles were as hostile to the Jews as the Germans were, but recently I have become aware that there were also many Poles, especially in the rural areas, who protected Jews during that scary time. Whose truth?

I travelled alone down to Czechoslovakia where I stayed in Prague for two weeks. Sleeping in a university dormitory which was rented out in the summer months to traveling youth, I met many interesting people and was interviewed on Voice of America about what it was like to be a young woman travelling alone. The producers of the program thought that it would encourage other young Americans to visit Eastern Europe to hear that I had been comfortable in my travels.

In the hostel I met Eliot, a young Jewish Englishman. His visa ran out before mine, and we agreed to meet in Vienna and travel together to Yugoslavia where he had family. When I arrived in Vienna, Eliot hadn't reserved a place for me to stay so I ended up sleeping in the Westbanhof train station. It was probably the scariest night I spent in my travels. We homeless people slept on cots arranged in a large open room. I worried about my suitcase lying next to my bed. The authorities threw us out early in the morning and I found Eliot and we left for Yugoslavia.

We were hitchhiking and doing fine until we reached the border. He dealt with arrangements in Austria because his Yiddish was understandable to those who spoke German. I had to deal with people on the Yugoslav side in my broken Russian. At the Yugoslav border, we were stuck, although we had no difficulty going through immigration and getting visas. The local people would not take hitchhikers. After many hours we talked someone into giving us a ride to the train station in the next town.

Eliot had family on the island of Krk, so we headed for Lubliyana. From there we could take a ferry to the island. We wanted to spend a few days on the coast, so we needed to find a room. There was an agency that directed visitors to vacant rooms in people's homes that could be rented by the night (an early version of Airbnb). Now my language skills were required. I explained to the clerk that we wanted two rooms for three days, using Russian, I thought. After some tries he understood what I wanted, but he asked me, "What language are you speaking?" There is enough commonality in Slavic languages that I was understood, but I spoke so badly, I suppose that he couldn't tell which one I spoke. It was probably best that my Russian wasn't good since my appearance was so Russian with my long blond braids, I probably would have been less welcome than I was as a bumbling American.

Eliot kept kosher, so we ate a lot of eggs and tuna fish. One night I suggested we eat in a restaurant and he ordered the "fish." Someone at the next table pointed out that it was "inkfish" (squid). Uh, oh, not kosher! I got to eat both meals. I had left my raincoat on the train. Knowing I had several more months to go in Europe I was very worried about not having a coat. When we got back to the train station, they had kept it in the lost and found. I was very impressed by the honesty.

From Yugoslavia, I went to Geneva by myself where I thought I might get a job with the International Labor Office as my father had contacts there from his time in Germany at the end of the war helping to reestablished labor unions as part of the Marshall Plan. After interviewing for the job in my very rusty French, I was waiting for a phone call telling me whether or not I got the job. Instead when the phone rang, it was my mother who asked me to meet her in Paris. She was trying to decompress after the stress of the NCNP convention in Chicago. I didn't regret leaving Geneva, even though it is a beautiful city. I was afraid of working in an environment where I would have to speak French on a daily basis.

Mother had had a difficult time with the NCNP conference. There had been a lot of infighting and she was exhausted. The issues of racism and representation overwhelmed people's ability to listen to each other and make choices based on the greatest likelihood of success. The left has often been hamstrung by in-fighting where the participants forget the bigger picture in an attempt to feel powerful. This was 1967 when so many groups were working to be liberated, but couldn't see their common interests.

I agreed to meet mother in Paris but thought I would go to Italy first. I visited Florence which I loved and Rome which I hated.

I had telling interactions with men in both cities. In Florence, I met Mario who was very flirtatious and took me to places I would never have seen otherwise, but respected my setting limits on our intimacy. In Rome, I was followed and catcalled till I stopped one man to ask him why he was being so obnoxious. He told me that catting after unattractive women paid off because they were so flattered by the attention they would allow him to do things that attractive women wouldn't. That was a horrible slap in the face.

I met my mother at Orly airport outside Paris. She rented a car and we drove through the countryside. I learned why the Impressionists painted the way they do: the light is really like that! But my mother had no soft edges. She was constantly telling me what to say and what to do. After three months of muddling through on my own all over Eastern Europe, I was not prepared to be told what to do every minute.

Mother didn't speak French and kept saying, "Kathy, tell the man…"

One day in a hotel I told her to "fuck off."

She was outraged and mortified that I had cursed her out in English in a public place.

I said, "If they could understand English, I wouldn't have to be translating for you." And stomped away. She made me promise to see a psychiatrist when I got back to the States.

Before she left Paris, she set me up in a pensione with all young French men from the provinces who were staying there to attend school nearby. I was to take French classes at the Alliance Française. Most of the other students at the Alliance spoke better English than French, so we hung out together after classes and spoke English and wandered around the city. The French men I ate my meals with wouldn't slow down in their speech enough for me to understand them and they just laughed at me when I tried to speak. I did get to visit occasionally with my French friends from the Soviet ship, but the party that Juliette gave where I got to meet her friends was a farewell party. I was perfectly glad to leave Paris and go to England for a couple of weeks before leaving for Liberia where I met David.

Liberia is the ugliest and most hypocritical place I have been. One of their most important national holidays is the day an indigenous girl warned the Americo-Liberians that they were going to be attacked. The Americo-Liberians were therefore able to annihilate the indigenous people first!

It was also horribly hot and humid, rainforest jungle. David lived in a small village several hours drive from the capital where he was teaching school. The book *Zinzin Road*, written by another Peace

Corps volunteer, tells the story well. I spent my days waiting for evening when I could stand under the jerry-rigged shower (a bucket with a hole and a shower head hanging above my head) and cool off enough to sleep.

After a month in Liberia, we spent David's "vacation" in the Canary Islands. We didn't get along at all. He was suffering from hepatitis, and could hardly stay awake. The Canary Islands seemed like another place filled with hypocrisy: tourists with lots of money benefitting from the poverty of the indigenous people who lived in shacks built against the sides of unfinished hotels. We visited a volcano there. That was pretty. Later when I played Pele in the Healing Theater play I found the photos of me sitting near the volcano with my hair loose over my shoulder and thought, "I could be a young Pele." But I wasn't fierce or independent enough at that time. I was still caught up in thinking I had to have a husband to be grown up.

It was a hard time and I can't understand from this perspective why I would have considered marrying him after that time together. He had no initiative which proved true when he returned to the States about a year later. The only thing he was clear about was wanting to stay out of the army and not have to fight in Vietnam. My mother helped him by getting an orthodontist to provide him with braces which couldn't be managed by army dentists so he didn't pass the physical.

I returned to New York City in January 1968 to begin taking graduate classes in political science at Columbia University. That was the year that Mark Rudd led a movement to take over the campus for Students for a Democratic Society. I was in a hospital bed with a fracture to the lumbar vertebrae that was a result of a bicycle accident.

I was riding my brother's bicycle through Riverside Park. I wasn't that stable on it as it was the first ten speed I had ever ridden. Suddenly, a young boy on a bike ran into me from the side. I fell down hard and was screaming in pain when a police officer came and called an ambulance. Since I was a student at Columbia University, they took me to that hospital. I had a compression fracture of the lumbar vertebrae. I was in the hospital for over a week and then in a brace for a few months.

Therefore, I couldn't participate in the takeover of the University. That summer as I was limited in what I could do by the back brace, I chose to stay in New York City to make up the incompletes I had earned in my graduate classes and began volunteering with AFS/International Scholarships, where I ended up working for three years. I never continued at Columbia after that summer, but I did take a typing course which has been useful to me ever since.

Even though I was engaged to David, that summer I corresponded with Eric. He was serving in the army in Washington, DC and like me, engaged to be married. I had a dream about him and wrote to him. He wrote back and asked if he could come and visit me in New York. By now, Eric had his signature handlebar mustache and cowboy boots. He had given up his belted blue jacket that matched the color of his eyes for a military uniform, but he still had the sparkle in his eye and thoughtful comments to share. My parents were in Amagansett and I was alone in their apartment.

I didn't know at the time that I had malaria from my time in Liberia. I only knew that every so often I would have a terrible fever and get slightly delirious. We went to see a play by Tennessee Williams in Greenwich Village and I felt fine when we started, but before the evening was over, I was feverish and disoriented. It didn't keep us from making love.

Meanwhile, the NCNP had collapsed with the death of Martin Luther King in April and mother ended up being in charge of the national fund raising campaign for Eugene McCarthy (no relation to Joseph McCarthy, but confusing to many people). With Howard Stein, Chairman of the Dreyfus Fund, she raised one million dollars from June 1 to September 15 of 1968. When she died in 1985, I found the entire card file on every donor to that campaign. The files had been stored in the closet of the room I had slept in as a child. I was surprised they were still there since she had cleaned up her apartment of all useless junk before she died. Was I to find some use for this information or was it that she just couldn't let go of that experience even after more than fifteen years?

Mother was in Chicago again for the Democratic Party Convention in 1968 as part of McCarthy's campaign while I was outside protesting. I had spent time that summer canvassing for McCarthy in Wisconsin but didn't have the status to be inside the hall as she was. That convention was very tempestuous. Thousands protested outside the meeting halls and police were brutal. I met up with one of my international buddies from college, a young man from Nigeria who wasn't able to go home because of the fighting there. He hadn't heard from his Igbo relatives for years and didn't know if he would ever be able to go home. He certainly wasn't going to risk being arrested in this melee. We were careful.

This was the first election I was old enough to vote in. In 1968 you had to be twenty-one years old to vote. That was changed to eighteen when young people said, "If we can be sent to die in Vietnam through the draft we should be able to vote for those who make those decisions." When I went to the polls in New York, I wanted to write in McCarthy. I got to the head of the line and asked, "How do I write in?" The poll worker didn't know. Voters lined up behind me began to get upset at the hold up. One said, "That is Teresa Liss' daughter." They all started cheering me on and insisting that the poll worker let me write in. They knew my mother from her campaigning in our apartment building.

❧

In the fall of 1968, instead of continuing with graduate school, I took a job at AFS, working with foreign students living in American homes for a year and going to high school. It was a wonderful job. David came back from Liberia that winter and we found an apartment on 21st St. and 8th Ave. in NYC. It was a quick time in my life. I travelled to Indiana and Illinois where I had students placed and got to know the mid-West. I learned about TPing and proms and the kind of student life I had never known in my New York City high school. I worked with young people from all over the world and made many friends. I also got to know a lot of wonderful people in the mid-west who were committed to world peace through understanding and to supporting these young people.

I rode my bicycle to work on 43rd Street and Second Avenue and carried it up the three flights of stairs when I got home. The apartment was only two rooms, a living room with a kitchen alcove and a bedroom. There was a sliding barn door between the rooms and the kitchen sink was too small to wash a full size dinner plate. I washed dishes in the bathtub.

I didn't bring AFS students home for a meal because I was afraid they would think badly of me for living with a man I wasn't married to. My mother said, "Don't get married; just keep living together. He is not mature enough to be a good partner for you."

We got married anyhow. Mother arranged for a judge friend of hers to legitimize our relationship. David and I wandered in Central Park on the day of the wedding in preparation and got stoned on marijuana. We returned to my parents' apartment for the small brief ceremony and then we had a reception for mother's extended family at the Plaza Hotel. I guess I wasn't really sure it was the right thing to do since I left the reception in a cab, nauseated and throwing up.

During my time at AFS, I got close to many of the forty or so students a year I placed in American homes in Indiana and Illinois. David and I decided to visit Europe and spent time visiting five of the students I had worked with in the Netherlands, Germany, Norway and Yugoslavia. Since David was of Norwegian ancestry, we stopped in two homes in Norway, one in Oslo and one on the coast. When I opened my "Pandora's box" of old letters, I found many letters I had saved after I left AFS from students all over the world. They influenced me as much as I influenced them.

I first recognized my prejudice against Germans when working for AFS. My first year, the youngest student was Klaus Rausche. He was also in the group on the bus I chaperoned at the end of the school year as we travelled back across the US to the port of embarkation. It seemed to me that Klaus was always right next to me. One day we were riding in a packed car and he was truly squished beside me. I asked, "Why are you always near me?" He said simply, "Because I like you."

How could I resist? So when I went to Europe with David, Klaus was one of the five AFSers I visited. We only spent two days in Germany because I really wasn't comfortable there, having been raised with a prejudice against Germans in a Jewish family who lived through the war. My mother was liberal in many ways, but one time she had thrown a German visitor out of our house. She had also objected to my buying a VW saying, "It had Jews rather than pistons to make it go."

⋞⋟

David hated living in New York City. He hated his work as a VISTA volunteer teaching in a school in Harlem. It was nothing like being a Peace Corps teacher in Liberia. There was no appreciation, no reward of getting close to his students. Basically he went on a sit down strike and refused to go back to school for almost two weeks.

Frustrated, I asked him, "What do you want?"

Not looking at me, he replied, "To go back to graduate school in anthropology."

I agreed we could do this, but I would get the final say as to which town we moved to. He applied to three New York State colleges and I chose Buffalo because I had just been there for AFS arranging for an end of year conference and knew that I could use my AFS connections to find work.

The first year in Buffalo I took a job as a secretary in the Department of Counselor Education at the University. The one woman professor had written her thesis on the vocational development of women and before the days of computers, I retyped it many times on an old IBM Selectric typewriter. What did that say about the consciousness of this professor?

I cut out an editorial from the first edition of Ms. Magazine that talked about a woman wanting a wife to do all the things a man expected his wife to do. I hung it on the wall by my desk with a postscript in my handwriting saying, "And then I want a secretary." I did learn quite a bit about counseling from talking with both professors and students. I resented that they didn't think I was as intelligent as they were because of the role I was playing. I even took courses at the State University College in counseling. I fully experienced the exploitation of low paid workers and the lack of respect just because of the role that one is playing and the gender one has. Whose truth?

I was the primary bread winner for our family and did all the housekeeping and cooking while David was going to graduate classes in anthropology and reading lots of science fiction. Eventually it seemed he was reading more science fiction and less anthropology.

In December 1972, my mother invited me to join her on a trip to San Francisco where I had two friends who had lived with my parents at different times in the New York apartment. Pat was my best friend in college and stayed with my parents in New York City when I was in Europe and Africa immediately after graduation. Tim was my best friend at AFS/International Scholarships and he and his boyfriend stayed in my parents' apartment while they were working in New York before moving to California. Again, my mother was deeply engaged with my friends while I was absent.

Mother had given up on dad joining in her travel plans and asked me along to San Francisco. We stayed with Pat. We were at a party at Tim's house when we got the call that my father had died. He was at a Democratic Party meeting and stood up to speak and fell down dead. Mother spent the evening changing our travel arrangements to leave the next day and I spent it filling her cigarette packages with marijuana to take back on the plane. David didn't join us in Amagansett for the funeral and burial.

Despite her constant demeaning of dad to me, when he died, mother mourned. In her typical way of not being able to express feelings directly, she injured her leg and had to spend a couple of weeks in bed. After almost forty years together, dad's death was a real loss for her. For me, it was a wake-up call about not staying with a man whom I didn't fully enjoy.

Before dad died I had met Joseph at the North Buffalo Food Coop. I had helped to start this coop next to the campus of the University of Buffalo. One day I was hanging out where we had set up couches in a conversational arrangement. A tall striking red headed man in his mid twenties strode in with a box containing jars. He was introduced to me as "the honey man." Curious, I asked him, "What's your interest in the Coop?"

Sitting down next to me on the couch, Joseph said, "Every week I go to a farm and pick up the honey which is sold here. What are you doing here?"

Very attracted to this handsome man, I replied, "I am working in the Department of Counselor Education at the University as a secretary while my husband works on a graduate degree in anthropology. Are you a student here?"

"I'm a sophomore in English and psychology."

"You seem a bit old to be an undergraduate."

"I went into the service after high school and served in Korea for two years. Now I'm married and my wife, Paula, works as a technician in a medical office."

We shared our interests in alternative life styles. I was very involved with putting together a People's Yellow Pages for the town that was published by the *Buffalo Rainy Day Sun.* The booklet says in its introduction, "One thing everyone who worked on this project agreed upon was that people working together can create and control their own institutions. We see this publication as proof of that." To carry out this project, we formed the "Buffalo New Community Council." I also had a radio show on the campus public radio station where I spoke about my vision for a more cooperative and democratic system to replace the competitive world I was living in. Joseph, too, wanted to be part of something larger which was why he had taken on responsibilities for the coop. He had visions of a better society that he shared with me. We exchanged contact information.

He stayed on my mind and I fantasized about him after my father died. I thought, "Why not invite Joseph and Paula over for New Year's Eve?" David and I were close to another couple who lived in a housing coop. Ed was in the anthropology department and Rene was a social worker. I thought the six of us could have an interesting evening. Ed and Rene, Joseph and Paula and the two of us got together for a quiet evening in our apartment above the garage walking distance from the main campus. At some point in the evening, we were all lying on the queen sized water bed watching "the ball drop" on television. I was lying next to Joseph and we began touching each other in promising ways. His fingers were light on my bare skin. He smelled delicious from the pipe tobacco which he smoked which reminded me of my father when we lived in Maryland. I felt the heat from his body. As things progressed, the six of us redivided so that I was with Joseph, David was with Rene and Ed was with Paula. Uh, oh! The only pairing that lasted in those days of "open marriage" was me and Joseph.

My father's death had left me thinking, "Why did my mother stay with my father for so long complaining about him and now that he is dead, she is mourning him?" I knew I did not want to end up in the same situation. And I clearly was headed there. David was a very sweet man, but he was not ambitious. His main interest was in avoiding the draft and getting out of New York City which, as a small town Wisconsin boy, he found overwhelming. At 6'4" he towered over my 5'2", as did Joseph. Both were fair in complexion and reminded me of my father in appearance. But Joseph was much more ambitious and intellectually stimulating.

David had retreated to his study where he read science fiction that relied on cultural differences to make a good story. This was not going to get him a master's degree. This was not going to give me the opportunity to follow him to back to Africa. I had imagined that the way I would get to travel to Africa was to accompany David while he did anthropological research. Despite my feminism, I couldn't see a way to get there independent of a man.

Joseph was working hard on his poetry and studying psychology which he saw as leading to a career in counseling. He was far more exciting. He had a vision for himself. This was a person I could hook up with and realize my vision of having a working partnership with a lover, even if it didn't include travel to Africa.

As the spring progressed, Joseph and I spent more and more time together. One time I was with him in our apartment when David came home unexpectedly. Although we had agreed on an open marriage, he was very upset and retreated even more. Joseph and I began spending our time together at his apartment where Paula's work had a more regular schedule.

By my second year in Buffalo, my contacts through AFS helped me to find a job as a study abroad coordinator at State University College. Again I was immersed in a world of people with different norms and beliefs. Often international students said to me things about America which were uncomplimentary, and I was completely comfortable hearing those things because I generally agreed with them. I enjoyed the work in the International Studies department and being on the campus at State University College. Moreover the job was only part time. This gave me much more time to visit with Joseph.

I walked into Joseph's sunny living room to find him smoking his pipe and reading poetry. The sun beams filtered through the windows lighting the room with a soft glow. I smelled his pipe tobacco wafting in the air. We talked about our common interests, poetry, psychology, books we were reading, movies we had seen. It was a stimulating "yes/and" conversation where our ideas built on each other. I felt seen and appreciated for my intellect. Sitting together on the couch, he began to caress me. As always, I responded with enthusiasm.

His hands were seductive, fondling me in ways that I enjoyed more because I saw him as so beautiful and our verbal interactions were so stimulating and connecting. It was always an exploration. He was discovering me as I was discovering my own eroticism. We moved into the bedroom, just a mattress on the floor. He kept petroleum jelly next to the bed for interesting experiments. Had he used it the night before with Paula? I didn't care. I was entranced. Whatever he wanted to do sexually, I accepted. He was very inventive.

He not only taught me about ways to be sexual I hadn't experienced before; he also taught me to change the spark plugs on my car and change a tire. When I practiced the latter, he sat on the curb and coached me. Someone walked by and chastised him for watching while I did the work, but I appreciated that he allowed me to learn by doing without taking over.

This was also the 70s where I became involved in the women's movement. Here I was being totally absorbed in a crazy extramarital affair and also going to women's consciousness raising meetings where we talked about our empowerment and looked at our cervix with a speculum and mirror. I think I was not the only one who confused women's liberation with the right to be as promiscuous as men in our intimate relationships. I resented the characterization of women as less interested in sex than men and believed that the freedom to exploit the weaknesses of the other gender was liberation. Since men were taught that it was masculine to sleep with any woman who was willing, I could use that to feel better about myself by noting how many men had chosen to have sex with me. I was no longer "fatso Lisso."

The third summer we were in Buffalo, David and I went to Amagansett to visit my mother. At the same time, Paula had decided she was tired of supporting a husband who spent his energy with other women. We let Joseph stay in our apartment while he was waiting to get a place of his own. He picked the tomatoes of our landlord thinking they were ours. When we returned, we had to apologize to our landlord for the mistake. Joseph went on to his own place.

But I was scared. Scared that Joseph would find someone else to be in a steady relationship with if I wasn't available whenever he wanted to get together. I was afraid I would lose him as I had my father (first by his emotional withdrawal when he lost his job and then by his death before we had reconciled). Joseph clearly had a history of multiple relationships and would have the opportunity to connect with other women. I decided to separate from David. While I was looking for a place to move into, I lived with Paula for a couple of weeks. She had a beautiful palomino horse she had stabled close to Buffalo and we went riding together. The stable had an older horse that I could ride. She looked lovely with her long light blond hair matching the color of the horse as they rode through the fields. She was very sweet and gentle just as the horse was. But the horse stepped on my foot one day when I walked too closely behind him and I fainted from the pain. It should have been a warning.

I enjoyed much of my time with Joseph. He was very competent but never took over. I felt like an independent woman who could take care of herself and not have to depend on a man to make my life work. I was living in my own apartment and making my own way in the world. Describing Joseph in the play I did years later, I talk about how he has the best of everything, "His leather couch, stereo, yellow 240 Z. I love his hairy chest, lean muscular body. We walk in stride with each other. He takes off his glasses to be closer to me when we have sex. I enjoy his curiosity; the sense that he is discovering me. It makes me feel beautiful. He calls me 'earth mother.'"

By now, Joseph was a senior. I was still working at State College. He began seeing other women even though I had moved away from David to be more available to him. I felt I had to accept this as we had started out non-monogamous. The hurts I felt when I knew Joseph was with another woman led me to put this poem by Robert Graves on my refrigerator.

> *SYMPTOMS OF LOVE*
> *Love is a universal migraine*
> *A bright stain on the vision*
> *Blotting out reason.*
>
> *Symptoms of true love*
> *Are leanness, jealousy,*
> *Laggard dawns;*
>
> *Are omens and nightmares*
> *Listening for a knock,*
> *Waiting for sign:*
>
> *For a touch of her fingers*
> *In a darkened room,*
> *For a searching look.*
>
> *Take courage, lover!*
> *Can you endure such grief*
> *At any hand but hers?*

What did I have to believe about myself in order to accept this painful relationship?

Eventually, Joseph decided he wanted to go to graduate school. We had no discussion about this. It was clear I wasn't figuring into his plans. So, I decided to apply to graduate school myself. This was my fourth attempt to get a graduate degree having hated each of the three previous programs. I chose The School for International Training which had an experiential degree and seemed much better suited to me than the regular classroom program. I was lucky. The international studies program I worked for at State College was disbanded (primarily to get rid of my boss who was not well liked) and I was able to get unemployment insurance for the six months I was in Vermont.

Meanwhile, Joseph was accepted to a Masters in psychology program in Atlanta, Georgia. We were going to be apart whether I stayed in Buffalo or not.

&

Mother lived another thirteen years after my father died and continued her political work, mostly by supporting Democratic candidates for local offices. She continued to organize fund-raisers using her connections to people of wealth and notoriety. Some of her successful campaigns including Joyce Burland as Suffolk County Legislator and Bill Ryan and Bella Abzug, New York Congresspersons and Ted Weiss, New York City Councilperson. There was a point at which the Suffolk County Democratic Party checked with her if she would support a candidate before moving forward because they knew that if she was on board, they could raise the money needed for the campaign.

I recently sent to my brother two prints by Jimmy Ernest (a famous American artist, son of Max Ernest) which he had offered to auction for one of her fund raising events. They have personal inscriptions to mother. She was especially good friends with his wife, Dallas, and travelled to Sedona, Arizona to stay with them more than once. She was well connected. Along with the theater, film and television people she had come to know while running the Inn in Amagansett, she had her academic and political luminaries on the left she worked with on her causes.

By the time I left Buffalo to go to graduate school, I had gotten some distance from my mother. She had met Joseph and liked him a lot, but was also supportive of my creating a career for myself. She had a Masters degree and thought it would be a good thing for me, too. I was financially independent of her by then and so she had fewer strings to pull. I had a substantial amount of international travel under my belt and several years experience working with international students. It looked like majoring in International Administration made sense.

"If we are to achieve a richer culture, rich in contrasting values,
we must recognize the whole gamut of human potentialities,
and so weave a less arbitrary social fabric,
one in which each diverse human gift
will find a fitting place."

- Margaret Mead

CHAPTER SIX

THE GRADUATE PROGRAM I ATTENDED AT THE SCHOOL FOR International Training (SIT) in Brattleboro, VT began a very intense period of change for me. I turned twenty-eight just before starting the program. It was the completion of four seven year periods of life, said to be a turning point in people's lives. After several months in the program, I wrote to the director of the program I worked for in Buffalo and said,

"I want to facilitate growth and learning in others such that they will be better able to take personal responsibility in working together to produce synergistic effects. I bring to this certain skills: an ability to organize and manage information and ideas, to find and use resources, to initiate and take responsibility for programming and for producing some changes...relinquishing my desire to have authority, control, whatever; while still feeling a sense of responsibility for the end product...The end product does not have to be what I first imagine, simply to represent growth."

That commitment to catalyzing growth in myself and others has stayed with me for a lifetime.

I talked with a friend from that program recently as I was rereading his letters and remembered how significant those months together were. We agreed that it was one of the most intense times of our lives and the bonds formed among the 22 Intercultural Training (ICT) students were so important in learning the value of community. We were all so different from each other, but we blended into a strong group.

One big lesson for me was learned in the process of our "community meeting." The "course" was called "community development." We were to come up with a project that cost no more than $2,200 that would serve as our "community development" project. The staff did not participate in our meetings. It was up to us as a group to make a decision. One day after we had chosen a facilitator, she called on Earl. I started to speak. Earl said, "Is your name Earl?" I was squashed. It hasn't stopped me from my childhood pattern of interrupting, but I try harder not to do that.

Another issue was, "What exactly does 'community' mean?" Could we do something just for members of our group? Did it have to be for the whole SIT community? Or should it be for the Brattleboro community? For some reason we didn't want to ask the staff or perhaps they refused to answer the question. In any case, early on one member of the group wrote up a whole proposal of what we should do. People immediately resisted, feeling left out of the process. We discussed the possibilities for weeks and finally chose something very like the proposal, but it couldn't be decided by just acclaiming the suggestion of one person. Everyone needed input and the one hour a week meetings were too short to decide quickly. This increased my understanding of the importance of process.

The project we chose was to work with the local schools providing programs about international subjects. I don't remember the details, just that having a car, I was involved in much of the presenting because I could get into town. I believe this made me feel more connected to the town of Brattleboro than I would have otherwise. The contra dancing I learned during that time has become a large part of my life and where I find community now.

We lived together on campus, sharing rooms, meals in the cafeteria, partying together. One of my best memories was listening to David Elliot sing the songs he wrote. I have the lyrics to many of them still and can hear his voice in my head as I read them. "You come to me, head hanging down, looking like some child...I want to see you smile." I believe this was written with me in mind. I felt able to be vulnerable there and let people see my feelings. I even have a picture of me reading poetry in the "coffee house" we created for ourselves and other students. To share something as personal as my writing publically was a big step for me, since I had grown up with my mother always correcting my writing.

Another highlight was working as a team to create the intercultural communication course. Several of us who were particularly interested in process and training worked together with staff to design the exercises and activities we used to teach our classmates about cultural differences. We got to practice by presenting to our peers and used the exercises which had been used by the school for years in training Peace Corps volunteers before they went overseas. I increased my self confidence in presenting in public and came away unafraid to speak in front of groups, something I understand now to be a great fear of many people and a skill which has served me well over my career. I wrote in my journal,

"The effective transition from one's own culture to the host culture is the result of the process of altering one's behavior (but not values) which permits one to feel at ease with oneself in the host environment by being able to meet one's own basic needs and by being able to communicate readily and comfortably with host nationals without loss of one's original cultural identity."

One of the exercises was too scary for me and I avoided it by some medical excuse. Each student was dropped off for 24 hours in a town with which they weren't familiar. They had just the coin it took to make an emergency phone call. They had to reach out to people in a place they had never been before to find a place to sleep and to get fed. The ways people dealt with this varied greatly but almost everyone felt that it was an exercise that led to greater self awareness.

It is interesting to me that although I chose not to participate in this in Vermont, I found myself in that position when I arrived in Nairobi, Kenya for my internship. Luckily I had money in my pocket and the name of a hotel where I could afford to stay for a night before finding my way to the site of my internship! I wasn't willing to sleep under a bridge in Vermont or in Kenya. I have been privileged throughout my life to have enough money to cushion myself in difficult circumstances.

For some reason I can't remember, several of us got involved in a project to help people make career decisions. Larry Crockett was teaching at Windham College and he taught us a system of decision making based on identifying your skills, values and interests. We wrote up a proposal to develop it into a class for the ICT program. Recently I found a vision board I created for myself some years ago. Using what I learned at SIT, it is centered on "my work" and defines it as including, "teaching about conflict and cooperation; working cooperatively with others; promoting dialogue and win/win solutions; non-violent solutions for social change; supportive and empowering colleagues; I am supported in my work; flexible hours; stimulating; fun. I am the facilitator of the new polity." And perhaps most importantly, "Mother approves!" Even after she has been dead for 30+ years, I still wish for her approval.

Another learning from my time at SIT which I wrote in my journal and has carried through to the rest of my life was, "One reason I prefer talking with people with whom I disagree initially is that it requires that I clarify my and his values in exploring the disagreement. Often one discovers agreement, but in the process I have come to understand my own values and those of the other person better." This fits well with becoming a mediator and facilitator of controversial issues, which is what my career eventually became.

From that time to this, I have believed that communication is key to continued survival of humans. I quoted Robert Theobald, economist and futurist, "Controlling and benefitting from cybernation will be possible only if we learn to communicate more honestly and efficiently than we do today." What I say to begin most conflict resolution workshops is, "We can develop all the technology imaginable, but if we don't learn to communicate with each other in compassionate and collaborative ways, we will destroy humanity."

In evaluating my strengths I enumerated these, "self-reflective ability—able to assess and reassess my abilities and performance and the resources available for continued self development and adaptation to new circumstances." I included perseverance, reliability, follow up and through, organization and leadership, ability to learn and to find and use necessary resources. I was aware of my limitations, particularly needing approving feedback.

It is interesting to me in rereading my "independent study project" where I wrote about how I have grown as a facilitator how much this influenced my life after graduate school. I wrote about the characteristics which got in the way of my participating effectively in groups, which I now see as mostly Jewish patterns: interrupting, pushing my ideas forward before people are ready and then getting hurt when they aren't accepted and withdrawing. I write about increased self-confidence from actually leading exercises and activities with groups which has become the basis for all the work I did subsequently, whether it was career development or conflict resolution. I learned so much at SIT. It was such a supportive environment. I felt so welcome and seen.

The notes I took in my notebook and journals during that period help to reflect my thinking. I wrote,

"As I become more 'emotionally mature' I feel I am better able to delegate responsibility and use my self-confidence to temper my enthusiasm and energy. I tend to be rather serious about most things; however, I can generally get sufficient perspective on a situation to see the humor in it unless it threatens my essential sense of myself. The more a situation feels like an emergency, the calmer I become."

My motto at the time was, "Not to decide is to decide not to." Looking at making life choices I wrote,

"Having made the choice to enter the stream, unwilling to choose to stop and pull up on the side. See a fork coming—choice —shall I paddle on one side or the other? Shall I not paddle at all and just see where I go? Does it make any difference? I can see such a small way further downstream anyhow with all the bends in each fork. On what basis would I make a choice? From here each fork looks equally appealing, though I realize they will lead in quite different directions. I suspect each will lead to the sea sooner or later. Perhaps one will be wider (more other streams joining it) one may be smoother (lacking the excitement of shooting the rapids). Even if I see some signs of the immediate future choices, that tells me nothing of what may come a mile, a year, further along. Is there any point in paddling?"

I was struggling with making choices, particularly about which internship I should pursue. In the end, I chose to go to Kenya with Friends World College for a year. I knew that Joseph was not happy with my choice and that I was risking the relationship by being gone for so long. He didn't end up going to graduate school for an entire year after I started in Vermont. For the six months I was at SIT, he didn't get involved with anyone else. We visited with each other a few times, sometimes in Buffalo, sometimes in Vermont.

When I told him I was going to Kenya for at least six months for my internship, he was very unhappy about it. But I knew going to Kenya was the right thing for me to do. I was torn. I still thought that being with the right man was important, but I had yearned for a way to spend time in Africa and this seemed like the right opportunity. David seemed like he might be able to carry me there in his tail winds. Here I was having the opportunity on my own.

The last time Joseph visited me on campus at SIT, he started a flirtation with Terri, whom I considered my best friend on campus. I found a letter I had written him at the time in which I said,

"She found herself unable to extend to you the friendship she would have liked because she felt so threatened by the evident sexuality of your come on...Your behavior this weekend reaffirmed my belief that in the end it jeopardizes my friendships to allow you the opportunity to know my friends. This is unacceptable. I realize that because of our intimacy, you no longer find it rewarding to flirt with me—there is nothing left to conquer. However, I see no reason that I should have to suffer watching you exude that honey at others...You expect to be given great leeway in pursuing your sexual appetite, but don't realize that that activity can effectively alter the environment such that other people's freedom to relate as they wish is hampered."

I have re-read letters sent to me while I was in Kenya from friends in the ICT program and can see how we supported one another in our very different situations—from David S. who was working for Warren Wilson College in Swannanoa, near where I live now to David E. who was in the Pacific Islands living in a hut. The relationships I formed in the program have led me in many directions, but probably most significant later experience was when my friend, Terri, told me to go to Insight Training. She had been instrumental in arranging for the Teacher in Space when the shuttle blew up and a big part of her recovery was doing Insight. It became a big part of my personal growth also. That's for another chapter.

I made friends at SIT whom I love forever. I can see now how when Terri and I were in conflict, it was just a matter of two Jewish New Yorkers meeting head on. Staying connected with the two Davids is so sweet. Finding the songs written by David Elliot is lovely. He got me. And accepted me as I was. Knowing I had the relationship with Joseph during that period helped me not be desperate for a lover; so I was able to be friends and colleagues with men in ways that were difficult when I wasn't in love with someone.

"Leaving that which you love breaks your heart open.
But you will find a jewel inside,
and this precious jewel is the opening of your heart
to all that is new and all that is different,
and it will be the making of you—if you allow it to be."

- Jacqueline Winspear from "Leaving Everything Most Loved"

⟋⟍

CHAPTER SEVEN

I WAS AN AMERICAN IN KENYA KILLING MYSELF BIT BY bit and being reborn as I tried to find my soul in this stunning and challenging land of beauty and struggle, contrasts and contradictions. Here I learned that truth is in the paradox. The question of "whose truth?" was transformed into "how can I embrace all of reality?" The either/or I had learned from my mother with her progressive ideas eliminated the possibility of both/and. Kenya was a place of both/and.

Arriving in the Nairobi airport after many hours flying from Belgium, I came through immigration with my bags full of what I needed for a year. I looked around for someone with a sign saying, "Kathryn Liss." There was no one. I expected to be met. I wasn't. This was before cell phones and e-mail and I had no way to connect with Sam Kamui who was the director of the program that had offered me an internship.

After assuring myself that there was no one looking for me, I looked at the multitude of drivers competing for customers who would pay them for a trip into the city, dozens of black faces eager to make a few shillings. This was my second time in Africa, but the first time in East Africa. I knew I had to find my way into town somehow. "I guess I have to pick one of these drivers," I thought. "This is not the welcome I expected."

As someone who needs to be prepared, I had talked with people in advance who had visited Nairobi. I chose a driver and asked to be taken to Brunner's Hotel where I had been told by previous travelers I could get a reasonably priced place to sleep. Brunner's was a traditional English hotel from when the English ran the country. It had big oversized upholstered chairs in the lounge area and a dining room serving traditional dull English food. Later, it turned out to be a regular stopping off place for me. By paying a small amount of money, I was able to rent a clean bathroom with a tub full of hot water and towels and soap. Bliss!

On that arrival day, all I wanted was a bed. Once registered and having paid in the Kenyan shillings I had exchanged my dollars for in the airport, I was delighted to fall into the clean white sheets of a soft bed.

On awakening, I realized I had my first challenge: how to find Sam Kamui. I knew that his wife worked as the librarian at a small private college outside of Nairobi. I got help from the concierge and was able to place a call to his home. No answer. Now what?

I asked the concierge how to take the bus to Mrs. Kamui's college and if he would store my bags till I got back. I had very little money and didn't want to spend it on another taxi ride. He gave me directions to the bus stop which took me to the campus. I wandered around until I found the library and Mrs. Kamui. She was sitting behind the checkout desk in the library wearing a western style dress, busy helping a student check out a book. She was able to tell me where to find her husband. This was the only time I was to see her in the whole year I was in the country.

I went to the building where she had directed me and found Sam calmly engaged in writing a report. I expected him to apologize for neither meeting me at the airport nor making any arrangements for me on my arrival. There was no apology forthcoming.

Sam was a man of average build, about 5'5. He made no direct eye contact and seemed uncomfortable with me. He had gone to college in the U.S. and returned to Kenya, finding it hard to get a job in either place. He was physically unimposing.

We got in his aged Toyota and drove to Brunner's where I picked up my bags and we headed for Katheka Kai. It is about an hour's drive and I felt obliged to make conversation. He seemed reluctant to initiate speaking. I needed to know more about what I was getting myself into.

Leaning back in my seat, I asked, "What would it be helpful for me to know about the college and the students?" (Thinking, why do I even need to ask this question? Is this the way he treats students, leaving them at the airport without a way to get to the campus? How would I have found Katheka Kai if I hadn't found Sam? What kind of a start is this to a year in this country?)

Not looking at me, Sam said, "Well, things are going along. We have about a dozen students presently in the Kenyan center." (I thought, "He doesn't know exactly how many students he is responsible for?")

I was feeling frustrated already but tried to keep the conversation going. "Can you tell me something about the students who are here? What is going well? What problems should I be prepared to deal with?" Watching the unfamiliar cityscape go by, I was thinking, "Why do I have to keep prompting him? Why doesn't he just tell me what I need to know?"

We passed the tall buildings of Nairobi and moved into the countryside. It is beautiful county once outside the city. We passed the Ngong Hills where Karen Blitzen lived when she wrote *Out of Africa.* We travelled down the Nairobi-Mombasa road for about thirty miles before turning off to the left toward Machakos, the nearest town to where I would be staying on the coffee plantation called Katheka Kai.

Sam gripped the wheel tightly as he drove, "Most of the students are placed in projects. Bruce is on Katheka Kai with his leather working project and Lawrence is back on campus finishing up writing his journal. There are some teaching in Harambee schools and a couple who have gone out of Kenya and into other parts of East Africa. We'll pass Bruce's place on our way up the dirt road to the school's campus."

"What are the issues you have had with students?"

Reluctantly, Sam told me, "You know, we have had problems with students using marijuana. It is illegal here and students buy it and use it and then get in trouble with the law."

This really concerned me because I also used marijuana at this point in my life. I said, "Really, what have you done about this?"

Sam's reply was typical of his response to any conflicted situation, "I have told them that they absolutely cannot buy or use marijuana."

Eventually, we turned off the paved road and drove two miles up a dirt road past fields and groups of round thatched roofed houses. Sam pointed out Bruce's home and shop. At the crest of the hill, we stopped in front of a large square building, the former main house for the European coffee plantation owners which the college rented to house students as they arrived in the country and got oriented. The house was a typical plantation house, white stucco with a broad veranda overlooking the entrance road, planted all around with flowering bushes. There were several steps up to the porch and Sam carried my bags up there, suggesting that I explore the various buildings and decide where I would like to have my room before settling my bags down. This was where I was to live for the next twelve months.

I looked out from the veranda back the way we had come and could see across the wide plains all the way to Mt. Kilimanjaro with its snow covered peak shining in the sun. We were on the crest of a small hill. Below were the fields and homes of the people who had worked this land for generations.

On my arrival, Sam gave me a letter that said,

"I assure you that each one of us (on the college council) will be more than ready to assist you, so please, don't hesitate to ask. We'll also do all we can to make every effort to make things as convenient to you as possible so that you can render more effective services to the Centre and hope that you can bear with us any unavoidable inconveniences that may be existing or might arise." [It also included the warning] "The government and the people of Kenya have extended a warm welcome to visitors from other countries to enjoy all the attractions available in the country as long as one does not break the laws of the land, as so is you."

Whose truth? Where was he or someone from the college when I needed him on arrival? Just how welcoming was this going to be?

The sky shone its bright blue and I thought, "This is going to be a very different year than I have ever spent before."

On my first morning, the quiet rays of sunrise brushed their fingers across me and I was awake. In the cool morning air, I was drawn to the east. Across the purple bougainvillea the dark hill hid its brilliant gem. The soft fingers reached up and touched nearby clouds with pink and gold, slowly spreading to the larger clouds overhead. Finally, the sky was bright and glowing; the cocks began to crow, the chatter of birds subsided momentarily and the first sliver of sun himself showed over the horizon, slipping ever more rapidly into view, its brightness pulsating against the black outline of trees on the top of the hill. I wrote in my journal, "God is with us." From that morning on I recognized that there was much beauty not made by the hand of man and to explore the possibility of a power greater than human.

⋙⋘

The day before, in order to choose a room for myself, I explored the buildings that the college rented from the coffee cooperative which now managed the plantation. The coop retained one small building of the compound for their office. There were several buildings some for sleeping, for office, for library, for cooking, for gatherings, most of them were around an open area which was planted with grass and flowering bushes. One, Swahili House, was off at a distance and this was where the students generally slept.

I chose a room next to the office and across from the library. It had one of the few bath tubs. When I wanted to bathe, I had to heat water in a metal tub on a jiko (a small metal container filled with coal) to fill the bathtub. It was a project. It was easier to just take a cool bath. Similarly for washing clothes. The toilet was across the open courtyard to the library. When students weren't around, I could keep the door to the toilet open and see the moon rise as the sun set on full moon nights.

Next to my bedroom was a small space in which I was able to keep a two burner propane stove on which I could cook something to eat. I learned to love eggs fried in butter on a piece of bread fried in the same skillet. When we ate as a group, we went to the main house. Food was prepared in a separate building (as is often true in hot climates) just behind the main house. In the mornings, when students were there for orientation, there was a cook, Gitaka, who prepared ugali (sort of grits) with papaya. There was a small refrigerator that ran on propane gas as did the generator which provided DC electricity to make pulsing light in the evening. It made a tremendous amount of noise and I learned how to turn it off but not to turn it on. It was more pleasant to read and write by the flickering light of the kerosene lantern than the pulsing light of the twelve volt DC bulb.

The room we ate in was large enough to have a table that a dozen students could sit at all at one time. When it was coffee harvesting season, it even had room for a big pile of freshly picked green coffee beans which we jumped into like children into a pile of orange and russet fall leaves at home. We used the space for language classes during orientation and dinner when there was a group around. Gathering together in the main house gave us a sense of community and allowed me to stay aware of the dynamics of the group. At night we played Hearts as a cooperative group. Whenever someone was about to win or lose, we worked together to keep the game going by passing the Queen to whomever needed it.

When it wasn't orientation and only a few students were on campus, I instituted a policy of having one student take responsibility for the evening meal each day. He or she prepared food for everyone to eat together in the dining room. This added to a sense of community which made living there much more pleasant. That person collected a few shillings from each person staying at the center and went into town with the combi (our VW van) to collect groceries for the day. They got vegetables from the market and staples like rice from the "dukas" or small stores selling dry goods. The meat was sold so fresh that the carcass was hanging in the butcher shop. The butcher cut a slice off by request. There was only one kind of bread and the flour was not always well sifted so that one found small bits of chaff in it. There was one kind of cheese. When we decided to make "pizza" which we craved, it was a strange concoction. The recipe book we had was very limited as well and didn't always match the ingredients we had available. My favorite thing to make was pound cake over a layer of fresh pineapple. We could get a pound of sugar and a pound of butter and a pound of flour and as much fresh pineapple as we could possibly eat.

Friends World College is a Quaker school using experiential learning as an approach to education. Like me, the students were required to find projects which gave them an opportunity to learn about the culture, nature and themselves. My job was to help them find those projects and then to evaluate the journals they kept to award college credit. I also kept records, including how we used petty cash. This was the area in which Sam and I had the most conflict. Our conflicts always left me feeling bad about myself and generally unresolved.

The college requires that students spend time in two

cultures not their own in order to realize that we live in a world of possibilities. However, you couldn't just mix and match cultural elements. Certain behaviors and beliefs were attached to each other in ways that were indivisible. Changes in one element required changes in other elements. Sam and the students and I were clearly from two different cultures. It was my task to bridge the gap and make things work for everyone. As a Quaker school, consensus was the decision-making process, but as Kenyans, the Faculty Council felt they should have the last word. That created the overarching conflict.

Most of the time there were some students at the school. Students were supposed to come to Katheka Kai to get oriented to Kenya, learned a little Kiswahili and go out and do projects in the country, keep a journal and then come back to have their observations evaluated. It was up to me to read their work, decide what courses they should get credit for and then send them on to their next part of the world or back to the U.S. for those who were only doing a semester abroad. Theoretically, except for about a month every six months, I should have been alone at Katheka Kai.

However, I was rarely alone. I called it Kathryn's home for wayward boys and girls. There was usually someone or other who needed a break from the foreignness or who was finishing early or had some medical need or whatever. They came by for a few days or longer and stayed on the campus and we shared the use of the kitchen. Sometimes it was students from the college and sometimes it was a Peace Corps volunteer who needed a break and had met a student who told them this was a place for respite.

One student, Bruce, had a hut built by the indigenous community near the home of our driver, Musyoko. For his senior project, he set up a leatherworking studio where he taught the local men to make leather handles for the baskets their wives wove so that they could be sold in the developed world for women who didn't carry their goods on their heads like the Kenyan women did. I could walk down to his house on moonlit nights to have company when there were no students living on the school's compound. He spoke the best Kiswahili and had been in Kenya the longest of any of the students. He was a great resource for me.

I noted that Kenya was a land of contrasts: no one with whom I felt I could be childlike, lean on, nuzzle against—yet always finding myself like a child, naïve, not understanding the language, unable to express myself, shy to intrude, feeling I don't have enough information to make a decision. Then I sensed my responsibility for situations. I was asked my opinion as an authority figure, expected to support students and expecting myself to be a model of responsible behavior for the students.

I could see that Kenya is a land of contrasts. From my point of view early on I saw that the blacks were so generous and had nothing; the whites were so selfish and shared nothing. I found myself giving a great deal (patience, time, things) to the Americans who asked for it and nothing to the Africans who waited to see what they could expect from me. All seemed to want things, feelings, responses from me, but none wanted what I most wanted to share with them, a close, caring intimate relationship in which we could grow together by learning from and about one another. Each seemed on his own trip and I could fit it or not. Sometimes I felt as if I spoke a different language from the students. So many things seemed unclear.

I began to write poetry to express my feelings,

Tight dark asses thrust cocks forward
Toward round swaying African women
Smooth hairless skin on arms
Faces unspeaking, expressionless
Young, pale men parading broad chests
Muscled arms to hold tall svelte women
Sensing eyes on long tan legs.
Salt and pepper beards of administrators
Concluding affairs on Nairobi streets
What's behind those faces?

Those bodies do not open to me
People knock against me
My body quivers, wanting
What?
Tenderness in abeyance
No eyes seek my soul
Where do I begin?

Twice students got into really bad trouble at the college. Sam, the director, who lived in Nairobi didn't want anyone using illegal drugs. His approach to control was to forbid what he disapproved of and assume that his rules would be followed. This was folly.

One night early in my stay, we were all sitting around playing Hearts and someone brought in a batch of brownies. I love chocolate and I ate my share. Suddenly I felt really weird. I went outside trying to find my way across the garden area that separated the buildings. I had been given a stronger drug than I had ever experienced before. It didn't occur to me at the time that it could have been marijuana in the brownies. I was looking for the toilet and couldn't get oriented. This was the first time I experienced marijuana in Kenya. It was incredibly potent. I was scared. That was when I decided I needed to take responsibility for the use of drugs at the school and see that people knew what they were getting into. I wasn't that much older than the students I was working with. I was twenty-eight when I arrived and they were in their early twenties for the most part.

I required that students only smoke marijuana on the campus so that they were less likely to get caught. (Remember Sam's admonition in his welcome letter about living within the laws of the country.) I kept the marijuana in my room which was the least likely to be searched. Students came and hung out with me and we smoked a joint or I had a couple of tokes at night before going to bed. I have found throughout my life that I have a lot more influence for the good by knowing what people for whom I have responsibility are doing and discussing with them ways to make it less dangerous than by making rules which won't be abided.

The second difficult situation was when a student got pregnant. Ellen was dating a local Indian young man, Sri. Indians make up the merchant class in Kenya and there was a large Indian community in Machakos. Sri found Ellen very exciting. He rode his motorcycle up to Katheka Kai to take her into town many evenings. Ellen came to me one day and said, "Kathryn, I'm pregnant and I don't know what to do. You know I can't have Sri's baby. He is betrothed to an Indian woman."

Ellen and Sri were certainly NOT going to have a child together. Abortions were illegal. This was very upsetting to me as I, too, had no idea of what to do. I suggested, "You should go see Dr. Jaffrey and ask him what you should do."

Dr. Jaffrey consulted with our students regularly and helped them find placements for their projects. He, too, was Indian and lived in Machakos. Ellen went to Dr. Jaffrey and together we worked out an abortion for her. I visited her in the hospital where she was recovering. It was all very hush-hush and I doubt Sam ever knew. Ellen and Sri continued to have a relationship and from then on she lived in Machakos rather than at Katheka Kai until she went back to the States.

There were some students I became very attached to, especially those from the group that came after I'd been there for six months. By then I was grounded in the environment and had persuaded the college council to let me start the orientation with having students stay in Kenyan homes where people spoke English for a few days before they started learning Kiswahili. I think that went well.

Jono, Barbara and Paula all came in the second wave in September. I was especially close to Jono and Barbara who were an item for a while. Then Jono was with Paula with whom I also got very close. We hung out mostly in my room next to the office and talked late into the night by the light of the kerosene lantern. Although I felt I could talk with them about many things, philosophy, life choices, even relationships, I never felt we were the kind of peer friends I would have if I were home, not so much because of difference in age, but because of the differences in roles. Certainly the second six months were easier than the first, but still I felt alone much of the time and spent many hours ruminating on the meaning of my life as well as supporting them in figuring out their own.

The first trip I took away from Katheka Kai was with one of the students, Lawler, to an area near Mount Kenya. Lawler had spent weeks on an island with no other people than her colleague Mary. They were doing a biological project recording the egg laying behavior of sea turtles. She modeled for me paying close attention to the environment around me. While we were there, we rode horses into the bush and got quite close to giraffe which were not put off by our odor as it was covered by the smell of the horses. We saw a magnificent waterfall which became my touchstone of an image of a place of retreat and peace for me for many years after. I wrote the following,

Waterfall tumbling down the side of the hill
Into the brown pool before me
Lying on my back in the crackling leaves
And twigs from seasons past
The sun already having burnt
My nose and cheeks from three midday hours
Riding a horse across shadeless plains
Here by the stream, the trees
Form an awning as they sway
In the breeze alternately
Shading and exposing me
To the bright rays.
Cobwebs formed in the spaces
Between twigs, branches cast no shadows.

Leaves shimmer as the light passes through.
The sound of the cicadas
Competes with the rushing water
My generator in the open, they
Do not produce light.
When riding across the open plain
There are two things you must beware of
The thorn tree which in its two hundred varieties
Distracts you on one side with the brilliant
Orange or green trunks and limbs
And on the other stabs you
With a low hanging branch as the horse
Passes smoothly under.
Then there are the animal holes
Which your mount steps in if
You are too busy watching giraffe
Or guinea hen trotting
To catch up with the others.

Later, I travelled with Barbara to Dar es Salaam. We could hitchhike as far as Mombasa, but after that, we had to take public buses which were crowded and unreliable. The bus that was scheduled to arrive at 11 a.m. showed up at 4 p.m. A lot of time waiting in a nowhere place.

Barbara was a stunning young woman. Tall and shapely with blond hair, she attracted a lot of attention which she did not like. People approached her and wanted to get close to her and she put them off. It was interesting to me to see the challenges of being beautiful were different from but similarly confusing as being short and pudgy. She only wanted to be loved for her good thinking and lovely soul while I sought approval for my looks. Isn't it a strange thing how we all get hurt but in different ways? Truth in the paradox.

I certainly learned as much from my students as they learned from me. We sat around in the evening and discussed all kinds of things, but in the end, I still felt less engaged with people than I was accustomed to and found myself looking inward more and seeing a bigger picture of the world in which there must be a higher power to explain all that humans had not created.

I struggled with relationships throughout my time in Kenya. It was a time of exploration of my relationships to myself, to men, to people in general and to a higher power. I didn't have to wait, as I had expected when I was married to David, to travel on the coattails of some man. Actually, I had left my man, Joseph, behind and the tug from him was a confusing force. I knew from my visit to Liberia with David that I wanted to go to East Africa, where there are cool breezes at 6,000 feet above sea level rather than the hot and humid jungle of West Africa. I had also known several Kenyan students when I worked at State University College in Buffalo. But being with Kenyans in Kenya was different from being with Kenyans in the U.S., even if they had been students in the U.S. at one time, as several of the men I got to know had been.

Probably the Kenyan I was closest to was Musyoko, our combi driver. Musyoko's compound was about a mile down the road from where I lived. He had three wives and more children than I could count. He was a young man by U.S. standards, probably in his early thirties. About 5 "10', he walked with pride. His dark skin shone with good health and he was generally cheerful and thoughtful. Always kind, he had clear boundaries and would not drive on Sunday which was his day off. He always wore a green hat called a kofia and a vest when he was driving. Unfortunately, he was not particularly mechanical and generally couldn't make repairs on the vehicle.

Musyoko. He was probably close to me in age. He lived in a group of houses called a "compound" that were occupied by his wives and children. As a "big man" (not in size but in influence) who actually had a money income, he had built a square house with a metal roof for his first wife, and left their previous round wattle house with a thatched roof for the second wife. The floors were all swept mud as was the clearing around each house. Each had a charcoal fire in a jiko in front on which was perched a black metal pot. Here the day's food was constantly cooking (the Kenyan equivalent of a crock pot): maize and beans grown by the women. During the day the women took whatever children were not in the Harambee ("pull together") school to the fields where they cultivated their crops.

Musyoko claimed he didn't speak English, but he understood much more than he would say. Instead of telling me I needed to learn Kiswahili, he came to me and asked if I would teach English to him and a couple of other men from the coffee co-op. So respectful of my role as "teacher." They called me "mwalimu," the word for teacher in Kiswahili. In the Wakamba language they called me "mwendi" (loved one). This was a lot better than being called Fatso as I had been in Amagansett, but it still marginalized me, set me apart from other people as I experienced when I visited Musyoko's compound for a party.

In our conversations using a mixture of English and Kiswahili, we learned about each other. I asked about his multiple wives. He stumbled through a response with words and gestures. "I chose my first wife. She said she needed help around the compound and chose another younger woman who was willing to follow my first wife's direction. I built a separate house for the second wife. I couldn't have another wife until I was able to provide her with her own home. The women share the tasks of caring for the children, preparing the food, tending the fields of maize and beans. If I am to have other wives, it will be at the request of the wives." Most of our conversations required lots of explanation with limited vocabulary.

After I had been there six months, Musyoko and I went to the Nairobi airport to pick up the next batch of students. On the ride back, the students were chatting with each other, commenting on what they were seeing, speculating on what their lives would be like for the next six months. That was really when I began to suspect that Musyoko could understand a lot more English than he let on. He listened to the conversations and heard how each student was relating to the others. He never interjected in the conversation. The students carried on for the whole hour and more that we drove from the Nairobi airport to the campus on the coffee plantation.

Later, Musyoko took me aside and told me what he thought would be useful for me to know. We were standing outside my room in the small grassed in area away from the students as they took their belongings into the Swahili House to set up their rooms. He told me with a serious and assured look on his face that one young man, Ford, would never make it in Kenya and that Jono would do well. I was surprised and wondered how he could make that judgment and whether it was accurate. I wished that we had enough vocabulary in common for me to follow up with questions about how he had come to that conclusion. Later, I saw the accuracy of his prediction as Ford turned out to be a total pain in the ass and Jono became a beacon for me and someone I stayed in touch with for many years after we all left Kenya.

One day, Musyoko invited me to a party being held on his compound in celebration of someone's wedding. I wrote this in my journal afterward,

"I watched once and then tried to serve, but everyone criticized me. I started in the wrong place, didn't serve enough, forgot to put in meat. Stood around the kitchen a lot but only two of the women would help and give me directions. They couldn't figure out why I couldn't repeat, but I never knew which house to bring the food to. Finally, we ate in the kitchen. The cooks had less than their share.

The women sit on the ground with their legs straight in front of them. Young people bumping to records. Men aggressive. Women shy. So much I can't get it all down...Musyoko knows more about cross-cultural training than I and I told him so. He said he wanted me to come because he knew I'd learn so much. I wish we had more shared vocabulary."

Friends and family came from all over to enjoy the food and fellowship. When I arrived at the compound, he was playing maitre d' and told each person where they should go. He sent me to join the old men because my status as a teacher entitled me to that position. I sat for a while in the room with the old men, but no one talked to me. They were talking in Kikamba and I could understand nothing. They didn't even try to talk to me in Kiswahili, although I probably wouldn't have understood anyhow. There was a lot of beer being drunk and cigarettes smoked and the energy in the room wasn't comfortable for me. These men were the most respected, so they got to sit in Musyoko's square house. The room was arranged with the straight backed chairs against the square walls. It is difficult with this arrangement to have a one on one conversation. There were other buildings on the compound where his wives and children lived. They were round with thatch roofs. Each building hosted a group of people similar in age and status. Some groups were in outside areas, still segregated by age and gender.

Periodically a woman walked into the old men's room bringing a plate of food to a man. After a while, I was frustrated and bored, so I asked one of the women to take me to where the adult married women (who were generally my age) were working preparing food. It was hot around the cook fires and there was a strong smell of goat meat. There were big pots cooking over the open fires of jikos. The pots contained goat meat, vegetables, and maize and beans, the staples of Kenyan diet. Women were moving around, joking with one another. I tried again to interact and still felt like an outsider, but at least the energy was more convivial.

One woman asked me if I had children. I said, "No" and she replied, "Pole sana." This means, "I am so sorry." This was a conversation I had consistently with women in Kenya. The fact of being almost thirty years old and not having a child was a sad thing for them. It left us very little to talk about as their children were the reason for their existence. Caring for children, seeing that they were fed, healthy, and educated was what was most important for these women.

The women cooking were up and busy most of the time, but when they took time out, they sat on the ground with their legs extended straight out. No woman would ever sit cross-legged as an open leg position would imply openness to sex. I sat with them, but it was very uncomfortable to sit without a back rest with my legs extended on the mud ground. I couldn't imagine how they could do this for long periods of time.

There was a man running around with little chits with the name of the person and what they were eating. I was glad when they sent me to take a plate of food into the men's room and I could move around off the ground. But when I brought the plate in where the men were sitting in chairs, I didn't know to whom to give the food even with the information on the little chit. The men teased me for being so foolish. They complained that I hadn't put in the right amount of meat and I felt very uncomfortable again. There was a specific order in which the men should be served which I wasn't following.

While I was out, I saw that the only mixed gender space was occupied by the young adult unmarried men and women. They had on high life records and were dancing together in a separate area. Children were somewhere out of sight while the older youth partied. If they had food, I didn't see it. There was probably beer being drunk, but I couldn't tell.

Failing to figure out where to deliver the food, I returned to the kitchen to have the women laugh at me and decide I was basically useless and let me just stand or sit around while they continued their work.

Eventually when everyone had been fed, the women got to eat together. They had less than their fair share, but they were used to this. First the men got served, oldest first, and then the children and finally the women. I was fascinated how this was similar to what I had learned at SIT when we had a third world meal based on the Indian tradition. I had felt angry there when the women did all the work and the men ate most of the food. However, here in Kenya, I was more accepting.

I had already spent time with the woman who led the women's learning circles who had explained to me that what women need to learn in Kenya is not the same as empowerment for U.S. women. I had heard from a western NGO officer that if we wanted women to use birth control, we needed to assure them that they would be taken care of in their old age. Children were their social security. The woman who was paid by the government to help other women, mostly taught the women better nutrition and ideas for how to make some money of their own.

Much of the suffering was due to overpopulation. Kenya had the highest birthrate in the world at that time. They were also suffering from drought; too many trees cut for making charcoal to cook the maize and beans which were slowly softening over the round metal jikos by every woman's hut. Too many children, too few fathers. Too little rain falling without the trees to recirculate ground water into rain. The women set the food to cook slowly over the fire while they went off to cultivate the land, wives of the same husband working together to feed their children. The men did business. They are responsible for making currency.

The roles of men and women were clearly different and defined. No Kenyan woman would drive a car and no Kenyan man would make a meal. Men were assumed to be polygamous and women learned to support one another in the home. I never could figure out how they dealt with jealousy, but then in a society where people married to create stability and love wasn't the motivating force, expectations were quite different than for USers.

Money is needed to buy shoes for those who wear them, tin roofs for the now square houses of those who can afford them, and mostly to pay off the debt Kenya incurred to the World Bank when the White settlers abandoned the land they had stolen and returned to Europe. When Europeans came to Kenya they found "empty" land between small villages. They appropriated this for themselves, built square houses with tin roofs and began planting orchards of coffee and oranges. These orchards required more water than fell from the sky, so they dug wells and used diesel fuel to pump the water up. They had the international currency to buy the fuel and sold their produce on the international market. The labor came from the people living in those small villages. The men became addicted to the pittance they were paid in currency for their labor for the wazungu (Europeans). But then came Mau Mau (in the 1950s). People were tired of their country being run by outsiders and they rebelled. The White people got scared and decided to leave. But they wanted compensation for their investment, the orchards and wells that had been their idea, even if done with local labor.

So, the newly African government borrowed the money from the World Bank to pay the Europeans for their contribution and western bankers made a profit called "interest." The Kenyans whose land and labor had been appropriated and developed were now responsible for continuing the production of exportable crops to earn the international currency to pay the bankers their principal and interest. Of course, the diesel to run the pumps to water the orchards still came from abroad as well, and must be paid for in international currency. There is no money left over to pump water for the fields of maize and beans or to buy fuel to heat the food eaten in the homes of the women whose husbands labor all day to maintain the orchards. But they keep having babies hoping that some of them will live to support them in their old age. And more and more do. And the forests turn into charcoal for the jikos and no rain falls.

The hand of man; not a light touch. Development is not always a blessing. Do we prefer shoes and tin roofs to clear skies and ice covered mountains? Is it worth the loss of community and family to produce coffee for Europeans indulgence? Are we choosing our outcomes as a world society or are we simply accepting the unintended consequences of greed? Who gets to choose? How are our choices made in this era of global economy? Whose truth?

Musyoko's main role was to drive us into town every day to pick up the mail and get fresh water in our jerry cans. When I stepped out of the combi, small children followed me calling "Mzungu, mzungu, unafanyaji?" This means, "What are you doing, white person?" They really didn't want an answer to this question, merely to be able to interact. I couldn't have answered it anyhow. What was I doing there anyhow? Discovering myself in new ways. Again being marginalized, but now by being elevated instead of being demeaned.

Once leaving the combi, the first place I went was to one of the coffee shops. The children followed me around and stared at me across the open space. I learned not to let it make me uncomfortable. I ordered coffee and a mandazi (sort of a doughnut hole) and they watched me eat. Here in the land of coffee, I got a cup of hot milk with a container of instant Nescafe to turn it into café au lait. The coffee beans had been shipped to Europe and processed and sent back. Never in all my time in Kenya did I see perked coffee.

Next, I investigated what I could buy in the open market in the central town square. Mostly women milled around in colorful khangas (sarongs). Some women wore only two of these one wrapped above the breasts and the other over it at the waist. Some women wore blouses above the waist-wrapped one. Almost all had a pattern which made a bullseye of their butt. Very rarely did the color of the khanga have anything to do with the color of whatever else they might be wearing. After some embarrassing failures, I learned to tuck the top in at the waist so that it didn't fall down unexpectedly.

Several women sat with their produce in small piles on top of khangas. There were pyramids of red tomatoes, green mangoes, orange papayas, yellow bananas, brown potatoes. Shoppers walked around the space deciding which produce looked the most appealing. There was rarely a variation in price although if someone's potatoes were smaller, she might give more for the same amount of money.

The students and I shared the cooking so I didn't need to buy food every day, but I enjoyed touring the options. I spoke to some of the women in Kiswahili.

"Miss, wouldn't you like a nice fresh pineapple?"

"How much?"

"Only three shillings."

"No, I'll give you one. It doesn't look fresh."

"Yes, ma'am, it is just picked this morning."

We both know we will settle for two shillings as that is the common price. The banter is part of the pleasure of shopping.

One day I was accosted in the market. A tall slender attractive man approached me with a lascivious look on his face. He asked what I was doing in Kenya and I tried to explain in Kiswahili that I worked for an American college that had no curriculum and no teachers. He said that he was a "mganga." (We translate mganga as "witchdoctor" but that is inaccurate. He actually was an herbalist who grew his own medicines and was on his way to learning allopathic medicine.) Despite the difficulty in communicating, he invited me to his home. Perhaps he thought I could help him get further education.

I felt very unsafe with him alone, so I said, "It would be very interesting for my students to learn about what you do. Can I bring them with me to visit you?"

He agreed that they could come, too. We went together to speak with Musyoko to make arrangements. He and Musyoko discussed when would be convenient for Musyoko to take the day to drive a bunch of us up into the mountains to Muthoko's home. Muthoko gave him directions and they agreed on a time and day.

On the appointed day, six students and I climbed into the

combi and Musyoko took off. We drove for a couple of hours up into a much less developed area in the mountains. It was another opportunity to engage with the beauty of nature as we drove over dirt roads that opened into views of hills and valleys. Some of the areas we drove through were also parched and dry from the drought. There we saw stubbly fields of stunted maize.

When we arrived, we were greeted by Muthoko and welcomed into his home. He showed us around the grounds pointing with his long graceful fingers to the gardens where he grew his herbs. He told us that his hospital treated 150,000 patients a year. He made it clear he was quite wealthy. We could see people sitting outside around the property. He explained the hospital was part of the compound and that the patients were inside and their families waited for them outside, sometimes for days.

He settled my students in his living room and took me to another room which was his apothecary. Three walls were covered in shelves with jars and jars on every shelf with herbs in them. He tried to explain to me what they were all used for. He opened some of the jars with his strong hands and asked me to smell the ingredients, but I couldn't identify them. He tried to explain what they were used for, but we had no language in common. Despite all his knowledge, he didn't speak any English and my Kiswahili was never more than rudimentary. I understood very little. Standing close to me, he bent down to kiss me. I decided it was time to rejoin the group. Moving away, I said, "I know what you want and I won't sleep with you, so let's go join the students in the living room." I could hear dance music being played through the walls.

The students were listening to high life on an old record player. It was the typical Kenyan square room with chairs placed against the walls so that there could only be one conversation in the room at a time. No one was dancing, so he encouraged them to dance and asked me to dance with him. We did a dance, but I felt embarrassed in front of my students in this very open day time space.

It was one thing to go dancing at the bar called "Small World" at night where the light was dim and many people were dancing. It felt awkward here in his living room in the middle of the day.

We sat back down and tried to have a conversation. Suddenly a woman brought a goat in led by a rope. In Kiswahili the mganga said, "I present this goat to you."

I thought, "What am I supposed to do with this? How are we going to transport it in the combi?" I imagined fitting it between the seated passengers and the next row of seats. Uh, oh.

I didn't want to embarrass myself by asking what I was to do with the goat even if I thought he couldn't understand my English. I asked Bruce, who probably spoke the best Kiswahili, what was going on with the goat. He wasn't really able to tell me without embarrassing us.

The awkward conversation continued. The mganga came in and out of the room. Straight backed wooden chairs are not very comfortable for long. I was ready to leave after a couple of hours of this when suddenly women came in bearing shallow bowls of goat stew!

Imagine my surprise! At least I didn't have to figure out how to transport a goat back to Katheka Kai. We politely ate the goat we had so recently seen alive. I generally didn't eat red meat, but when offered it as a symbolic gesture of hospitality, I felt compelled. Soon after we ate, the students and I were ready to leave. There was no repeat invitation.

I don't know why Muthoka invited me to visit his home. Was he being welcoming to a foreigner? Did he want something from me, an opportunity, a connection? Other men repeated his lecherous behavior. Being a woman who as a girl had been called Fatso, I was flattered by the attention. It was the one time in my life that I was encouraged to gain weight, where a round woman is seen as a sign of wealth and beauty.

༒༝

The most difficult interaction I had was with a politician, Musa, who picked me up hitchhiking. I had learned that the key to not being forced into sex when hitchhiking was to keep my legs crossed at the knees at all times. Kenyan women never sat flat on the ground with open legs crossed in yoga style. Musa asked if I would go on a date with him and a friend of his to a bar. He was a good looking man, spoke good English and was running for office. I had seen his posters plastered everywhere and I thought it would be interesting to get to know him.

We had a couple of beers and talked with the friend and the friend's date. Eventually, I said, "It's time for me to go home."

"No," he said, "We will stay here tonight. There are rooms above the bar and my friends have already retired there."

I was surprised and upset. I wasn't having it. He said, "You agreed to come out with me so that means you agreed to have sex with me." The bar was closing, so we had to retire to the room above to continue the argument. Ascending the stairs I could see his assurance that he would win, being a politician. His steps were firm and decisive. I was hesitant and reluctant, dawdling and holding back.

At the top of the stairs, we entered a small room. The only place to sit was on the bed. I tried to stay standing, but eventually, gave in and sat down. This made it even more uncomfortable. We spent several hours arguing about whether he would take me back to Katheka Kai. I was increasingly tired and just wanted to sleep. In the end, I lost. I wanted sleep more than I didn't want sex. It was the one time in my life when I clearly in my own mind did not want to have sex with a man and felt pressured to the point of acquiescence. The next morning was awkward as we had to face each other over breakfast. He still thought I would go out with him again and came by at Katheka Kai (we had no phone). I told him firmly "No."

My struggle with my feelings that, as woman, I needed a man to feel complete took on new dimensions. It was holding me back and represented a limitation in becoming all that I could be, but it was still operating and even more so in a culture where women were not generally educated, and often seen just as the bearers of children and keepers of the house. Whose truth?

I wrote in my journal,

"Sometimes I wonder why I'm in Africa. I so dislike most of my relationships with Africans; they seem like such radical compromises with my own values. At the same time, I miss peer relationships and most of all I miss being in love. Perhaps even I were home, I would be, as I so often have been, without a lover, someone I really care for – but at least I would have a wider choice of friends and acquaintances. There is such a limited choice of associations because of the transportation and communications problems. As I said to one student, when I start calling a man a good catch when he takes me home within an hour of when I want to go, I've certainly changed my standards. It's a cold day in hell."

❦

Sometimes the experience of Kenya was so exotic that there was nothing from home with which compare it. The first time I visited a Masai community, we had heard that it was the time of year when the young men transitioned to manhood. My students and I wanted to see the ceremony. A group of us went in the combi with Musyoko driving. We had to drive a long time on the paved road and then a considerable way on a dirt track that forded a stream without a bridge. As we approached the stream, we saw a rhinoceros bathing. Musyoko told us we had to be very careful not to draw his attention or he might charge the vehicle thinking it was a predator. We were as quiet as we could be in an old VW bus.

We were in the middle of the stream and I saw out the window that the rhino had lifted his head and looked towards the bus. I heard him snort. Musyoko told us that rhinos have very poor eyesight and all they detect is movement. As he said this, all I could see was the long horn attached to a two and half ton animal. I thought, "what would it be like if that came crashing through the side of the bus." I don't think we would have stood a chance.

When we arrived at the location for the ceremony, we found a lot of outsiders. White people had come from all over to see the Masai, much as people today come to the traditional dances in Cherokee near where I live now. The land was dry and dusty. The cattle were in their fenced in bomas and the young men who were participating in the coming of age ceremony were walking around through the crowd.

The men stood tall and proud as Masai men do. They seemed handsome to me, even with their strange hair, long and twisted. Draped with just a red cloth, their black asses flashed in the sun. They held a knobbed stick (staff) between their crossed legs. I guess it gives them the balance to stand there for hours quite still as that is what they do. I was shocked to see how this staff had a large bulb on the top which made it look like a large penis standing upright between their legs.

The women were weighed down with beaded jewelry and didn't seem as handsome. But they seemed 'right' with their stretched out earlobes. They all had a particular odor which I rather liked. Both men and women pierce their ears and place ever larger objects in the holes until some of them can put a tin can in the hole. For me, it didn't look attractive, but different cultures have different ideas of beauty. The difference I experienced in this Kenyan culture was so much more dramatic than I did with the Wakamba it was striking and made them seem more of a curiosity than possible friends.

That made it even more startling when a young man approached me and reached out to touch my hair. A tradition of becoming a man was that the boy had to cut his hair off. Up to that time, the boy's hair had never been cut so it was a great relinquishing. I had my waist length hair and the young man found it fascinating and wanted to touch it. His hair was a completely different texture but I wasn't comfortable enough to reach out to touch his as I knew viscerally that losing it that day was a tender place. Once this young man had been successful in making contact, many hands stroked my head throughout the day. I accepted it patiently glad to have the close contact with these exotic young men with whom I could not communicate otherwise. They were always kind and polite, as curious about me as I was about them. We had very little language in common as they don't usually speak Kiswahili, so our connection was through this fragile bridge of touch.

One older man invited me and my colleagues into his house. We couldn't quite understand why, but we were eager to see the inside. The houses are made from cattle dung shaped into a long rounded mound about the shape of a Quonset hut, but much smaller and lower. The "chief's" house was so small and low.

Leaving the bright African sun behind, we ducked our heads and pulled the cloth covering the doorway aside. I suddenly found myself in a smoke filled, dark cave. Unlike the Wakamba, the cook fire was inside. My eyes started watering. It was rectangular with some division of space. The fire was in the center. There were no windows; the door was arranged to keep out air, eyes, and light. I had trouble breathing, and found it oppressively close. I wondered what we were doing here. Why had we been invited in when so many other white people at this event were not? What did they want from us? We never found out.

They offered us their traditional ceremonial drink: cows' milk mixed with their blood. Masai traditionally do not kill the cow to get the blood for their drink. They take blood from the cow like they take milk, a little at a time. They only eat what comes from animals, nothing from the earth. Although I had no judgment about this, I wasn't willing to participate myself. I was as afraid of disease as I was worried about how bad it would taste. I knew this was rude, but my health was more important to me than what they might think of me.

Emerging from the hut as soon as we felt we could, the

ceremony was about to begin. We visitors stood in a large circle around the young men who were participating. Most of the coming of age ceremony involved the young men competing for who could jump the highest from a still position. This is a useful skill for hunters who want to be able to see across the plains to find game. Each hunter took a turn to jump as high as he could, his red and white checked clothe swirling around him. There was applause for each attempt. Eventually a winner was chosen although I couldn't tell how they determined who had jumped the highest. This was only part of the ceremony as each young man was required to kill a lion by himself before or after this event.

On the trip back to campus, I was nodding off. Suddenly I felt the vehicle collide with something and was immediately wide awake. We had hit a nyama (gazelle) in the road. After some discussion in Kiswahili between Musyoko and Sam which I couldn't understand, Musyoko picked it up and put it in the back of the vehicle. Now I thought, "This is great, I get to ride back to Katheka Kai with a dead animal in the vehicle with me." Sam, our director, was worried that we might meet a police blockade and it was poaching to kill a gazelle. I was afraid it might carry a disease. Gitaka, our cook, made a stew. We ate it. I had indigestion. Whose truth?

When I got back to the campus, my hair smelled of henna oil from all the touching of the young men's hands and there was (as often was the case) no running water available from the taps in the sinks. I had just washed my hair the day before, too. My mouth felt like the dusty road we had travelled on as I hadn't drunk enough water being afraid it hadn't been boiled.

I looked out the window from the bathroom where I couldn't get water from the tap and saw a man outside watering the flowers and the pathways. He got the water from the tanks (that caught the rain water) but there was no water for the faucet in the kitchen to wash the dishes. I wrote in my journal "For most simply through paradox do I usually discover the truth." This epiphany became a pivotal point for me. No longer was I operating on my mother's admonition to be extreme in the pursuit of righteousness. I could see that there are many ways in which truth may reveal itself and many truths from many points of view. Who says that watering plants is not more important than washing henna from my hair? Who says that we must eat a varied diet or decorate ourselves in a particular way?

All Masai do not live like those who participated in the ceremony. Many have also taken on much more western ways. The second time I visited Masai land, I was helping choose a family to host an AFS student from the U.S. for the summer months. I had met Solomon, the AFS/International Scholarships representative in Nairobi. He was glad to have my experience to help him to find and qualify families. We visited a Masai family who had a modern house. Even there, a boma was a major feature. We sat with the family in the living room of their house with a tin roof and multiple separate rooms and discussed what it would be like if they were to host an American student for two months.

The mother and father did most of the talking. Their daughter also expressed her eagerness to share her life with an American. Solomon and I said that the visitor would need a varied diet and opportunities to visit places in Kenya outside Masai land. They did end up hosting a student for two months and it seemed to work out all right. I don't know what she ate, but I again refused the hospitality of drinking their traditional milk. Not all traditions are lost in modernization.

Later, I was picked up hitchhiking by a Masai man who had taken up business. He was in a western suit and driving a Mercedes. I was shocked to notice that he was grossly overweight after taking up a western diet as well as his other western ways. Sometimes we bring more harm than good.

Through Solomon I got to visit a number of Kenyan households of people of moderate wealth—sufficient to host an America teenager. It was so different from what I experienced at

182

Katheka Kai. I was so used to our "enough" lifestyle it was confusing when I stayed in homes with hot running water, art on the walls, and a cleaning staff. The older people who had accumulated some wealth were different from the younger graduates of foreign universities as well. They were more likely to hold on to their money than to spend it in bars drinking beer. They stay in smaller towns and their children stay with them even when grown. They stay connected to the earth and growing things. I noted that they have flower gardens where the Nairobi houses have maize growing. Perhaps the more rural wealthy know they can get their maize from their neighbors. I was also surprised at the willingness of the Kenyans to barge in on people at all hours of the night and morning and expect to be served chai (English style tea with milk) and a snack.

One of my challenges was that I was supposed to be doing research to underpin the masters' thesis I was to write to complete my degree. I, like my students, needed to get out into the world surrounding Katheka Kai. I decided initially that what I could most usefully and easily do was to learn about Kenyans who had studied in the U.S. and who were now back in Kenya. Since I had worked with international students before going to graduate school, I assumed that understanding what would best serve them in their readjustment would be useful to me and others in the future. It was also easier to imagine having meaningful conversations with them than with those who had not travelled outside of Kenya. However, my discomfort with figuring out how hospitality worked got in my way. I could never tell if I was intruding on someone or if he was honestly willing to get together. And what questions was it all right for me to ask? I ended up not using this research for my master's essay because I wasn't able to collect enough data to make any meaningful conclusions. But I did meet a lot of Western educated men.

The one way to get away from the center in the evening was to go dancing. Sometimes a man with a car came and picked me up. I always insisted on taking other students. We went to a dance hall called "Small World." Mostly it was a place to drink beer, but there was often music and dancing. People were surprised at how well I could do the African popular dances. I had learned the high life from African students when I was in the International Club at University of Wisconsin.

One night I went to the ladies room. A woman came in and said, "How did you learn to dance like that?" I said, "I have always been a dancer." I don't mind moving my hips in sensuous ways and I can shake my upper body with abandon. But I wasn't comfortable dancing in the small dark spaces of Katheka Kai homes. At night sometimes we could hear the drumming and once we went to investigate, but sat quietly watching from the edge of the crowd rather than joining in the dancing in the center. It was traditional dancing in a small dark space lit only by a fire, quite different from the western experience of dancing at Small World.

❧

My time in Kenya was pivotal. First it is a dramatically different environment both in the natural world and in the cultural sense from anything I had experienced before. In addition, my time was unstructured in ways that forced me to look at who I am and how I fit in the world. I was a resource to the students in ways that gave me value I hadn't experienced before. I met people and read books which allowed me to appreciate myself in new ways.

Politically and economically, I was most impressed by how colonialism affected Africa. Kenya at the time had one of the highest birthrates in the world and overpopulation was leading to famine. The need for material to burn to cook food in the indigenous compounds was such that much of the tree cover on Katheka Kai had been cut down to provide charcoal. The overcutting of trees disrupted the water cycle so that it was hard to grow much of anything. Drought prevailed.

In order to get the land back after the English had left in fear for their lives during Mau Mau, the Kenyans had to pay the departing English what the English thought their investment was worth. The World Bank had financed this project. To have the international currency to pay the World Bank, it was necessary to grow something that the world wanted: coffee. However, coffee trees need lots of water. There wasn't enough rain, so irrigation had to be done by pumps which required diesel fuel which required foreign currency. Thus there wasn't irrigation for the food crops which people depended on. Understanding this political/economic reality helped me to see the effects of colonialism.

At the same time, I was experiencing the natural beauty. When it did rain, there were often rainbows. We could see them because we could see over great open distances across the plains. I said, "Look at the sky" with great wonder that it could be so blue and the Kenyans replied, "It's just the sky." The beauty of the environment which was clearly not created by the hand of man, brought me to a new understanding of "a power greater than myself."

Living in Kenya, I became aware of my environment in ways I never had been aware living in the States. My observations on the land and ecology changed me in ways that frame my concerns about environmental degradation today. I travelled from the coast to the far west and saw the variety of environments from sea to mountains to the Rift Valley.

Approaching the precipice I looked down on the broad expanse of the valley with round clear places encircled by the houses of the Masai minyatas. As the sun moved lower the variations in height over the previously level valley became apparent. Shadows defined the edges of the different layers. Dry and brown, it was a wonder people could survive in such an area.

On the other side, Kikuyu land. Green and fertile, homes hidden by trees, spread out, fields cultivated up to Nairobi. Marking the edge between Kikuyu land and Akombani—the land of the Wakamba people—again, dry, brown, flat though with attempts to cultivate it.

The plateau stretched for hundreds of miles in every direction.

Toward the west, the sudden drop of the rift formed millennia ago was clear. Perpendicular to that, one could draw a line from Mt. Kilamanjaro to the south to Mt. Kenya in the north. Both barely visible in the haze. In the sloped valleys between the peaks there were dense forests. Green and lush.

We took a trip to the Abedare Mountains, also west of where we were living. We camped out in tents and saw the tracks of elephant and watched a leopard walk through the camp. The Kenyans with us slept in the vehicle. They thought we were nuts to sleep in tents. They wanted the protection of solid walls.

Driving west from Nairobi, the Rift was dry and brown and the harvest was recently in. The dry air made for a clear view and Mount Longonut seemed to be next to us along the road. The jacaranda trees were in bloom all over the town, but those in Machakos were all gone. I felt I didn't understand seasons in Kenya!

On our way to the mountains, we passed through new territory. I was impressed by what I saw. First large farms, recently harvested of maize and wheat. Then lovely forest covered hills where pine trees were grown to be made into paper. In one place there was a serious fire with orange smoke pouring out and into the clouds. Then there were large pastures where people related to Masai grazed their cattle without fences. In the forest areas, the shambas (farms) were marked with fences made completely of upright wooden poles so close to each other they needed no connecting wires at all.

We saw Mt. Longonot—century old black lava left wide tracks down the soft short green growth on its sides. Only quiescent, not extinct, it projected itself toward the heavens from the bottom of the long low Rift, God's sculpture, found art. Everywhere there were bits of nature cum art that arrested me, like a tap on the shoulder from God to remind me of my own transiency, the impermanence of this earth. Only the barest essential of my Self could ever live on past my most brief sojourn in this material reality.

Since colonization, even the trees had been cut and replanted in rows of sameness, evenly spaced, and of similar height to remind us of the inescapable laws of nature. I noted that even as man strives for reason—to be more godlike—he stumbles on his lack of trust in his intuitive knowledge, the true gift of nature. I wrote in my journal that, "Only living within and accepting this paradox can we truly appreciate Wholeness, truly approach Truthfulness and Reality. The beauty is in discovering what has been there all along: not in having it pointed out and explained before you even perceived that there was something to question, but coming to it at your own pace, in your own way."

The natural environment of the Indian Ocean coast impressed me even more. On the coast, the cultures mix just as Kiswahili is a mixture of the indigenous Bantu languages with Arabic as a result of trade along the coast. Deeply black skinned women darkened by working in the sun wear khangas wrapped above or below their old worn out breasts. On the bus I could see that they stuffed fabric under the khanga at their waist to hide the real shape of their hips even while they left their breasts bare. In the city, they mixed with Islamic women wearing black bouibouis that covered themselves from head to toe and with white women wearing short skirts above the knee. All live together in peace. Another truth found in the paradox.

Where I stayed in Mombasa, the sea lapped quietly against the shore, the full moon hung above waiting for the pastel pink sky to quiet toward blackness before sharing its own glow with the clouds. It formed a brilliant ring and cast its bright path out across the sea to the breakers rumbling against the coral reefs. All the fascination of a new town dissolved in the beauty of nature, stark white sand beaches felt like flour in my hands, between my toes, watching bathers having one last swim in the warm salt water. The air was rich with oxygen and the smell of salt filled my empty lungs. The hot sun sent me to the relief of a shower only to bring forth another purifying sweat from my pores. Cleansing, healing, deepening. I wanted time to slow down and cradle me in this gentle warm cocoon. Sleep, the true rest, could

187

carry me safely home. Two butterflies yellow and black, like a pair of brilliant khangas flying round and round one another in a mating dance entranced me.

I wanted to share this with someone I loved – or have it all to myself. Once again I remembered how good it is to be lonely alone, rather than lonely with others. Alone, loneliness is deep and black as the sea on a moonless night. With others the air crackles around me demanding my attention without filling my heart. The vacuum inside draws in the pain of lost souls which writhe and wriggle inside me and stir the old, not yet forgotten hurts; imagined desertions of friends no longer lovers.

I wrote, "It's true that my real self has had to struggle to emerge from the façade which pretends to need people, has sought company as a way to escape facing Self. As I become less afraid of my essential, central, unchanging connection with nature and Reality, I rather like being alone, feel no need to join people just because they are there and only choose to be with people if they have something to offer."

Being alone had always reminded me of being in my room in Amagansett with only my plastic horses, a book to read and chocolate to eat. Now, I found that being alone gave me the space to be with something greater than myself. I found that noticing the natural environment brought me closer to something some call God and I could best appreciate this power when I was alone and in a natrual environment.

In the morning I saw the moon slip behind the palm trees to the west. One day past full, just the slightest scoop from round. As the pink glow of sunrise over the sea turned the sky from black to pastel blue with grey blotches of soft drifting clouds the last star twinkled out of sight overhead. The Indian Ocean at high tide lapped steadily against the shore bringing in masses of dry black sea grass to tangle itself around my ankles and caress my feet sore from walking on too much coral. Already the bright patches between the clouds made paths on the reflecting surface of the water as the moon did less than twelve hours ago, leading me out to its brightness. People began to awaken and move around. The charm of single experience waned as I realized the clouds would obscure the sun's emergence and I desired more sleep. The waves breaking on the reef became a white line as well as a dull roar. Ocean has always been a healing place for me and the Indian Ocean was a new scene with familiar power to bring my spirit into alignment.

In July, I traveled to Embu, deeper into the western countryside with Solomon and twenty AFS students. Several times I felt I wasn't particularly enjoying myself, but there wasn't anywhere else I wanted to be. I thought, "I seem to still have expectations from people and to rise too quickly to anger with other people when I should be more in control of myself and recognize that my anger with others is only a reflection of my anger at myself for opening myself to disappointment. Any way I feel at any time is only a product of my own creation. I seem to be more easily upset the more accustomed I become to this environment. When I think I know, I think I can control my environment to meet my needs, but I never really know and thus I can never control, but only move with the flow of the river, guiding myself to avoid the obvious snags and extricating myself when I err and get hooked on a hidden obstacle. It's so hard to keep a perspective. I always have to give in some ways to have a full experience. Compromise is the heart of maturity."

As I reflected on the unfamiliar environment, I also reflected on my place in the universe and what was important in my relationships with people. I can see in reading my journal how at this turning point in my life I was shifting from the either/or perspective I had been raised with to the both/and perspective that eventually brought me to mediation and conflict resolution. I can see in these passages how my recognition of the vastness of what has not been created by man has brought me to seek something greater than human individuals, community, a oneness of humans with each other and with all life. I see the nugget of my present life where I prefer being alone or with a group with common purpose to being with individuals who bore me.

The beauty in Kenya has been severely affected by the hand of man. When I was there we could see the smoke from the "gare la moshe" (vehicle of smoke) or in English, railroad train, trailing behind as the large engine pulled its following cars the 6,000 foot rise up the mountains from Mombasa to Nairobi, along with car exhaust altering the blue of the sky. The desire for industrialization pushes beautiful places to exchange what nature has provided for the manufactured products of what we call "civilization." Having returned to Africa after more than forty years, I have learned of the changes to culture and society that the money economy has wrought, as well. Among other things, more educated men are choosing to have only one wife because children are now expensive, not an asset as in agricultural times.

When I was there in the mid-70s, Machakos had several shops in addition to the open market. It startled me to see what people thought went together. Tuna fish with batteries. There was so little on the shelves. There might be a few cans of one item, no choice of brand. The chocolate was months old and had melted and reformed many times before being bought. Forty years later, things have developed to where there is more available, more choices in products in larger towns. When I came back to the States in 1976, I noticed how grocery stores only had groceries and drug stores only had things related to health but lots of brands of everything to choose from. The cereal aisle of grocery stores overwhelmed me. Today in the States our stores are more like those in Kenya with a diversity of common products that we would never have seen together back then. How long will it be before the African sky is no longer so brilliant and the animals so plentiful? What constitutes improvement? Is all "progress" a good thing? Where is truth?

❧❧

In Kenya, I made my first connections to a spiritual faith, "Believing makes fine people. They've always attracted me. And the areas I've felt I've tapped into on this are poetry and nature. I want to write about this experience through poetry filled with nature metaphor."

This poem written sitting on a hillside in Mombasa reflects the connection of nature and spirit:

I strive to be
            Transparent
Energy
A cool breeze on a hot Mombasa day
The blue sea sparkling in the sun
Beyond the green algae
Baobub tree casting its shadow
Puffy clouds on the horizon
To the east lies India
Not Europe

I strive to be
            Transparent
 Energy
The warm heat radiating
From a fire of acacia branches
High in a cloud of the Abedare mountains
In the cool rainy season.
Animals roaming wild
Living lives without thought.
No past, no future
Only now.

Thou art the energy
Which connects us all,
The tie which binds me to mySelf
Thou art beauty, light, goodness.
I reach out to touch you and find mySelf.

A sailboat man-made
Enters the channel
From the vast sea
Wind blows, filling the sail
I am that wind
Assisting you into port
I open my legs and you flow down that channel
To safe harbor
Acceptance for who you really are
I am the death that awaits you
At the end of your journey
And the life that takes you there

I am the beauty which brings you joy
And the intensity of your pain
When the joy is absent.

You are the sun winking
Through the baobub tree
Taunting me to emerge
And expose myself to its intense rays
To be scorched,
Penetrated.
My soul exposed in your brilliance
Finally to become
     Transparent
 Energy
Returned to Thou totally.

During my time in Kenya, I started reading about psychosynthesis in Assagioli's *Act of Will* and much of my thinking was shaped by looking at "sub personalities" and "disidentifying" with parts of myself that weren't working. It started my thinking about the difference between "being willing" and "willing something to happen." That theme followed me for many years. I struggled with how much I should take charge of my direction and considered "steering downstream" to be one approach. When I returned to the States I followed up on this interest in humanistic psychology and spent a month at a personal growth center called The New England Center for Personal and Organizational Development.

I also learned to pay attention to things people did in a ritual way. I wrote, "I love ritual. It's such fun. It's a game where I have to guess the rules...If I play real well...we might even learn from each other.I'm pretty positive about what I'm doing: something that's fun, that's going to let me do more fun things in the future and has already allowed me to do a few...I can feel good about myself and how I handle myself."

I met a Baha'i woman, Celia, with whom I became friends. She had a big influence on how I thought about religion. I especially appreciated that she provided me with a place I could stay overnight in Nairobi. She was a missionary who was in Kenya to convert people to her religion, but she was also very accepting of me and told me that I "belonged to Baha'i" whether or not I ever joined her religion.

In my journal, I quoted from Eric Fromm the *Art of Loving,*

"The mature stage of love is where God ceases to be an outside power, where man has incorporated the principles of love and justice into himself, where he has become one with God, and eventually, to a point where he speaks of god only in a poetic, symbolic sense.

"The mature person who 'loves god' thinks truth, lives love and justice, and considers all of his life valuable inasmuch as it gives him the chance to arrive at an even fuller unfolding of his human powers—as the only reality that matters is the only object of ultimate concern."

After quoting this, I wrote,

"God is not some outside figure whom we worship in order to

receive favors. God is a name for the immutable truth and reality that exists within each of us and which we perceive to the degree to which we break down the categories which constitute the barriers to our true perceptions of ourselves and appreciation for our sharing in that universal consciousness.

"I do not like the Aristotelian duality which is based on the logic of the excluded middle. I have always had more affinity for Plato, Kant and Hegel: the philosophy of an absolute truth which man cannot perceive but only approach through objective, rational faith, synthesis and an open heart and mind—a confluence of intuition and reason."

This kind of philosophical thinking ran through all my writing during that time. I told myself that I have to be careful not to be too exclusive in my associations that I might meet some really fine people in very strange places. I must learn to appreciate what's there.

I was glad Daniel was there. I met Daniel in the hostel in Nairobi. He was unlike other people I knew, belonging to a cult I had never heard of before and can't remember the name of, and he challenged my thinking. I believed that engaging with him affirmed that I could make meaningful contact with people wherever I went. I believed I wouldn't forget that making good contact with interesting people would be like riding a bike and I thought I wouldn't forget it (though I have often enough). It made me believe there are people in the world who appreciate me for what I am. I liked being her. I believed I was solid in the center—only the edges changed.

I found myself articulating how I wanted space and closeness, shared values rather than wanting to create social change for a larger group. Daniel saw himself so much more in terms of educating larger groups of people, social issues, political change. I still felt guilty. I judged myself through my mother's lens as being too indulgent, too concerned with a comfortable life style for myself. I knew that the world I wanted to live in requires work and building institutions to serve those needs. I also saw myself as profiting from those institutions and just assumed that there are others who could profit from those changes as well. I had no drive to impose those institutions on anyone. If they found them attractive and satisfying, good. If not, I didn't want to force it. I asked myself, "What happens to the institutions if I'm wrong and people don't subscribe, participate in them?"

Then I quoted from M.L. von Franz,

"Genuine liberation can start only with a psychological transformation. To what end does one liberate one's country if afterward there is no meaningful goal of life – no goal for which it is worthwhile to be free? If man no longer finds any meaning in his life, it makes no difference whether he wastes away under a communist or a capitalist regime. Only if he can use his freedom to create something meaningful is it relevant that he should be free. That is why finding the inner meaning of life is more important to the individual than anything else, and why the process of individuation must be given priority."

I did a great deal of reading while I was in Kenya and since all I had were the books in the college's library, much of it was quite serious and thoughtful. I kept a list of the books I read and looking back on it am quite impressed by how much of what I think now was shaped during those months.

I had moved from my thinking that I had to have a man in my life to be whole to appreciating being alone where I could be in contact with a power greater than myself. I wrote this poem in my journal:

I remember a Sunday
When I was stoned
In my empty dining room
No one answered his phone
The rug was soft
Sun played with the pattern and warmed my feet

The stereo played what I chose
I screamed "I don't want to be ALONE"
To my journal
Today I search for the ache,
The "I want" that I feel.
It is
Aloneness.
Enough of people, places, things to do and see and think and say.
Enough of everything
Except time and space
Alone.

Close to the end of my stay in Kenya, my relationships at home again came into prominence. My mother came to visit with her friend, Suzy. I wrote, "The rain falls heavily, clouds part to reveal the sun, covered again, and moist air rises from the rich green earth. Everything laden with the wealth of water. Colors muted as through "soft eyes." Hills spotted with the lavender of jacaranda, as it is on the dry earth in front of the kitchen. The lilac smell transfixes as one walks through...Thoughts drawn toward the U.S. as I picture my mother departing from Kenya, read Nin's diary of New York. Feeling unclean, unhealthy, untogether, tired, restless, waiting."

I said I spent more time in gift shops when she was there than in the whole rest of my year in Kenya. Mother asked me to travel with her to Mombasa. I said, "No, it is too close to the end of my stay here and I need to be available at school and with my students."

I wrote in my journal, "She loves me a lot. She wants so much to be with me. She wants me home to love and to hold her. It takes so much out of me. I am so reminded of my obligations. And of how little time I have left in this country. I love this country...I can never be good enough, generous enough, giving enough for mother. Can I be for someone else?"

I was also struggling with how it would feel to see Joseph

again. Thinking of him having finished his exams, I wrote

At 8:30, the two day past full moon rising behind the clouds
Now stands overhead glowing off the tin roof
Of my happiness
A glow of self knowledge
Reflecting off the intellect
And expressed in written clarity
A sureness I want to share with you tonight.
Certainly finished with those threatening trials
And now free to re-find
Center that connects with mine.
I felt you in the moon rise
Body relaxing, anxiety dissipating into the shared
Glow of the moon
Happy holidays.
My love is with you
A good new year to come
See you soon.
Touch you, too.

On New Year's day, I got a telegram from Joseph saying he wanted to talk with me on the phone. The day I got the telegram, I saw the most beautiful double rainbow I have ever seen. The display went from one side of the plains to the other, completing 180 degrees of brilliant color. I was transfixed. What did this mean?

We had no phone where I was living and town was about 10 miles away, but I had a Kenyan friend who worked in a place with a phone and let me use it. I sent Joseph the number. I suggested he call on January 12th when I would be back from my side trip to Tanzania

The facility was about three miles away. I could only get there by foot. Walking stoned on marijuana for over an hour across the parched empty land with only occasional acacia trees to provide shade, I wondered what he would have to say to me. The sun was hot. Even the gazelles and giraffe were not out on that hot plain. I saw deserted compounds of huts mixed with occasional occupied homes. I wasn't walking on the road, but cutting across country in the general direction of Machakos, the nearest town.

Sitting in the office, wondering why I was there I waited an hour. I gazed at a green hillside with goats and round huts. I distracted the staff member who thought he smelled marijuana. The phone rang. "Hello," I said, "Where are you?"

In a sleepy voice, he said, "I am in a hotel in Ohio on my way back to Buffalo with Mary. We stopped here overnight. I flunked out of school in Atlanta and we're driving back to Mary's place in Buffalo."

I thought, "I walked across the hot plain for an hour to hear this?" But I said, "What are your plans when you get to Mary's?"

Still sleepy, he replied, "If you will come back to the U.S. now, I'll find a place of my own and we can see what we can make of our relationship. If not, I will move in with Mary. In any case, I will meet you wherever and whenever you ask."

"NO," I said strongly, "What can I say that I haven't said before? I am not ready to leave here. I need to wrap things up and close my relationships with people here. I doubt I will ever come back here and this has been an important part of my life and can't be closed in a moment."

"Well, then, I am moving in with Mary when we get to Buffalo."

"Okay, I will be back toward the end of February. I hope to see you then. Goodbye for now."

"Goodbye."

Luckily my boss, Sam, showed up as I was walking back along

the road and I got a ride back to the school. I was disappointed and scared that I would lose the relationship with Joseph, but I also felt that staying till the time I had intended to leave was important for me.

I came away from Kenya seeing myself in new ways, appreciating myself more; seeing life from different perspectives. I recognized that the either/or my mother had presented as the truth was only one version of truth. I learned to appreciate the bigger picture in which there was a spectrum of possibilities. This allowed me to see more options both for myself and for the world. Inclusivity brought me closer to the world I was seeking than "my way or the highway." I recognized through a new connection with nature that there is more to reality than what man has made. It took several more years of experience before I fully realized what this would mean for me. Like the Jews coming through the Red Sea, it still took forty years of wandering in the desert to get to the Promised Land.

In February, when I arrived at the airport in New York City, my mother greeted me with another telegram from Joseph which she must have opened. She was excited that he wanted to wish me a pleasant homecoming. I was troubled that this temptation was again being set before me when I had resolved that the relationship was over. My mother persisted, letting me know she thought this was the best man I had ever been with. She was charmed by his witty personality and good looks as she had been by my father when she first met him. She hadn't been monogamous in her marriage, why should I let his philandering bother me?

Eventually after a couple of weeks of struggling with my feelings, I spoke to him on the phone. He was hiding our communication from Mary which made it really difficult. At first, he said he would come on a particular Saturday but when that day came, he backed out. Now I was pursuing and begging. He finally did agree to visit.

The doorbell rang. I went to the door and opened it. Gasp. He still had that power over me that came from his good looks, height and beautiful red beard. I knew the body that resided under his flannel shirt and well fitting pants. My body responded. But we were in my mother's house. We moved from the foyer to the living room. Joseph and I sat on the couch a respectable distance apart while mother sat in one of the upholstered chairs. The conversation was superficial. Eventually, mother went into the kitchen to make some dinner for us all. I tried to talk with Joseph about what was going on between us, but it was stilted and uncomfortable. That was when he told me he had promised Mary he wouldn't have sex with me. I was confused. Suddenly he was monogamous?

When bedtime came, he slept in my brother's old bedroom. I lay in my bed awake, thinking of the juicy opportunity for sex which was just down the hall. I obsessed over how I had shared him with others. Why should Mary have him to herself? What was so compelling about her that he would agree to those terms? Eventually, I climbed out of bed and walked into his room. He was asleep naked and I crawled into the bed next to him. He responded to my touch and we had sex. It was awkward and unpleasant. I felt debased and hurt. He only bothered to satisfy himself.

The next morning as we sat at the breakfast table, we didn't really talk with each other. He left for Buffalo and Mary. I figured it was over—again. But then I got letters from him. We continued to correspond as we had for all those months I was in Kenya. I continued to yearn to receive the next letter, to have it say something reassuring, loving. He continued to use me as someone with whom he could explore his ideas, expand his mind.

While I was in Kenya one of my students had encouraged me to move to Atlanta where the college had a representative placing students in internships. Since Joseph had been in Atlanta for some of the time I was in Kenya, I decided to go there in the unreasonable hope that he would return there. He never did. Eventually, we stopped writing each other and he slipped from my mind.

"Having children makes you see the world
in a completely different way.
When you're responsible for those little lives,
you can't slough it off or forget about it until later."

- Linda Ronstadt

CHAPTER EIGHT

WHEN I CAME BACK FROM KENYA, I WAS LOST. WHEN ONE goes to a new country, one expects to be disoriented, needing to learn new behaviors, finding difference where one anticipates continuity with already established norms. However, coming home one expects to find things as one left them. They aren't. People have changed; you have changed. I had changed.

For one thing, I wasn't willing to live in a cold climate six months out of the year. After Buffalo, New York, Madison, Wisconsin and Brattleboro, Vermont I was headed south. One of my students, Jono, had strongly recommended I check out Georgia where there was an outpost of Friends World College which was overseen by Toby Ives. Jono thought I would find many things there of interest and I thought I would find the challenges of living in a different culture rewarding as I had in Kenya. I anticipated that the South would be a different culture and it was; not in the way I anticipated.

The journey to Atlanta took four days. In March after completing the last month of the graduate program in Brattleboro, I drove stopping to visit friends along the way. It was a startling contrast to leave wintry Buffalo and move through the climate zones into spring in Georgia. By the time I got to Tennessee, the redbud trees were in bloom and I was entranced. Atlanta was in full bloom with azaleas and dogwoods showing their pinks, whites, purples. This was great! Driving my blue VW bug through the ever more brilliant floral display, I knew this was where I wanted to be.

I arrived in Atlanta to find that Toby was in the process of separating from his wife, Pam, and heading toward a round the world tour. He was happy for me to stay in the collective household in Inman Park where they were living and later to use his cabin in the rural north Georgia foothills as a place to retreat and write my dissertation. He helped me make some early connections which quickly expanded into the progressive relationships which were my home for the coming year. I eventually moved into a different collective household across from the zoo in Grant Park.

The people in the collective had come out of Young Life, a Christian based intentional community which supported the work that eventually became Communities in Schools. It made enormous difference in the lives of inner city youth. Our household consisted of six adults and four children. Two of the children were Jeanne's natural children. She was the woman who owned the house. Two others were adopted by her and her ex-husband, Neil. I particularly was drawn to Kristen who was Korean and about ten years old. She reminded me of my brother and his struggle with racial difference and adoption.

This was 1976. The U.S.A. turned 200 and I turned thirty on July 4th. I had written Eric with my address. As a reporter, he could get reverse phone numbers and got the number where I lived. He called me the day before my birthday. He had just been assigned to Chattanooga and his wife and daughters hadn't moved yet. Would I like to come visit him for my birthday? I did. When I saw where he had chosen to live in a very ordinary suburban neighborhood and contrasted it to where I had chosen to live, in a progressive collective household, I understood why we weren't together.

It was at a workshop in Atlanta that I first recognized myself as nurturing. I had always thought of myself as "strong." But I had never seen myself as a caretaker. In the workshop when we were asked to list the adjectives we felt related to us, I realized that both as a foreign student advisor and during my time in Kenya, I had actually been nurturing young adults. Even though they weren't young children, I could see that perhaps I could parent a child.

I began looking for a co-parent. While I was in Kenya I had heard over and over "pole sana" (so sorry) when I said that I had no children. It was clear living in the collective house that being a mother was not going to be any easier just because there were other adults around. No one took responsibility for the four children other than their mother and occasionally their father who lived across the park. Yes, we shared the meal preparation and shopping and cleaning. But childcare was left up to Jeanne. She had to deal with their individual needs, their schooling, their clothes, their bedtime and all the other trivia of parenting. That wasn't going to work for me. If I was to become a mother, I needed someone equally invested in parenting.

Through Jeanne, I met Howard Kress. He was the co-president of the first interracial pre-school in Atlanta. We met at a fund raising party for the school. He had two sons, Howard and Brad, who had attended the school. He was separated from his wife who had worked for the election of Jimmy Carter and been given a job working in Washington as a reward for her efforts.

We made a date for the following week. He invited me to his house as he didn't have childcare for his two sons. He lived in a townhome community in Sandy Springs across the road from Western Electric where he worked designing telephone substations. When I arrived, he asked if I would like to see his sons. I agreed. We walked up the stairs to the room where two boys, Brad 7 and Howard III 9 lay asleep in bed. His obvious pride in his children was compelling. He showed me a note from Howard's teacher, which used a phrase that was so southern and unfamiliar to me that I knew I was in a different culture. It was only one of many adjustments.

It looked like Howard could be a reliable co-parent.

Within a year of my arrival in Atlanta, Howard and I bought a house in Candler Park and moved in together. Candler Park, adjacent to Little Five Points was a transitional neighborhood at that time before there was rapid transit. Little Five Points is a commercial district and at the time was just starting to develop services for an "alternative" community. There was a food co-op run by Ananda Margies and a community credit union. Some neighbors took over the bar on the corner and turned it into a welcoming community space. Our neighbors were mainly Quakers who had a meeting house down the street where we, too, attended for a while. It fit my need for community.

Our house had once been a single family home which had been turned into a duplex. We restored it to a single family house, tearing out walls, putting in a staircase to the upstairs where we built two more rooms, one for the television and one for Brad. Young Howard had a room on the main floor. The second kitchen turned into a washroom with clothes washer and dryer and a door to the outside. We decided to modernize the old fashioned bathroom with a clawfoot tub. As do-it-yourselfers, we took out the old plumbing fixtures to prepare for the modern tub and shower. I took one end of the tub and Howard took the other. He said, "One, two, three, lift." His side raised. Mine didn't. It was a vivid lesson for me that I couldn't do everything a man could! Our neighbor came over and the two men lifted the tub and took it outside.

My favorite room was the kitchen. I repainted every wall of the house, and I chose a bright orange for the kitchen. Later, I hung posters from the Soviet Union on all the cabinets. It was a great space with a counter along one wall where people could sit on stools and hang out while I cooked. My best conversations took place in that room. It was where I talked on the wall phone with my mother on Sunday afternoons. It was where girlfriends hung out while I made a meal and we talked about our children. That house was where I experienced the normalcy of American middle class life in the 1980s. It was when I most resembled the image of a young adult white American woman, raising a family and working part time.

What was typical of me was that I chose to do that in a culture significantly different from the one in which I had grown up. Not quite as mean to me as living in Amagansett, but still quite challenging.

There were many things about living in the South which were challenging to a New York Jewish woman. Being culturally different in Kenya people had discounted my "inappropriate behavior" because I was a foreigner. However, in Atlanta, people expected me to be "like them" because we are all "Americans." I wasn't like them. The patterns I had learned growing up, speaking up for myself, being direct in asking for what I want, speaking over others, are considered "rude" in the South. I was constantly being corrected or shunned for being inappropriate. It was painful. I definitely didn't "fit in," again. However, I was older than when I had experienced this in Amagansett and had more resources. Atlanta was changing, becoming more cosmopolitan. There were people in the international community there with whom I was able to make comfortable relationships.

One new experience for me was to own our own home for the first time. Our house had a big backyard. When we moved in, it was filled with kudzu, a southern scourge. The tangled vines made it impossible to use the yard for anything so all four of us, Howard, his two sons and I, spent untold hours pulling up the vines. Eventually, we had them all rolled into a huge ball, taller than any of us, and needed to bring it in front so that it would be collected and carried away by the city. We couldn't move it. In the end, we tied a rope around it and pulled it out with Howard's VW van. In order to keep it from growing back, we had to mow the lawn weekly for several years till the roots finally gave up. Later, when Howard was looking for ways to reduce energy usage, we built an experimental structure in the yard which piled stones in a glass covered box. The box faced south and heated water which was circulated into the house to heat it in the winter. It was much less attractive than our neighbor's tilapia pond in a greenhouse.

One of the things I liked best about living in Candler Park was that people were experimenting with alternative social structures as well as economic and technological approaches. We created a weekly potluck group which met in one another's homes. Several of our neighbors worked together to buy a bar in Little Five Points and make it into a community watering hole. I was on the board of the food co-op, Sevananda, and we had a community credit union. The potluck group made a comfortable community of like-minded people. Several of us collectively bought an old defunct gas station on the corner and fixed it up. One member turned it into a jewelry studio and shop. Howard became the president of the neighborhood association and we felt well embedded in the community.

During this time, Andy Young ran for mayor of Atlanta. We supported him. One of our demands was that the effort to build a road through our neighborhood to connect I-85 with Emory University be stopped. Young said he opposed the road. However, when he became mayor and continued to support the road as homage to Jimmy Carter, we all felt betrayed. After the election, Howard stood up in a meeting and took off his t-shirt with a saying that supported Young's candidacy and flung it at Young saying, "You're a liar." In the end, the demographics of the neighborhood changed. As middle class professionals moved into the neighborhood, the city was no longer able to build a road where they had already torn down dozens of houses and cut down hundreds of trees. The space that had once had trees and homes became used for a park with walking and biking trails. The road now only goes through the "Old Fourth Ward," a traditionally black neighborhood that connects I-85 with the Jimmy Carter library. That compromise was fashioned at the Neighborhood Justice Center where I was later trained as a mediator.

When I first came to Atlanta, I got a bit of pay from Friends World College for taking freshman students to explore options for experiential learning in the South. I began taking short term assignments. I became friends with an African American woman from the northeast, Rita. She invited me to use my skills and knowledge as a vocational counselor to work with the young VISTA volunteers she was shepherding into a real job. I participated in the retreat she was organizing in Alabama. I turned up at the appointed time and place in my little blue VW bug. While we were in Alabama, a group of the trainers decided to go out for dinner in "town." We were a racially mixed group, but I thought nothing of it. It was 1977 after all!

We arrived at the restaurant and were seated with some unfriendly looks. Our order was taken. Sometime later, all of the white people at our table were served. We asked about the rest of the orders. Reluctantly, they were produced, completely uncooked. Raw and partially thawed fish was not acceptable. None of us knew what to do. I was in shock, mortified to be white and unable to eat what was set before me. I can't remember whether we paid or not, but we left hastily.

It was an eye opening experience for me. It was so embarrassing, I don't even remember discussing it on the car ride back to the retreat facility, but it has been etched in my memory. My feeling was that the black people involved were not surprised and what appeared to me to be lack of outrage only made it worse for me.

I had several jobs in Atlanta. My first full-time job was with the Women's Center of the YWCA. One of my friends from Quaker meeting worked at the YW and told me they were looking for staff for a vocational training program. The YW had been given a grant to create a program to help women return to work after raising their children. Five of us were hired to implement the program. I used what I had learned in Brattleboro to get the job of supervising the counselors who would work with the clients. Susan Hester was the director. I thought she walked on water. There were two other counselors and an administrative assistant. When we were looking for an administrative assistant, Susan chose a black woman with dreadlocks. She thought they were braids and that anyone who could do such intricate work would make a good administrative assistant with attention to detail.

My job was to develop the workshop format that provided the clients with a framework for making career decisions. Then the other two counselors worked with them individually to flesh out their plans, write a resume, and apply for jobs. It was a time when there was a big push for getting women into non-traditional jobs and we got advertisements for job openings for engineers and other professions which women had not previously been able to enter. What always amused and annoyed me was that they said they were open to women, but required so many years of experience it was impossible for a woman to meet the criteria for employment. Women hadn't been in those professions fifteen years before. How could a woman have fifteen years of experience to qualify for this job? Was this "affirmative action?" Whose truth?

I left this job to work at Oglethorpe University as director of the student center. I took the job because it included working with the international students which I had done before. My boss was John Thames whom I liked and respected. I had made good connections with the people who worked with internationals and we had formed a support group that I enjoyed participating in. I felt this was what I had been trained to do in my masters program and this was where my heart was. However, I didn't particularly like the aspects of my job which entailed finding bands and entertainment for the general student body. I also found that I had a lot of empty time on my hands where I was required to sit at my desk waiting for something to happen. Despite my practice in Kenya of learning "creative waiting" when in the U.S., I wanted to be DOING something.

During that time, I decided I it was time to get pregnant. I was scared that having a baby would mean even more empty time on my hands. In order to assess whether I could handle the life change that having a small child would entail, I left that job and tried developing a business doing career counseling. Eventually, trying to market myself was too challenging for me so I took a part time job at Georgia State University doing career counseling. This ended up being a very reasonable way for me to mother a baby. I had been with Howard's two sons now for a couple of years, but a baby was something completely different.

Shortly after Sasha was born, I got a job teaching cross-cultural communication at the newly established magnet program for international studies at North Fulton High School. This was really my first foray into using my educational credentials. Having appreciated the experiential learning at the School for International Training and written my Master's thesis on experiential learning, I had an opportunity to use this approach to teach. I learned a great deal. It was also a good job to have as a new mother, since I could work mornings and be home around lunch time to pick up my child from Bessie, the babysitter across the street. Eventually, Sasha went to the preschool that had brought his father and me together.

I loved teaching, the opportunity to discover ways of sharing information about cultural difference and communication styles. I gathered books and materials and experimented with ways of setting up a classroom which would be most effective. I learned the limits of what can be done within oppressive structures like the public school system. The year I decided to let the students make the rules and enforce them, my supervisor took me aside and told me I would have to return to being a disciplinarian or lose my job.

On the other hand, my role expanded over time and I was able to teach two courses: intercultural communication and global issues. Then I also became the person working with service learning opportunities and was able to use my experience with career development and my contacts in the growing international community in Atlanta to place students in internships during their senior year.

The school attracted students from many backgrounds, Cuban-Americans, Vietnamese-Americans, African-Americans, European- Americans. And they had classes in Chinese and Arabic languages. I wrote and published my first article about teaching in a multicultural classroom. It was published in both the International

Schools Journal and the Association of Secondary School Principals Journal. It led to my being invited to consult with some international schools about how to use a multicultural classroom to enhance learning.

I was free to design my own curriculum in intercultural communication and global issues based on my experience at SIT. The director of the program knew me from our time in New York City with AFS/International Scholarships where we had both worked. She wanted an experiential program for this magnet school which was designed to keep some white students in a school system rapidly turning all black. Eventually it became an International Baccalaureate school. Since 1991 this program has continued at North Atlanta High School.

One aspect of the school was to give students an opportunity to travel overseas and experience another culture. The first time I chaperoned a group was to Jamaica in summer of 1985. The school was trying to create a sister school relationship since Atlanta had a Sister City relationship with Montego Bay. However, we didn't stay in Montego Bay, but in Kingston. This city is not a place one wanted to be in the summer! It was hot and sticky and getting to the beach was not easy. I stayed with the school principal who lived alone and was busy during the day during the week preparing for the coming school year. My students were scattered around the city and I rarely saw them so I had to fend for myself most of the time. I was determined not to do that again.

The next chapter of my life was started by one of my students, Lisa. She was an exchange student to Denmark before coming to my class for seniors where they did service learning. I understood her challenges about coming back "home" and placed her in an internship with the Neighborhood Justice Center, one of the first mediation centers in the country. Lisa said, "Kathryn, mediation is just for you. You will love it. You should go be trained as a volunteer mediator." This formed the foundation for my next career.

Mediation was the antithesis of my mother's principle: "Go way out on the left to balance the crazies on the right." However, it was just what I needed to balance the conflicts I experienced with Howard. Although I had taken counseling classes at Georgia State University and been rebuffed by Howard for using "I messages" which sounded phony to him, I knew I needed to learn more about conflict resolution to keep from creating situations which turned violent.

∾∾

When I was pregnant with my son, Sasha, in 1979, I went to visit my mother in New York City. She was living alone in her huge seven room apartment. She said that because it was rent controlled and a smaller place would cost even more money. Sitting on the couch in the familiar living room with all the furniture I had grown up with, I told her "I'm pregnant."

She said, "You are too selfish to be a mother."

I was shocked and hurt. I can only think now that she was projecting her own limitations as a mother on to me.

Sasha has been my greatest joy and my greatest heartache. When he was born, I held him and thought, "I created this new life." It broke my heart open to feel that connection and responsibility.

When Sasha was about two, I decided it was time for him to give up the bottle which always hung from his mouth, like a large pacifier. I thought, "This is nuts." I was embarrassed to see him looking so foolish. He spent his mornings at the baby sitter's across the street and it didn't seem fair to have her have to be the one to get him to sleep without a bottle, but I was teaching at that point, so I thought I would wait until it was Christmas break to try to change his pattern. I was sitting on a stool in the orange kitchen talking to his father.

"I think we should have Sasha give up the bottle over Christmas vacation when I can put him down for his nap as well as at night."

"I'm okay with that," Howard said.

Sasha was listening and left the room, bottle hanging from his mouth. His dad and I continued to discuss the possibilities. A few minutes later, Sasha reappeared, walked over to the trash can and threw his bottle in.

"I guess we won't have to wait until Christmas," I said.

This is when I should have learned that Sasha would do things in his own time. Not understanding his differences, I felt great pain and confusion. Even now, seeing him as a grown man struggling to find a life that includes other people I find myself being too controlling, trying to make a round peg fit into a square hole. As an adult, he said, "I say no at first because when I say 'yes' all the time, I get into trouble. If I say 'no,' I might miss out on something, but I won't get into trouble. Now I am learning to say 'Let me think about it.' That seems to work pretty well." He says he works like a Chinese finger trap: the harder you pull to get out of it, the more it resists.

One of the institutions that made our neighborhood in Candler Park work well was that the potluck group spawned a babysitting cooperative. Everyone started out with an equal number of "chits" representing a half hour of babysitting for one child. We could call another member of the coop and ask them to take our child for a couple of hours. If they agreed, we left Sasha with them for two hours and paid with four chits. Later, to earn chits, we had their children over. There were some families who weren't willing to deal with Sasha's differences, but we could always count on other families to be accepting. Some people just couldn't understand why someone who was so articulate could say such socially inappropriate things or respond to other children so unacceptably. Mostly he kept to himself both at school and in social situations, but sometimes he got frustrated and refused to cooperate.

When Sasha was in pre-school, we were told he needed counseling because he didn't fit in. The counselor told us if we parents could get along better, Sasha would be okay. She told us that she had never seen a couple with higher tolerance for emotional pain. We were hurting each other on a regular basis. Howard kept having affairs with women. This was, from his point of view, permissible because when we first got together, I wanted an open marriage and I had continued to have occasional contact with Eric. I tolerated his relationships for a time and then I got fed up and gave him a choice of "her or me." Ultimately, our relationship was more about mutual revenge than about mutual support.

❧❧

Mother was not happy when I chose to move to Georgia. She thought the south was a terrible place filled with racism and stupid people. However, over the years she adjusted to coming to Atlanta once a year and I visited her at least once a year, usually in the summer when we could go to the house in Amagansett. Moving to Georgia was as far away from her as I felt I could go. I considered settling in San Francisco where I had still had the friends with whom we had stayed when dad died. But I thought that being three times zones away from mother would be difficult. Being in Georgia allowed me to be driving distance away from her.

In 1981, I was visiting in Amagansett with Sasha, Howard and my two stepsons. We drove up there in the VW van with all our camping equipment. We were en route to Toronto for a family vacation. My son was a year and a half old and I felt like I had finally become an adult.

We woke to a beautiful sunny day. Howard was feeling magnanimous and offered, "Let me make breakfast for everyone."

I asked young Howard to set the table. I brought the silverware, cups, mats, napkins, etc. to the Dutch door and passed them through. He set places for five at the picnic table on the porch. Sasha sat in his high chair. Mom and I sat outside with the boys waiting for Howard to bring the food. The smell of bacon cooking wafted out on the warm morning air. The sun was bright but not yet hot. The garden was filled with brilliant flowers. Mother and I talked about the garden. She always loved pansies and they were brilliant in their purple and yellow glory. I admired the flowering butterfly bush was now grown almost up to the second story windows. Her chaise sat under the red leafed Japanese maple waiting for her to spend the afternoon reading.

Howard came out with plates in his hands filled with the eggs, toast and bacon. He set them down in front of Sasha, Howard and Brad. Mother was outraged, "What are you doing? I should be served first!"

Howard was completely taken aback. Appalled, he went back inside and finished preparing the food for the three adults, and vowed he would never return to her house again. We never did as a family.

There came a point when I decided I was not going to accept any more direction from my mother, I was standing in the orange kitchen in Atlanta. Talking on the phone with her as I did every Sunday evening, I told her about the project I was working on. She responded with advice on how I could do it better.

Angry, I firmly told her, "If you don't stop telling me how to do everything better than I am, I won't talk with you anymore."

Not at all contrite, she asserted, "I have other friends your age and they don't mind the way I talk with them."

Taking a deep breath, I explained, "You aren't their mother."

She did modify her behavior, but it was too late. I could hear her criticism even when she wasn't speaking.

One of our points of conflict was that she felt we were so much alike. In 1985, she sent me a birthday card which said,

"For a swell, kind, warm, intelligent, well liked person...We have so much in common."

Not too long after, she wrote, for once not addressing me as "Kathy, darling,"

"We're a mother and a daughter, and that very closeness and affection results in an added burden and added stress. We are both aware of being strong and aggressive women. And we are both intelligent and passionate. At my age, I have quieted the surge of my aggressiveness—the passion has been somewhat spent. My illnesses in the past three years have seriously undermined what has been my zest for living.

"...In dealing with each other we must deal with the present. You see I have reached an age where I have had my full quota of pain and hurt; have learnt how to deal with it and have resolved that I no longer need to either seek it out or to accept it. I avoid it...I cannot cope with anger, either my own, or another's...We cannot look to each other as mirror images—with the same values—we come out of different generations, and there is no reason to agree or pattern each other in the same mold.

"...At NO time do I want to direct or control you. You are an adult, married and a mother. I respect you for your accomplishments. I love you because we are part of each other. And because we love each other, we must learn to be more careful with each other than we are with most people. You cannot on a visit to me tell me, in words, how much you love and admire me, while your voice, your body movement is cutting me down. Your anger shreds me – several times you made me cry. Didn't you know why I cried? You never told me why you were angry—I still don't know...I cannot sustain another visit from you until you understand yourself...

"We will have to find other ways of relating to each other. I have to protect myself."

I find it rather remarkable from my present perspective that she claimed she had no idea why I might be angry with her. Clearly, she wasn't aware of how much she had controlled me from the day she chose when I would be born. She said to me "I made you independent." Is it possible to "make" another person independent? Whose truth?

I think it was impressive that I could tell her that I admired her for the contribution she had made to society even though I felt I had been damaged by the way she parented me. Someone once observed she was an "altruistic narcissist." It was hard being her daughter and being expected to follow in her footsteps, never going outside the lines she had drawn.

I wrote her, "I am disappointed in how you are bringing your life to an end. You spend all our time telling me about your various maladies and weaknesses." She stopped sharing this information such that I really don't know what she died of.

The last time Sasha and I visited mother, she was in Amagansett. She had been having bouts of forgetting where she was or thinking when the clock said ten it was 10 a.m. when it was really 10 p.m. She went out looking for the newspaper and wondered why it was dark out. If she got lost, she would call her friend Suzy Barker to help her find her way home. She was feeling poorly and asked me to lie next to her on the bed and listen to her talk about her life. I spent most of my visit looking for someone to come and live in her house with her. I succeeded in this before I left. I found someone, but when I called to see how it was going and she said, "Oh, he left already." There was nothing more I could do.

I was teaching at North Fulton High School that fall. I was called to the office over the P.A. system. My cousin Victor had called to say that mother had died. She had some friends visiting for the weekend. They said she had gotten up in the morning, drunk a cup of coffee and gone back to bed. She never got up again.

She wanted a Jewish burial even though we had never practiced any religion. I had to find a rabbi. I called the one synagogue in East Hampton which only operated in the summer, hoping that the rabbi hadn't gone back to the city yet. He agreed to conduct the service. He came to her house in Amagansett. Sitting in the living room with the large plate glass window looking out on the woods which had grown up from the empty fields which had been there when we built the house, he asked me, "What were the Jewish values you were raised with?"

I said, "I don't know anything about Jewish values. I was raised to value all people, to do my best to make this a better world for everyone and to protect the democratic values of our country."

He said, "Those are the Jewish values of tikkun olam."

It was the beginning of my identifying as a Jew.

I spent the next day cooking all the food she had in the freezer. I planned to share it with people after the service at the cemetery. We buried mother next to my father in the Green River Cemetery along with many of the famous people whom she had cultivated as friends and donors to her causes. Wikipedia has a list of 30 names of famous people buried in that cemetery including Jackson Pollack. Hardly anyone except a few cousins from the city came back to the house after the service. I was left with a lot of cooked meat that I had no use for.

My mother died a week before her seventy-fifth birthday. My first thought when she died was, "she can't hurt me again." Mother's death allowed me to become my own person and to follow my dreams, without her criticism—except the little voice in my head which still says, "You could do this better."

Just as the death of my father changed my outlook on my relationship with men, over time, the death of my mother freed me up to become an adventurer, explorer, seeker. She left me an inheritance that allowed me to leave my job, build a dream house in a rural community and create a different life from that of a middle class housewife and mother living in the suburbs.

"Contradictions, denounced by logic,
are embraced by love, but not without a touch of suffering."

- Adi k. Irani, follower of Meher Baba

৵৵

CHAPTER NINE

I HAD BEEN TEACHING HIGH SCHOOL IN ATLANTA PART-TIME and yearned to live in a rural intentional community. I was seeking the cooperation and collaboration I had read about in Communities Magazine and seen when visiting places like Koinonia, the Highlander Center and Stephen's Farm with the students from Friends World College.

A couple I had befriended through the Quaker Meeting in Atlanta had purchased land and built a house in North Georgia close to the place I had stayed when writing my master's thesis. Howard and I bought twenty acres in their neighborhood, called Golden Hill, in 1984. A number of ex-urbanites had settled on subdivided land. Our acreage was in Banks County, known for being the largest county with the fewest people and only ninety minutes from Atlanta.

Our land was in an unintentional community, somewhere between a subdivision and hippyville. Our lot was furthest from the paved road across a creek and up a hill, a challenge for getting access. Howard built the bridge himself and we cut a path through the woods. He hated cutting trees, so it was rather winding. We got gravel laid and began building a house in 1986 using the money I had inherited from my mother.

There were already a number of families living on the two hundred plus acres. Each family had eight acres and our friends had set aside part of their acreage for a community building. We helped build a Quonset hut style building on that lot to be used by the whole community for gatherings. One of the men in the community, Larry P., owned a shop where he bent wood into curved beams that made the Quonset shape possible.

Before we built our house, we built a small octagonal cabin where I spent weekends when I needed to get away from Atlanta. We began by putting a tent in a barrel to protect it from the rain when we weren't there. But some hunters must have stolen the tent, so we built a "plywood tent." This was done in a day long "barnraising" by neighbors before there was even a road. We piled eight sheets of plywood and pieces of two by four on one side of the creek and hand carried the materials up to the crest of the hill. It was a beautiful day and people enjoyed staying around after it was assembled for the food I had prepared. I thought after all this cooperative effort it would be easy to continue our joint efforts in raising our children.

When Howard and I still only had the "plywood tent" on our land, we had meetings and potlucks in the community building. I thought that this building would become a school for our children as well as a place where we could bring in people from the outside for weekend workshops. This would meet a lot of my needs for stimulation and engagement.

Larry P. had architectural knowledge and was able to design a thirty foot diameter octagon; two and a half story house with arched beams supporting the roof. It was a joy to behold. Everything except shingling the roof was constructed by people who lived in the community. I prided myself that I was giving work to my neighbors and helping the community by providing income in exchange for their labor. The whole community worked on the construction of the house: Jan did the foundation of concrete block, Tony was the general contractor and found inexpensive materials, Genevieve and Willow worked on the beams, Klaus did all the cabinet work in the kitchen and under the eaves in the loft. I did the painting of the walls.

At the peak of the beams was an eight sided ring that supported the roof. Inside the ring was leaded glass in a sun shape with eight points that Howard commissioned from a friend as a 40th birthday present from the community to me. The house was 900 square feet on each of two and a half levels. The half story above was the master bedroom with a balcony overlooking the living room. On one of my trips to the Soviet Union, I brought back a large carpet picturing a mother bear and her three cubs in the woods. We hung that over the railing so that it provided privacy in the loft room. Under the eaves there were cabinets where we stored our clothes. It was lovely to lie in the bed and look up at the leaded glass in the apex of the beams. We were surrounded by beauty in the light wood walls and the dark stained curved wood beams layered to be a foot thick.

Walking in the front door, you could see all eight beams and the pinnacle where they came together in the leaded glass octagon with a crystal in the center that threw rainbows around the main room when the sun shone through it. It was like walking into a small cathedral. It was all open except for the one and a half sections that had the bathroom. There were large plate glass windows in two of the eight walls and a sliding glass door in another. It was filled with light. There was a long deck which reached around four sides, bulging out into a space big enough for a picnic table on the side by the dining area accessed through the sliding glass door.

Howard was very interested in alternative energy so we built the house with no power wires. All the electricity came from the sun with backup from a liquid propane (LP) generator. The liquid propane was stored in a tank where the road crossed the small creek and pressured to come up the hill to the house to fuel the cook stove, refrigerator, on demand hot water heater and generator. The photovoltaic panels were on a long pole which allowed us to turn them during the day to follow the sun. The only source of heat in the house was the wood burning stove which was next to a concrete wall in the basement allowing us to set a fire at bedtime and have the heat stored in the wall radiate throughout the night. The basement was partially bermed in. The first floor had three walls with glass facing south to capture the sun in winter, with an overhang to protect the space from too much heat in summer.

In the basement there was a large bermed room which housed the twelve RV batteries and inverter to take the power from the solar panels on the pole outside and turn it from DC to AC, so we could run ordinary electrical equipment from the system. We got our water from a spring down the hill and kept the pump turned off during the day to save electricity. In the evening, when the lights were on, we ran the pump to fill the pressure tank which supplied enough water during the day to flush the one quart toilets. It took effort and attention to keep things running, but we did live "off the grid." We even got photos and a write up in the *Atlanta Journal Constitution* about our alternative energy system.

Howard had good building skills. He built a pond on the creek by making a dam. He used the energy from the dam to run a ram pump providing water for the garden which was over the septic field. It was very prolific! Sasha ate the fresh peas right there while I pulled the weeds. We were able to grow much of the vegetables we ate in summer.

I loved walking in the woods. There were 200 acres of undeveloped forested land behind the house and I took long walks there when Sasha was in school. I especially liked to walk down to the small cascade at the edge of our property. I could lie in the hammock hung there between two trees and read a book listening to the water flow over the rocks. It was peaceful.

Golden Hill community consisted of about ten houses, each lived in by a family which had moved to this area toward a more self-sufficient life style. Each house was unique as was each household. There were a few single people and several families with children. I imagined that we would share childcare and communal homeschooling.

Genevieve and Larry E. had two sons, Silvan and Yoric with whom my son, Sasha got along well. Willow and Dusk had a son, Forest, a little older who turned out to be a terrible bully. He made life very difficult for Sasha. Dusk had no patience with a child who didn't obey him automatically. Dusk's heavy hand had a great deal to do with how mean Forest was. He ended up getting into trouble with the law. Forest had two half sisters who were older and they didn't hang with the younger children. In addition there was Amber, Tony's daughter, who was a bit younger. Tony also had a stepson, Jeremiah, who lived with his mother. He was the oldest boy and also was mean to Sasha.

The first year, Howard stayed in Atlanta with his son, Brad, who was finishing high school. Since Dusk wasn't willing to homeschool our children together and Gen and Tony weren't willing to homeschool at all, I was alone with Sasha many hours every day and we had a lot of learning to do about each other. This was when I began to realize how difficult he was. Although he was six years old, he would not dress himself or in any other way take care of daily needs. Trying to teach him math was a challenge. He was curious and read on his own, even picking up the *Encyclopedia Britannica*, which I had bought to ensure we had a source of information in this isolated place. But math was another story. I bought all kinds of gadgets which were supposed to make math more concrete, but none of it worked to engage him. Conversation went like this:

"Sasha, if you don't get dressed, you can't do anything else. You must sit on your bed and not read or play with anything."

No reply.

"Are you getting dressed?"

No reply.

"If you aren't dressed you can't move off the bed."

And he wouldn't.

Eventually, I would be so annoyed, I'd say, "Sasha, I am going into town to the library. If you want to go, you must be dressed."

Two minutes later, he appeared in front of me fully dressed, needing me to tie his shoes. His dexterity with fine motor skills was very poor and it took forever before he could actually tie shoes. Thank goodness for Velcro. He has never been motivated by trying to please anyone. He hates to hurt anyone's feelings, but won't change his behavior to adapt to other's norms or expectations.

The only channel we could get on the television was the educational channel and he would watch fishing if that was the only thing on. Having limited electricity made it fairly easy for me to limit his watching, so he watched anything that moved during the hours he had permission. Even as a toddler, his babysitter was amazed that he would watch the news just to see the moving figures on the screen. He now keeps the television on twenty four hours a day.

I had friends over. I could see that he was bothering them. I said, "Sasha, stop that. You are bothering that person."

He said to me, "No, I'm not" and asked my friend, "Am I bothering you?"

Of course they were "southern polite" and said "no, you're not bothering me." That left me no recourse. I couldn't argue with them that they weren't telling the truth and he felt that he was right. But he wasn't. Whose truth?

At the same time, Sasha was amazing at finding the person in the room who was most likely to be warm and accepting. He sidled up to someone who was willing to be physically close and tolerant of his differences. Sasha likes physical contact as long as he can be in a position to move closer or away when he feels the need.

Sasha was never much for being in the out of doors. When we were still just visiting at the "plywood tent" he wandered off into the woods and it took much searching to find him because he didn't reply to our calls. Later, Howard and I needed to bring supplies from the car across the creek; we left Sasha standing on the deck of the small cabin. Howard told him, "Don't leave the deck." Sasha takes everything very literally. We returned with our supplies and found him still standing on the deck looking very uncomfortable. There was a pile of feces lying on the boards and Howard was outraged.

While he raged at Sasha I thought about how many times I had told Sasha to "stay right there" in front of a grocery store while I ran in to pick up a few things. He was always standing there when I returned waiting for me. I felt powerless in the face of Howard's anger even though I didn't think it was helpful to rage at Sasha. Howard had already raised two sons and insisted there was nothing wrong with Sasha. I had never had a child before and didn't know what was reasonable to expect. I also was hesitant to engage with Howard when he was enraged because when he turned his anger on me it was scary.

The woods were an unknown and uncomfortable place for Sasha. He walked with me down to the waterfall where we could hang out playing in the creek, or followed me along the road to go visit a neighbor, but he never was one to explore alone in the woods. At one point after I started sending him to school, he did have a friend who came over from town and they did some exploring together, but he never went by himself. That was the reason it was so surprising the day we were working on the community building and he said he was hungry. I said that there were bagels in the freezer back at the house. He actually walked back there alone and got himself a bagel. He would never have done that for anything else. Bagels were his favorite food and he still prefers them to almost anything else beside pizza.

Sasha is fascinated with how things work. We walked around the zoo and he asked questions about how the gates worked that let the animals out of their indoor pens and into the outdoor spaces. I said, "Look at that big lion."

He replied, "How do they keep the lions apart? Do you see how the water flows into the trough it drinks from?"

Still today in the science museum we look at a display on

electricity and he is fascinated by how it is designed to demonstrate the flow of electricity from the power plant to the home. Best of all is the Rube Goldberg machine where at the age of thirty eight he can spend fifteen minutes turning the wheel to see how the different balls follow different paths causing different sounds as the ball bounces off different objects.

After the first couple of months in the octagon house, I couldn't bear to spend every day in the house with Sasha. I found a day care center where he could go in the afternoons. Gloria, who ran it, turned out to be a teacher of children with disabilities, and was very kind and helpful. When she moved her school to Commerce (almost an hour away), Sasha travelled with her there every day. Thus we got through first and second grades. But then she closed the school and we had to find a place for him in public school. Thinking that Habersham County was more sophisticated than Banks, I chose to send Sasha to Cornelia.

The third grade teacher was very kind. She told me when I checked with her after a couple of months that Sasha was doing much better. "He no longer spins himself around in the floor when he is upset," she told me. What a surprise! I had never seen that behavior. I wonder if he would have begun to demonstrate these behaviors if we had been able to homeschool. Certainly he hadn't been like this even at Gloria's school. Was public school just too stressful for him?

To be promoted to fourth grade, the school required Sasha to pass a test on which he had to answer eighty five out of 100 multiplication questions in five minutes. We must have done this hundreds of times using the kitchen timer. His teacher also must have tested him many times before he could do it. She tutored him in math over the summer and warned me that he was going to have a hard time with the fourth grade teachers.

The fourth grade teacher, Ellen Ivey, just saw him as non-compliant. She insisted that he change from writing in print to writing in cursive. Since his motor skills were not up to this, he just stopped writing. She thought the way to get him to do what she wanted was to punish him so she wouldn't let him go to recess. He loved that as he didn't have to deal with the other children and could sit in the library alone and read. She suggested I punish him by not letting him go to Scouts and baseball and I wouldn't as those were the only times he actually had to interact with other children and learn some social skills.

She insisted that we take him for therapy which we did. The therapist wanted to blame the difficult relationship between Howard and me rather than working with Sasha. She enjoyed Sasha's creative imagination and one on one found him charming. At the end of the year, the fourth grade teacher wouldn't pass him on to fifth grade even though he made one of the highest grades in the class on the end of year test. (Of course, his bubbles were so dark they made holes in the paper.) She said that he did well to "spite her." As if he cared what she thought!

When it was apparent that another year in Cornelia school would just be a repeat of this terrible experience, we enrolled him in school in Homer. It turned out that the fourth grade teacher there was very competent, on her way to a Ph.D. in education and was able to work with Sasha to get him to cooperate. When his behaviors became too difficult for other students in the class, she sent Sasha to the office with a note, not as punishment but as a way to get him out of the room. She reminded the children while he was out of the room that he wasn't trying to be difficult but that he had differences and they needed to not provoke him. She even changed the order of her curriculum so that he started with math he could do easily before having to take on some things that were harder for him.

That was probably his best year in north Georgia. I wonder if he felt as marginalized there as I felt in Amagansett. He says it wasn't so bad, but he did recognize he was being bullied.

❧

Sometimes I took the ninety minute drive to Atlanta. We were sitting in the orange kitchen on one of my visits talking about the future toward the end of that first year. I said to Howard, "If you don't move up to Banks County with me, I rather get a divorce."

❧❧

I was frustrated with living alone with Sasha and struggling to make a life for myself. I wanted a partner who would share the responsibilities of living in a solar powered house in a community which had proven to be less supportive than I had anticipated.

He agreed, "I can take early retirement and we can sell this house in Atlanta. I'll come live with you and Sasha."

It was hard for all of us living in this isolated place. Howard couldn't find work and spent most of his time with alternative energy projects, such as building the dam to use a ram pump to push water up the hill for the garden. He had his own medium sized octagonal out-building where he hung out to give us both space from each other while still being nearby. Even though he didn't have a job most of the time, he considered me responsible for the housework and for childcare. He enjoyed working with his hands and is very good at it, but we also needed income. He spent all the money in his retirement package in the first year.

Howard and Sasha argued all the time. They find it fun even today to argue, but I found it very stressful to listen to. Howard refused to acknowledge that Sasha was "different" and might need some intervention. Sasha had many behaviors that other people found difficult to be around. At that time, mothers were blamed when their children misbehaved and people looked at me as if I was deficient and that was why my child was odd.

Our neighbors had been a big part of the reason I chose to move to this community. I bought an additional eight acres of land contiguous with the land of the community building we had all built together. I imagined we could have workshop participants stay in tents on platforms on this land and use the community building for a meeting space. I decided to bring in international volunteers to help build the platforms and outhouses. I asked for four volunteers and got eight. That meant I had to feed and house eight people instead of four. There were some neighbors who helped with the housing and the volunteers cooked the food I bought in the community building. However, at the end of that summer, some neighbors organized to use our consensus process to choose to revert to voting and voted not to have outsiders use the building. I began to seek stimulation elsewhere. I began doing personal growth work. I also increased my involvement in exchanges with the Republic of Georgia. Both of these paths I will describe in detail in subsequent chapters.

With all the disappointments and my own changes as I became more empowered through my activities organizing exchanges with the Soviet Union and my engagement with Lifespring, it became clear that Golden Hill was not the dream I had had of living in community. I could see that I was being willful rather than willing. I had had a child that I wanted, but he did not fit in. I built my dream house, but it was somewhere I didn't get the support I expected. I moved into a community, but it turned out to be more of a struggle than I had anticipated. As they said in Lifespring, you can get what you strive for, but it doesn't always look the way you thought it would.

In our sixth year in Banks County, it turned out the undeveloped land behind our house was owned by a paper company. When they decided to log it, the dead bodies of the trees piled up behind my house crying out to me day and night in the rough voice of the chain saws and logging trucks. Eventually, the state bought the land and turned it into a hunting preserve, but the damage had been done. My favorite trails and streams had all disappeared into logging roads and fords. The stream beds were no longer my sanctuary. The copses of mountain laurel with their elven creatures were trampled and the hobbits all run off ahead of men with rifles out to shoot a deer or bear to prove their manhood.

That same year, Sasha was in fifth grade and had a very sympathetic teacher. She made it clear that Sasha would have a hard time in the middle school in Homer. Since I had not heeded that warning from the third grade teacher, I took her advice to heart.

Meanwhile, after a peak experience with the Atlanta-Tbilisi Sister City Committee and many Lifespring trainings, (which I will describe in subsequent chapters) I was ready to call the marriage dead. I had grown and changed and it was time for Howard and me to part company. We got divorced. It was time for me to return to civilization. Sasha and I moved back to Atlanta in August of 1992.

"I have never been especially impressed
by the heroics of people who are convinced
they are about to change the world.
I am more awed by those
who struggle to make one small difference after another."

- Ellen Goodman

CHAPTER TEN

I was in the car with Howard in fall of 1985. We were driving up to the mountains where we had the "plywood tent" that we used as a vacation place. He asked me, "Will you go back to Jamaica next summer if they ask you to?"

"No way! But I think they will ask me." I was clear!

"Where would you like to go?" he asked with genuine curiosity.

Without even thinking about it, I said, "The Soviet Union."

Although I had many experiences that enriched me while my mother was still alive, it was only after her death in fall of 1985 that I made what I consider to be real contribution in the world. I created the Atlanta-Tbilisi Sister City relationship which has continued until today. Doing anything with "Russia" was scary for me as it brought up fear of being called a Communist and not being able to find work, as my father had experienced. What amazes me today is that so many people can know that the Russians have dramatically influenced our national elections, and they don't seem disturbed about it. After hiding my identity as a red diaper baby for so many years, it is very confusing. I don't think Howard even knew at that time that my father had been blacklisted. Whose truth?

There were a million reasons why I thought I couldn't take students to the Soviet Union beginning with the fact that the cost of travel to Moscow was far greater than to Jamaica. One reason was that guests had to stay in hotels, not homes as we did in Jamaica. The airfare was much more expensive. And people were scared of the evil empire...

When I studied Russian as an undergraduate, one of the hard things for me was that all my teachers hated Russians and could see no reason to go there. When I spent the summer in the U.S.S.R. after I graduated from college, I had enjoyed the people I met so I knew there were Russians who loved their homeland as well as Americans love this country.

I had developed a unit for my high school students where we looked at the prejudice against Russians. I chose Russians because that was a group my students didn't know much about–other than they were labeled the "Evil Empire" by then President Reagan. Prejudice is most evident where there is lack of knowledge. The only Russians you could meet in Atlanta were immigrants who left because they hated the system there, like my language teachers in college.

It turned out, in my very ethnically mixed classes one commonality was that the Vietnamese refugees, the Cuban exiles and both black and white Americans could all find common ground in their contempt for those "dirty communists."

When I first started teaching the unit on prejudice I was scared of the possible repercussions of saying nice things about Soviet people and got laryngitis. I lost my voice for a couple of days. Since I couldn't talk, I devised a lesson that didn't require much talking. I had met a man who worked for Soviet *Life* magazine who had given me a subscription to the magazine full of color photos of Soviets living normal lives. I cut out these pictures of Russians and asked my students to write about "One day in the life of Ivan Ivanovich or Natasha Ivanovna..." the people in the pictures.

I saw a pattern emerge. If the person was working, the story's theme was "working hard from dawn to dusk, this miserable person..." If the picture presented someone participating in recreation, i.e. sailing, camping, on a motorcycle, the story's theme was always about planning or arranging to escape from their terrible life to a western country where he or she would be "free." What was even more amazing was when I demonstrated this lesson to adults in the Society for International Education, Training, and Research, I got the same results. Americans could not imagine Soviets living normal lives and enjoying leisure time, content to remain in their own country. I knew the only way to rectify this misconception was for Americans to meet Soviets who loved their homeland and were glad to be there.

I had been thinking about taking students to the Soviet Union when my mother died, and this idea became much easier to realize when I didn't have her looking over my shoulder telling me how to do it better. I made friends with a couple of visiting scholars from Russia who were taking post graduate classes at Georgia Tech, Vitaly and Gennady. I began negotiating with the Soviet travel agency, Intourist, to figure out where we could go and how many students I needed to make a group. A group of seven people was sufficient. Six students plus me. I recruited them.

As I looked into taking students to the Soviet Union, I learned how expensive it was to travel there. I also learned that the way to get scholarship money for young people was to be part of Sister Cities International. If we were a Sister City, there would be government funding for youth exchanges. However, the exchanges were homestay programs and the Soviet Union was not allowing foreigners to stay in homes at that time.

The Soviet Union consisted of fifteen republics. Russia was the largest and its capital was Moscow, which was also the capital of the Soviet Union. We were interested in going to one of the smaller republics in the southwest, Georgia. We learned that Georgians are to Russians as Greeks are to Norwegians. They are very different cultures with different languages and different histories but they have been in relationship for centuries because of proximity and the fact that Georgia has a long coastline on the Black Sea and Russia has always needed access to a water route that is not frozen half the year.

In the 80s, the only way you could enter the Soviet Union was through Moscow, so I arranged for our tour to start there. My main objective was to go to Tbilisi the capital of the Georgian Republic where I believed we could meet with Gela Charkviani. I had met Gela when he was in Atlanta with a Friendship Force group. (Friendship Force is an international exchange program started in 1977 and supported by Jimmy Carter. It is centered in Atlanta and creates adult homestay exchanges.) Gela worked with the organization in Tbilisi which was authorized to develop relationships with people from other countries. He is the son of a former head of the Georgian state and speaks English like an American. He also taught at the University in Tbilisi. He was a close advisor to Shevernadze, the head of state of Georgia from 1992 to 2003 and during that time became the ambassador to England. Gela is one of the most brilliant people I have ever met.

Arriving in Moscow, we stayed in an Intourist hotel, met our interpreter and began to find our way around. Some of my students were very adventurous and went out that first night to investigate. They sold their first pair of blue jeans on the black market while I was sleeping off the time changes. In Moscow my Jewish students and I got to meet with some dissident Jews who gave us their side of the story of religious persecution. At another time on the trip we had a local guide who was Jewish. He told us about how privileged his family was and that he experienced no harm from being Jewish. At that time, everyone in the Soviet Union carried an identity card which stated their nationality. Jewish was a nationality just like Russian or Ukrainian. Whose truth?

I also arranged for us to go to Odessa to see where my father was born. As it happened, it was shortly after the meltdown of Chernobyl and we had to pass near the area by train during the night. We couldn't see anything interesting, but I worried that parents would be reluctant to have their children so close to the radioactivity.

Luckily, none of the parents withdrew their children.

The trip was worth it as I got to see the synagogue in Odessa which was no longer in use as most of the Jews in the Ukraine who had not emigrated had been killed during the holocaust. Religion of all kinds was anathema to the Soviets who saw the power of the church as potentially an opponent and used Marx's statement "Religion is the opiate of the people" as a tenet of the Communism they claimed to practice. The synagogue was not in use for anything and the watchperson told us it hadn't been used in a long time.

In Odessa, we had dinner in the home of Vitaly's wife's family where we saw the contrast with the public spaces and restaurants that had been available to us. The food was vastly better than any restaurant. The norm in that part of the world was that you entertain guests in your home and restaurants were for foreigners or a meal when you didn't have time to go home, like fast food here. Although their home was small and having seven guests greatly cramped them, they were generous. They gave me a Vanishka, the male equivalent of the matryoshka (the Russian nesting dolls). The Vanishka covers a vodka bottle instead of having multiple babies inside like the "little mother."

When we arrived at the Iveria hotel in Tbilisi, I began to question my decision to spend ten days there. There seemed to be little to do in the town and the hotel only had three possible menus, assuming people would not stay more than three nights. The hotel itself was a high-rise with very little to recommend it and the Intourist guide from Moscow had little idea of what we might do for half our time in the U.S.S.R. The city itself is spread out along the Mktvari River with mountains all around. At that time, the air was dense with the smells of poor quality gasoline being burned by older model Ladas, the locally manufactured common car. The main street, Rustaveli Avenue, had shops with limited merchandise and one place for tourists to buy handmade items. There were a couple of museums that were poorly maintained.

The first morning, I went down to the lobby to see what I could learn. I was sitting there disconsolate having no leads even to Gela and Metropolitan David, another Georgian whom I had met in Atlanta but had never responded to my letters. Out of nowhere, along came a bevy of men in black robes. And wonder of wonders they were speaking English!

I greeted them enthusiastically, "Hello, who are you and what are you doing here?"

One man replied, "We are Orthodox Christian priests from the U.S. visiting in Georgia."

Delighted to hear this, I asked, "Do you know Metropolitan David?"

"Yes, he is our host. We are meeting him in front of the hotel in just a little while."

Joy of joys!

I went running out front and ran right into David. Dressed in his black silk robes with his long grey beard and black square hat, he looked like a Santa Claus in mourning garb. His cheery demeanor and jolly chuckle rumbling in his big belly made me feel instantly welcome. In my broken Russian I reminded him we had met in Atlanta. He invited me to meet him that afternoon in the lobby when he returned from escorting this group.

That afternoon we met on the upholstered benches in the lobby and talked for hours. His interpreter, Boris, was there. For a long time it was just David pouring out his heart in Russian. I sat fascinated, nodding where it felt appropriate and swimming in his extraordinary energy.

Finally, Boris said, "It's too much for me to translate!"

David said in Georgian, "She understands me."

Boris checked with me and I confessed "I only understand about one in ten words, but I love what he is communicating."

Who was this amazing man? I met Metropolitan (which means "bishop") David while I was teaching at North Fulton High School. It was known in the progressive community that if you wanted to show foreign visitors an American school, I was the one to contact. When the Council of Churches had a delegation from the Soviet Union, they called me.

As my students settled in their seats that day, in walked a motley crew of Russians and Georgians in various attire befitting their status. Some were lay leaders, wearing their brown suits typical of Soviet officials. Some wore ecclesiastic robes. David stood out from the group in his black silk robes and compelling rotund presence: he engaged the group's and my attention. I have no memory of what he said, but when it came time for me to follow through on my commitment to bring youth to the U.S.S.R., I knew I wanted to meet him again.

In my naiveté, I wrote to him asking if he would have youth in his congregation meet my youth travelers. David didn't write back when I asked if he could help me meet some young people when we came to Georgia, but in his book *Live for the Sake of Peace and Justice*, printed in 1986, he wrote,

"On one of my visits to the United States I met a young teacher from Atlanta Georgia. She showed a keen interest in the way Soviet people live and spend their leisure time and asked me many questions about it. Some time later I received a letter from her in which she says that her meeting with me has made her decide to include information about Soviet people and about the Soviet Union in her lectures on international cultural ties. Her students, she says, are convinced that exchange of visits and personal contacts are good way of getting to know people." (p. 35)

After I met with David that first day in Tbilisi not only did I get a great supporter who helped us have a marvelous experience in Georgia, I also got to know Boris. After David had poured out his thoughts to me in Russian, Boris then explained in English the gist of what had been said and added that he, himself, shared these sentiments and desires for peace. He also told me that he prefered to translate from Georgian to English without having to go through Russian. That was the end of my improving my Russian language skills and the beginning of a long friendship.

Many years later, I saw how little contact David had with ordinary people in his own community. He and I were walking together to his daughter's house in Tbilisi. A child ran up to me (I was clearly a foreigner), and asked incredulously in Russian, "Do you really believe in God?" It was hard for this child to believe that a woman of my age (40s) actually believed in God, as it wasn't customary for Soviet women to acknowledge any relationship to the church until they became quite old and death was no longer an enemy. It was dangerous to demonstrate an interest in religion in this Communist state. I really couldn't say at that point whether I believed in God; but I definitely believed in David!

After meeting with David, I still thought that Gela was the person I needed to talk with to get the Sister City to happen. He kept putting me off saying he didn't have time to meet with our group. When I finally got to meet with him he was much less hospitable than I had heard he was with others, hardly serving us refreshments and not playing the piano as he was reputed to do. He was known for his jazz piano playing.

I said, "We are here because we want to start a Sister City relationship between Atlanta and Tbilisi."

Gela replied, "Your mayor has been here, and he didn't mention this interest. You are a high school teacher how can you represent your city?"

This is an example of the differences in our perceptions of how things happen. For the Soviets, the only way to make relations with another government entity was through political contacts. For the Americans, we assumed that ordinary citizens were empowered to make international relationships. Overcoming this difference was an interesting project. Without Boris, it would never have happened. Which way is right?

After my meeting with Gela, I came back to the hotel miserable and ran into Boris in the lobby. Seeing my tears, he invited me to join him in the courtyard where we had some privacy. He asked me what had happened. He explained that Gela was having personal problems and I shouldn't take it personally. But it wasn't about a personal brush-off. I was afraid it was the tanking of my plans to become Sister Cities and not having funding for future exchanges.

Boris took pity on me and arranged for us to visit with the Patriarch of the Georgian Orthodox Church. It was quite an experience. First we visited the church where the Patriarch was holding services. There are no seats. Everyone stands the whole time. The clergy comes in swinging a censer hanging from three chains and filling the room with the odor of incense. Everyone sings the service. The small church adjacent to the Patriarch's residence is decorated with many icons of Christian events. I have lots of formal photos which were taken by the official photographer for the church. Even then when religion was supposed to be unacceptable, the Patriarch's official residence was ornate, filled with gold candelabras and uncomfortable antique upright chairs. Boris translated the meaningless polite kindnesses which were said on both sides. I was no closer to having a Sister City relationship. However, I was impressed with the wealth and respect afforded the church in a supposedly atheist country. More questions about "truth."

Meanwhile, David arranged a day for us where we got to visit a young children's program and a rural area where we picnicked by a rushing river. We also visited the outdoor museum of culture where you can see the various traditional homes representing the many cultures which all coexist in this country of only six million people. We went to Mtskheta, the ancient capital where one of the oldest churches is located. The ancient church was in reasonable repair in the midst of a tiny village with a few very old houses and one shop to buy trinkets. It is amazing what it has become since independence! It was designated a UNESCO World Heritage Site in 1994 and the "Holy City" by the Georgian Orthodox Church in 2014. As a tourist site, it looks like Disneyworld compared to the staid place it was in 1986!

One day on that first trip to Tbilisi, walking down the street, I was accosted by a young girl who spoke reasonable English. She invited us to her home for a meal. She and her mother lived in a room on the second floor of a large building with a kitchen and a bathroom down the hall. It seemed as if all the people who had rooms on the floor contributed to the meal that we shared and the gifts they gave us. I believe her mother hoped that this might lead to the opportunity for the daughter to come to the U.S. to study. This kind of hospitality was just a natural part of the Georgian culture. The Georgian origination story is about how God blessed the Georgian people with the most beautiful and fruitful land in the world as a reward for their hospitality.

On one of the trips I organized in the 80s, Gela came to our house in North Georgia. We were standing on the deck looking out over the woods. He said, "You think that you are free, here in the west, because you can choose between which color of tie you want to buy. We don't have so much stuff to choose from but perhaps we have more freedom." Whose truth?

One of the biggest issues between the Americans and the Georgians was over hospitality. Georgians receive guests with a "supra." This is a meal with twelve toasts led by a "tamada." Each toast is to a specific group or person. With each toast you were to drink your glass to the bottom. Traditionally, the wine was served in a ram's horn so that you couldn't lay it down with anything in it. Any time your plate is empty, someone put more food on it, expecting you to leave some to show you were full. Americans think it shows you liked the food if you "clean your plate." Georgians thought Americans were very greedy, because they kept eating. Americans thought Georgians were ridiculously generous because they kept refilling our plates. Whose truth? I quit drinking alcohol all together because it was the only way they accepted my not participating in twelve toasts.

The expectation was that if you said you liked something you saw, the host felt obliged to give it to you. Americans really struggled with receiving and certainly weren't willing to reciprocate. We think that saying nice things about something in someone's home is a way to start a pleasant conversation. When Georgians came to the U.S. they wanted their hosts to buy them things as gifts. There was a joke, "What do you call a Georgian in New York City?" Answer, "A vacuum cleaner." They were so eager to acquire all the goods that were available that they couldn't get at home.

Georgians have great humor. When the weather was not as good as one might hope for, Georgians said that "Shevardnadze sold the spring and the few warm days are international humanitarian aid." The changes of becoming a capitalist country almost outweighed the benefits of becoming more democratic. Although they were able to elect their political leadership, it didn't make up for many of the economic hardships they experienced as the country became as unequal as the U.S. And I am not sure that their democracy, as ours, hasn't become corrupted by greed.

On a trip to Georgia, Boris gave me a crystal ball which came in two halves that fit together with a scalloped edge and could be used as punch bowls. It sat on mother's antique wash stand which she had used as a dressing table. The drawer still smelled of her makeup. Howard and Sasha broke that crystal when they were horsing around one day. They were sorry. I was furious. Boris had said on giving me the bowl that this represented the way I was working to bring together the two halves of the world, Atlanta and Tbilisi. Breaking it broke my heart.

After my first trip to Tbilisi, I knew that building this relationship between the two Georgias was my path. I needed an identity beyond raising my child. Eventually, I was able to answer people who asked, "What do you do?" by saying, "I do exchanges with the Soviet Union." But first I had a few hurdles to overcome.

In 1987, I went back to Tbilisi with Howard and Sasha and we brought a quilt that was made by the American Quakers in their perennial quest for peace. Americans make friendship between countries through people to people exchanges. Soviets made all their relationships through institutions. It wasn't easy finding an institution to receive the quilt we brought. Boris helped me by arranging for it to be received by a school in Tbilisi which moved us along the path to becoming Sister Cities.

Eventually the idea of a Sister City was taken over by some white professional men, including a lawyer named Scott, whose wife had travelled to Georgia. Carleton Parker who was the head of all the Atlanta Sister City projects was adamantly opposed to my having a leadership role. He found my assertiveness as a woman terribly upsetting and did anything he could to oppose me. I didn't behave like a Southern woman and he was sure that my strength would not be welcome by Georgians. Carleton said, "Anyone but Kathryn." There was a terrible meeting held in the Quaker meeting house where I had worshiped for years. I sat on the staircase outside the meeting room while they discussed who should lead the group. Scott became the president of the committee and finally a delegation headed by the mayor of Tbilisi came to Atlanta.

When the delegation came, I was not allowed to be in the inner circle. A friend of mine was the interpreter. One day there was a meeting between people in construction in Atlanta and the delegation. I was allowed to attend. They were discussing which materials were the most economical to use. The American named one material and the Georgian another. The interpreter kept repeating just what the two men were saying. They were not understanding each other and disagreeing. Finally, I pointed out that the reason the Soviet man found a certain material less expensive was that he did not have to pay interest on his materials so the length of time it took to finish the building did not contribute to a greater cost. For the American paying interest over time made that material too expensive. Sometimes it isn't about the words, but about the norms.

One of the norms where we differ is where the most important person is supposed to sit in a meeting. The Americans were trying to get the mayor of Tbilisi to sit at the "head" (end) of the table. The Georgians were trying to get him in the middle, which they perceived to be the "head." It was a strange dance until finally someone made clear what the expectations were and the mayor was seated in the middle of the table with his delegation on either side facing the Americans on the other side. Who was right and who was wrong?

The delegation was invited to the home of a wealthy Quaker. I had been banned from travelling with the group, but this man knew my involvement and invited me to join them. Shirley Franklin, who was then the chief executive officer of the City of Atlanta, was at the gathering. She is a petite black woman with a forceful personality. Somehow the two of us ended up alone together in the garden. She told me that the delegation kept saying that they wanted to do a youth homestay exchange but the committee members kept holding back because no one on the committee knew how to make something like that happen. I said, "I do."

Over the strenuous objection of Carleton and with the support of Ms. Franklin, I rounded up a group of young people from Atlanta, and sent them to Tbilisi for a couple of weeks. After that, their host siblings came to Atlanta for a couple of weeks stay in their homes. This sealed the deal with the Sister City agreement. I was proud of arranging one of the earliest homestay exchanges between the U.S. and the U.S.S.R. As a result, I got involved with the Institute for Soviet American Relations (ISAR) and through that discovered the Earthstewards Network which also had sponsored one of the earliest youth homestay exchanges. The Atlanta-Tbilisi program was a small rivulet that joined a growing stream of exchanges and programs between the U.S. and the U.S.S.R. It didn't change history, but it certainly contributed to the changes that took place in the early 90s.

The school that received the quilt became a sister school with North Fulton High School and there were several exchanges. One of the teachers who accompanied the students ended up marrying one of the teachers from North Fulton High School and staying in Atlanta.

≈≈

Over time, my relationships developed, especially with Metropolitan David and with Boris. Metropolitan David had an amazing combination of humility with an expectation that whatever he wanted would be provided. He was charming and charismatic. Boris was always afraid he would be arrested for child molestation as children eagerly gravitated to his lap in airports and other public spaces.

He loved "stuff." When he visited me the small town in North Georgia where I lived and stayed in the one motel, there wasn't much to see and do. We went to a very junky flea market where he immediately engaged the sellers who responded to his cheery non-verbal gestures by giving him gifts of whatever interested him.

Giving gifts is a national occupation for Georgians. It is expected that when you receive guests they will leave with some kind of a gift. I noticed that the more opulent the host the less generous the gift. Shevernadze's daughter with her gold candlesticks on the mantelpiece gave me a simple gourd made into a pitcher. People with much less to spare gave very generous gifts of art or jewelry. After receiving many unwanted and useless gifts, I was delighted when Metropolitan David allowed me to choose what I liked from a gift shop. Although I never got to visit him in his home in Sukhumi (the capital of Abkhazia), I treasure the needlework image of St. George killing the dragon he bought me the last time I ever saw him.

He died before I had a chance to meet with him again. I heard of his death when I met with a group of Soviet visitors in Atlanta shortly after Abkhazia broke away from the newly independent Georgia. We were grounding ourselves in the "who do you know" when I mentioned David. My conversation partner said, "Don't you know, he died a few months ago." I wailed, scaring my American colleagues and demonstrating to the Georgian I was speaking with the depth of my connection to David.

When I saw Boris again, he told me that he had been with David the day he died of a heart attack. Boris believed that David died of a broken heart when his beloved region severed its ties with the rest of Georgia. The Abkhazians with the support of the Russians (in the winter of 1992-3) threw out the ethnic Georgians, relegating them to a long forced march through the snowy Caucuses Mountains to end up in the very Iveria Hotel where I had stayed on my first trip.

Later when I returned to Georgia, I saw the laundry hanging from the hotel balconies where whole families of displaced persons were living in one room waiting for space to be built where they could live. I bought the traditional round Georgian bread (thicker and bigger than pita, but very similar in shape) from a woman who said she had been a school teacher in Abkhazia but was now reduced to baking bread and selling it on the street corner.

After the changes in the economic system that took place in the 1990s, people did not even recognize their friends on a minibus because the norm was that the first person to alight paid for friends travelling further. People could no longer afford to spend double the fare and avoided noticing someone they knew on the bus. Has capitalism made their lives better? They certainly have more "stuff" available for sale, but only a few can afford it. Georgians are very enterprising and took to capitalism with enthusiasm, recreating inequality equal to that of the U.S. The desire for acquisition of goods absorbs the wealth that was previous used for generosity. The benefits of capitalism. Whose truth?

I was in Georgia when it was announced that elections would be held in which there would be actual choices of candidates. Our hosts were very excited to hear this news on the radio in the bus which was carrying us to Batumi. I said to one of my Georgian friends, "there will be a lot of hard times before things become better." He couldn't hear me. He was delighted at the possibility of change.

That day we stopped in a small Georgian town where we visited a police officer who was also an artist. He gave us an oil painting he had made with an inscription on the back wishing us peace between our nations. He lived in a remarkable unique house with a spiral staircase in the middle. I was surprised at the ability to have something so individualistic in this very communal society.

We arrived in Batumi, a resort town on the Black Sea, at dinner time. We were hurried into our rooms without partaking of the extensive meal that had been laid out for us. The next morning, it was still sitting on the table when we reconvened for breakfast. We asked why we could not have enjoyed the food when it was fresh and were told in hushed tones that there was a guest in the hotel who was a radical dissident and they didn't want us to encounter him.

It turned out this radical was Gamsakhurdia, who became the first president of Georgia after the dissolution of the U.S.S.R. He was a very nationalistic man who wanted to forbid anyone who was not ethnically Georgian to have citizenship, although only about 60% of the people living in Georgia were ethnically Georgian at the time. He lasted less than a year.

After 1991 and Georgian independence, I continued my friendship with Boris. He got a job with a Georgian bank and was their representative in New York. He lived in New Jersey for a year and I spent a night in his place. We decided we were like siblings. We could talk for hours on the phone. He made me laugh aloud with his dry satiric humor.

He always dressed impeccably but comfortably and presented himself as completely in charge of every situation. His diplomacy served him well in the various work he did. He always garnered support because he built trust by being reliable and honest even when dealing with less than reliable and honest people. It was through his efforts that I eventually got to meet the mayor of Tbilisi and establish the Sister City relationship. When Americans wanted to send that Quaker quilt as a gesture of friendship, he found a school willing to receive it. When we wanted to send a "peace delegation" he found a group willing to receive us. Boris wanted his wife, Nina, to have the experience of visiting the U.S. and when she did, she stayed in my home as part of the peace delegation.

As a gift, Nina brought me a weaving of a woman under a rainbow with a long Georgian style purple gown (my favorite color) and hair flowing down her back just like I wore my hair at that time. The woman's arms are reaching for the sky. The doves flying around represented my peace work. The dearest thing was that it was a woolen tapestry which I had sought when in Tbilisi and could not find. Boris had the weaving commissioned for me by a famous fabric artist. He gave the most thoughtful gifts.

Nina eventually became the ambassador to the Czech Republic and Boris has had several leadership positions in Tbilisi. The last time I was there was in 2010. It was August and hot. I was startled to see the improvements they have been able to make to their apartment now that the country is capitalist and there is lots of money for some. I was also disappointed by the gift Boris gave me on that occasion which was a green and brown felt blanket too large to carry and not at all something I would have chosen. It seems we have drifted apart and he no longer responds to my e-mails. It has been great loss to me and I can't really explain it. Was it that I had changed partners too often? Or that our status in our respective societies was now too disparate? Or that our belief systems had diverged too much? I'll never know for sure. Whose truth? That weaving is still my most prized possession even though it has faded with too much sunlight, just as our relationship seems to have faded. I miss him.

Why was Georgia so important to me? Perhaps my interest was first piqued when I met Vitaly and Genady the students at Georgia Tech. Vitaly was from Odessa, my father's birthplace, and I found him especially attractive. Vitaly reminded me of my father with his pale blue eyes and mild manner. I went out of my way to make them welcome including inviting them for Passover. When their wives visited the U.S., I had them over for a meal.

Later Georgia became important to me because I felt more welcome there than anywhere I had ever been. Not only is Georgian hospitality remarkable, but they also have a warm relationship with Jews in general. They speak of "our Jews" who came through the Fertile Crescent into Georgia around the east of the Black Sea. There are both Ashkenazi and Sephardic synagogues in Tbilisi.

From the mid nineteen eighties on Tbilisi became a major destination for people on Friendship Force and other exchanges. I wrote the booklet that Friendship Force used to orient Americans going to Georgia to stay in homes. I never did learn to speak Khartuli, which is what they call their language. The country is called Sakartvelo, in Khartuli.

After Georgian independence, I created a business I called "Megabroba and Company." Megabroba means "friendship" in Khartuli. I brought a group of Americans to visit as tourists and we stayed in a hotel. It was quite different from coming as "peace delegates." It was back to the pre-Boris and David days; no homestays, no hospitality, and the generosity with which I had become accustomed was no longer available as capitalism had conquered all.

❧

In the late eighties, I was very involved with a personal effectiveness training called Lifespring which encouraged us to set goals for ourselves. I decided that a meaningful goal was to create the opportunity to teach about American culture in Tbilisi. I knew that

Gela taught a course on the United States at the University in Tbilisi and that he was coming on another Friendship Force delegation. I arranged to meet with him. Waiting at a shopping mall where the delegation was going to have lunch, I was so keyed up I was afraid I would not be clear. Taking off my shoes and grounding myself by walking barefoot on the little strip of grass between parking spaces, I prepared to ask Gela to invite me to Tbilisi.

Gela wanted something different. He wanted to bring a delegation of performers to Atlanta. I thought if I gave him what he wanted, he would give me what I wanted. Little did I know what changes were upon us! I agreed to make his wish come true.

Simultaneously, I was trying to get to be a volunteer with Lifespring to staff their training in Moscow. I had only been in the program for a couple of years and did not qualify. As it happened, I was visiting Howard's sister in North Carolina when I got a phone call telling me that someone had dropped out of going to Moscow because they were concerned about the unrest in early 1991. I could go if I could get a visa. Of course I could get a visa. I contacted Gela and he arranged for me to get the necessary documents.

This meant that in addition to going to Moscow for the Lifespring Training, I also needed to go to Tbilisi where Gela took me all over to view the various performing groups he wanted to bring to Atlanta. It was an amazing trip!

In order to carry out Tbilisoba, I became the chair of the Atlanta Tbilisi Committee. After years of hanging back from appearing to be the leader, while doing all the work that kept things going, I now had the title. I thought Carleton would have a heart attack the evening when George Brown, who had been the titular head of the committee, announced that he was nominating me as chair. George knew I had been doing all the work, and thought I should also have the acknowledgement. This meant that when the delegation came, I took them to meet the mayor of Atlanta, Maynard Jackson. I was interviewed when the papers wanted to cover the story.

This is another pattern in my life, where I get the title because some feminist man sees the work I am doing and figures out a way to give me the credit I deserve, despite the culturally determined sexism which gets in the way. It had happened with the International Club at the University of Wisconsin and it happened again with the Sister City program.

In the end, we had forty people come to Atlanta for ten days in fall of 1991. We got sponsorship from Delta Airlines and Coke Cola. We housed people in the homes of Americans who did something in common: puppeteers with puppeteers, dancers with dancers, singers with singers, etc. There was a filmmaker who showed his films at Emory University. We had a chef who cooked at a restaurant a few times and prepared a big fund raising dinner at Callanwolde Fine Arts Center (a magnificent Southern mansion). We served the outstanding Georgian champagne I had asked each person to bring in his or her suitcase. The dancers performed at the Piedmont Arts Festival and everyone participated in the finale which was supposed to be the opening but the group was delayed in Moscow and didn't get there until after we were supposed to open. Oh, well.

In spite of this success, Carleton continued his opposition and managed to replace me as chairperson of the committee with a manager from Coke who had done nothing to make this happen. He even arranged to have the transition party at a time when I wasn't available.

As it turned out, Gela never brought me to Georgia to teach. However, Nugzar, who was the interpreter for the Tbilisoba delegation, did. In 1996 I made two more trips to Georgia. The first time, I was invited by Nugzar who was now the director of The Institute for Public Administration, a school for training people for management positions in the newly capitalist Georgia. The school was funded by Americans and Nina, Boris's wife, was teaching English there. Nugzar remembered me from the Tbilisoba events and Nina recommended me as a teacher of conflict resolution, which I had been doing at The Mediation Center in Asheville for the previous two years.

I went for two weeks and stayed in an apartment arranged for me by the school. It was a walk up on the sixth floor which taxed my energy. The electric power at that time was still intermittent and the hot water never worked properly. Boris was not there so Nina hosted me.

It was during that April visit that I met Zaliko and I got to spend time with him both at his farm and his house in the city. One of the students at the school had recommended him as an interesting person and I took the risk of contacting him. Zaliko initially impressed me because he was working to improve relations between Georgians and Ossetians. There was conflict over the shared border and disputes among the different ethnic groups which had lived together in peace under Soviet rule. Zaliko was part of a small delegation that was being brought together with a delegation of people from Ossetia with the help of Roger Fisher, famous for his leadership in the Harvard Negotiation Project. Zaliko said that he would be happy to talk with me about his work, but he was very busy and could only fit me in if I would take the drive with him to his land.

I drove into the mountains with Zaliko, whom I had met for the first time that day. When I stepped out of his Jeep onto the land he was planning to be a community using organic farming techniques, I cried tears of recognition. This was home. I fell instantly in love. Was it the man or the land, the food or the culture? I don't know but altogether it was love. The smell of lilac filled the air. I walked on the land and was deeply touched by the beauty of the majestic Caucasus Mountains and the brilliant blue sky. My heart opened and poured out joy into the sparkling sunlight, shining on the craggy mountains and dipping into the valleys channeling rushing rivers. All is beauty.

The land we visited was in Karsoni near the crest of a hill. His father and his son were taking care of the crops and animals, living in the "finished" basement, the rest of the house being incomplete. It was spring and the fruit trees were in bloom. I have a photo his son took later which looks like it was taken on that hillside. There is a tree in full leaf standing by itself with a snow topped mountain in the background. I felt as if I could touch heaven there. My arms reached up inviting a power greater than myself to carry me away. Tears came to my eyes as I stepped out of the car onto the land. I was where I belonged.

Zaliko became very important to me as he was interested in so many of the same things I was at the time and I really hoped he would get involved with the Earthstewards. I spent as much time as I could with him and when I sought a way to return to Georgia, I asked him to sponsor a project where we would bring people of different ethnic groups together in a workshop format I had learned that helps bridge those gaps. He agreed.

Even though I was teaching two classes at the Institute, (one English language and the other on conflict resolution) teaching only took up part of each day, so I wandered the streets and sought other NGOs which might be interested in hosting me to teach future workshops. Michael Clayton from the Institute for Soviet American Relations (ISAR) which now had an office in Tbilisi was interested. I arranged with him to come back, again for two weeks, and teach their affiliates conflict resolution skills.

On that October trip, I invited my friend, Martin, from Earthstewards, to come along. He and I led a weekend Essential Peacemaking workshop with participants mostly rounded up by Zaliko. In addition, I had several days with folk who were working with ISAR and a day-long workshop based on the prejudice reduction model I learned from the National Coalition Building Institute.

The experiences I had in Georgia and with Georgians changed my perception of myself. Not only did I gain a deeper understanding of the both/and perspective I had embraced in my year in Kenya, but I also deepened my understanding of the variety of ways humans can be different from each other. My experiences in both countries provided content for my recognition that there are multiple ways of making life work; that society can organize itself in a multitude of ways and finally that humans can create culture in life affirming ways if they are encouraged to become conscious.

"Through the blur, I wondered if I was alone
or if other parents felt the same way I did—that everything
involving our children was painful in some way.
The emotions, whether they were sorrow, love or pride,
were so deep and sharp that in the end
they left you raw, exposed and yes, in pain.
The human heart was not designed to beat outside the body
and yet, each child represented just that: a parent's heart bared,
weather forever outside its chest."

- *Debra Ginsberg*

CHAPTER ELEVEN

When we first left the octagon house, Sasha and I moved to Atlanta and I rented rooms from old friends near where we had lived. It was a rough year for both of us. Sasha went to a school that his half brothers had gone to, but found it much less hospitable. Although he was able to get back on the right grade level, the teacher did not appreciate his differences and the pressures to produce work left him confused and isolated. One day, the teacher did a sociogram and then announced to the class that Sasha was the only person with whom no one was friends! She tried to pair him with a young man who was developmentally delayed, but Sasha said it was, "Like talking to a tree." All the boy wanted to talk about was recycling. Sasha, too, has things he talks about despite his listeners' disinterest.

One day, Sasha didn't return from school when I expected him. He normally took the MARTA train back to our station and then a bus home. I called the school to see if he had left. He had. I drove over there to see if he was somewhere they hadn't looked. He wasn't. I drove back along the route he would have taken to the house and didn't see him. I enlisted Ed, our housemate, making him promise that he would stay in the house in case Sasha reappeared. It was before the days of cell phones and once I was out looking, I was cut off from communication. I was frantic.

About an hour after he should have arrived home, I went to the MARTA station on an intuition. As I got out of the car, he emerged from an arriving train coming from the opposite direction than he should have been. He saw me and walked over like nothing out of the ordinary had happened. I greeted him with enthusiasm and said, "I am so happy to see you. I was really scared when you didn't come home on time. Where have you been?"

Nonchalantly, he said, "I missed my stop and rode to the end of the line and came back."

It never occurred to him to get off and get a train in the opposite direction sooner than the end of the line.

He often came home with his lunch intact. The lunch period at school was so stressful he wouldn't eat with the other children. He also wouldn't eat on the train because there were signs that said, "No eating or drinking allowed." He was very careful to follow any explicitly stated rules.

Sasha went to Renfroe Middle School in Decatur that fall on the recommendation of my friend Haqiqa. It was not very successful. When he came home with all Ds on his report card and his shirt wet down the front, I knew we had a problem. I asked him, "What happened to your shirt?" He said, "I chewed on it."

When I told the principal how upset he was, she said, "The teachers thought they were being kind and taking into account that he has an IEP (Individualized Education Plan) and gave him Ds instead of Fs."

The school had recently hired a new special needs counselor who was a black man from the north. He was ill prepared to work in this southern school with major race issues. He didn't last and neither did we.

By great good luck, Haqiqa had taken a workshop in peer mediation from The Mediation Center in Asheville. The Mediation Center got a large grant in January 1994 which allowed them to hire new staff to train school personnel in peer mediation. I got hired.

I moved to Asheville to help set up peer mediation programs

in all the middle and high schools in the county. Sasha stayed in Atlanta with Larry, who became my third husband, for the first month while I got settled and found us a place to live. It was a difficult month for all of us.

I moved into a spare room in my new colleague's home in Black Mountain. Dee was generous in letting me have a place to stay when I needed it. We also shared an office where if we both pushed our chairs back at the same time, we bumped into each other. Luckily, she was a good collaborator and we both accommodated to make that first month work.

The team for our first training was a group of seven people most of whom hadn't worked together at this level before. There were the three of us hired specifically for the grant, two other full time staff of the center and two people contracted specifically for this training. Our first task was a three day training for seventy-two staff and faculty of the twelve schools in the district. I was new to them and new to Asheville and knew nothing! They sent me out to buy the food for the three days of training. Carrying it back into the office, I stumbled and twisted my ankle so badly that I hobbled for the rest of the training. I was in pain. I didn't have time to get it looked at so I just soldiered through. It was definitely a trial by fire!

The three of us hired specifically for this grant, Dee, Copper and I, went on to write curriculum to teach conflict resolution skills to grade levels K—12 with a common theme. We called the middle and high school levels TRIBE. Dee loved acronyms. It stood for Tell What is Up for You, Reflectively Listen, Identify the Problem, Brainstorm and Evaluate. I have used that paradigm ever since in teaching conflict resolution whether I am in the Republic of Georgia or the state of Georgia.

Many hours were spent on the floor of our tight little office creating piles of papers, each with an exercise which taught one of these skills, sorting them out into by grade level appropriateness. What was best for me with my background in experiential learning was that all of us were committed to teaching through experiences rather than by lecture.

My relationships with these two women have been complex and dynamic, sometimes very close and nurturing and sometimes very difficult. Using the skills we taught was very helpful. I learned so much during those years. I appreciate our collaboration as a model of how I want to work with people.

During that first month while I was in Asheville and Sasha and Larry were still in Decatur, Sasha got as sick as I can ever remember between living with Larry and going to a school where he felt they didn't understand him. It was a rough month. Haqiqa helped Larry out with Sasha, but everyone was very happy when I finally found a place for us to live and we could move in together again.

In February, Larry and Sasha joined me and we moved into a rented town house in Swannanoa, just outside Asheville. Owen Middle School was a place where I liked the principal who had been in the peer mediation training. I knew Mr. Jones would be thoughtful when Sasha faced problems, which he inevitably did. Kids picked on him at lunch and he threw food at his tormentor. Sasha was chastised but not isolated.

I knew that we needed to find permanent housing in the city of Asheville so that he could go to Asheville High School where his differences might not bring such negative attention. That July, we moved to West Asheville. Even then, in the middle 90s, finding rental housing in Asheville was a challenge. We were lucky to get this house on a quiet street except on Friday nights when the NASCAR track was still in what is now Carrier Park and the noise on Friday nights could be overwhelming.

It was actually before we even moved to West Asheville that Sasha began strange behavior. I was completely confused and scared. I had tried on diagnoses of ADHD and "developmentally delayed" and discovered that whatever specialist I took him to said that Sasha had that disorder. One of my colleagues at The Mediation Center had been trained in child psychology. I came to him saying, "My son is cutting up his underwear and tying up the furniture in his room with cord."

He said, "Why don't you look into the possibility of his having autism." So I had him tested at TEACCH, a state supported program for people on the autism spectrum. They gave us a diagnosis that actually fit.

The label, Asperger's Syndrome (AS), has helped, both in my understanding and expectations and in being able to get help. The diagnosis of AS had only been determined a few years before. We were lucky to be in North Carolina where there are free services for people with autism. Thank God for TEACCH! They explained, "It's just like being from another culture. You can't understand the language."

I said, "I've lived and travelled in many cultures, but I can always tell what people are feeling, whether I understand their words or not. He is from another planet!"

Yeah! I had a diagnosis that fit. I had books to read, resources to help. What a difference it made to be able to have realistic expectations.

Years later, our neighbor, Gen told me that she had known that Sasha was on the autism spectrum when she found him talking to a chair as a young child. She had taken child development in college when I was taking courses in philosophy. Gen and I were very close, but she thought that I didn't want to "label" Sasha, so she never mentioned what she believed.

Ron Larson, Sasha's counselor at TEACCH, went to Sasha's classes every semester and explained to his classmates that Sasha was not (as I had always said) the most contentious person they had ever met; he simply sees the world differently. Ron's explanation went like this: If you are looking out a window that Sasha has looked out many times before and Sasha is across the room from you and you say, "Sasha, what am I looking at?" Sasha will reply, "How should I know, I am not looking out that window." Sasha cannot put himself in your place; he cannot imagine what you might be seeing because he cannot imagine himself as being in your place. He is always and only in his own place. Neurotypicals call this "lack of empathy." Sasha says now that he feels too much of what other people feel and it overwhelms him and he shuts down. It may be so as he always knew who would be open to him as a child.

My relationship with the school counselor, Ms. Sutton, through the work I was doing in the school around peer mediation also helped to ensure that Sasha got the best education the school could provide. He got to be in English classes with Ms. Rutledge and Ms. Shaw who acknowledged his verbal abilities and (with my support) his writing abilities (that small motor dexterity was still an issue but I had been taking dictation from him ever since he dictated his dreams to me when he woke in the mornings in North Georgia). He had a science teacher who really appreciated his curiosity and channeled it into productive learning. But there wasn't much that could be done about his deficiencies in math. In the end, he had a disabilities coordinator that really loved him and even helped him when we enrolled him in college. He also had the opportunity to get support from Upward Bound. The director, Meg, was wonderful with him and he loved her a lot. He just couldn't understand why he couldn't hug her when he had learned that he could hug women, but not men. Role authority has never meant anything to him.

Eventually, we moved into a house that I was able to buy after selling the octagon house in North Georgia. There, Sasha was able to have the basement pretty much to himself and he made his man cave and developed his patterns of watching TV and playing on the computer which continue to dominate his life. He has never learned to do anything on time nor gained the executive skills to take the initiative to get what he wants. He has never cared about hygiene or having nutritious food and I doubt he ever will. Sasha's description of our relationship is, "My life was the Titanic and you were the Carpathia." I guess I saved some portion of him.

He says now that Asperger's is like always having a conversation in a chat room—you get the words, but not the feelings or nuances. As an adult, he spends most of his time in chat rooms with the television on. He gets into lots of conflicts on *YouTube* where he feels compelled to tell people how wrong their thinking is and then vents with me on the phone about how people can be so stupid.

After several years and two associates programs, he was able to earn a bachelor's degree in computer game design, but he hasn't been able to hold a job. He gets hired, but then he says or does something that upsets people. He was great answering the phone for people having to solve problems, but eventually he said, "What did you expect, buying a Ford, Apple, etc." (whatever he is providing support for.) He has no initiative and irritates people he works around. Just like having to bribe him with going to the library to get him to get dressed at the age of six, he has to have an incentive beyond money to keep his interest. He is very isolated. I feel sad when I think about his life. And at thirty-eight years of age with little job history, he is not an attractive employee.

Luckily, he was able to buy a house with money left to him by my mother and he gets social security as the disabled child of a retired person. I fear for him (and me) if the government cuts off or reduces social security for people with disabilities.

"I say Yes to my life, I say Yes to love,
I say Yes to a one world family,
I say Yes to a planet at peace,
I say Yes to all the children everywhere,
I say Yes to us,
I want my next act to increase the Yes in the world.
So just say Yes!"

- Danaan Parry's Daily Dedication

CHAPTER TWELVE

DANAAN PARRY HAD A HUGE INFLUENCE ON ME. I HAVE taken a great many personal growth seminars, but no facilitator was as flexible and creative as Danaan. He was a big man, about six feet tall and solidly built. His reddish brown hair receded from his hairline but was full in the beard around his face. His work was shaped by his decision to change from using his immense mind from being a scientist for the Atomic Energy Commission to getting a PhD in psychology and helping to heal the world. He called his signature work, *Warriors of the Heart*. I never took that workshop, but I did other work with him. He was the creator of the Earthstewards Network.

I first encountered Danaan when we were both doing homestay exchanges with the Soviet Union in the 1980s. I learned about his work through the Institute for Soviet American Relations established in 1983. They had a publication which reported on programs which brought people together from the two countries despite (or perhaps because) President Reagan had declared the Soviet Union, the "Evil Empire." Danaan's program brought U.S. Vietnam veterans together with Soviet Afghansti veterans to help them figure out how to survive the despair of fighting a lost battle between a vastly stronger power which was defeated by a much smaller and supposedly vulnerable nation.

In the 1980s, Soviet citizens were not allowed to stay in American homes, but with Gorbachev's glasnost and perestroika things began to open up and we were able to create youth homestay exchanges between young people from Atlanta (where I was living) and Tbilisi (the capital of Soviet Georgia). Danaan also created a homestay exchange through his organization, the Earthstewards Network. I was curious as to how his program functioned and when I had an opportunity to participate in one of his workshops, I took it.

Danaan encouraged us to have a clearly stated vision for one's personal direction. For many years, I had my "daily dedication" over my desk. On the back of the card, is typed Danaan's admonition. "Starting off your day with a clear vision about your Purpose can uplevel that day greatly."

He also taught that conflict is a cry for intimacy, that when we are in conflict with someone, it is because we yearn to be known more deeply by that person. At the time we met, I was just starting to work teaching conflict resolution and mediation. His thinking about these issues was a ground for my work. He worked on himself continuously, and taught from what he understood about himself. He had put himself in many conflicted situations, in Ireland (which was his heritage) and in the Middle East and the Soviet Union.

At the time I had the opportunity to take a workshop with Danaan, I was living with Larry. We had rented an apartment in Decatur, Georgia. I believed that to keep this relationship alive, it would be helpful to participate in some structured learning together. Danaan had created Essential Peacemaking: Women and Men (EP:W&M) as a program he co-lead with his wife, Jerilyn Brusseau. He, as I, felt that working together with a life partner would help the relationship. The program was pretty simple, readily reproducible and relatively easy to enroll people in. Larry and I went to Seattle to take the workshop and I was hooked. Danaan felt a commonality with Larry and invited us into his inner circle of trainers. I was delighted and honored.

It was very significant for me to learn about conflict from Danaan. There was an exercise in the weekend workshop where we first played out the behaviors that kept us from having our hoped-for relationships and then replayed them to show how it could be if we could overcome our hurts and be authentic with each other.

At the weekend in Georgia, the four of us (Danaan, Jerilyn, Larry and I) did one of these skits together. It went like this,

Danaan: "I think you should do this project this way."

Kathryn: "No, I know a better way." (So like my mother talking to me.)

We were thirty seconds into a roleplay and everyone was playing himself. We resisted each other into a total meltdown. It was clear that Danaan was threatened by my independent thinking and I wasn't going to give way. When we replayed it, we collaborated and treated each other with respect and were able to demonstrate how, without our patterns dominating, we could actually come up with some good ideas that we could cooperate on.

When we moved to Asheville and married, Larry and I led workshops in Asheville and north Georgia. We brought Danaan and Jerilyn east to lead the first weekend workshop in the southeast. We led a couple of day-long workshops to build participation. I wanted us to become authorized trainers for the weekend workshop as well as the day-long. This was, I believed at the time, the way for me to fulfill my dream of having a life partner with whom I could work. It didn't turn out that way mainly because Larry was uncomfortable with conflict and repressed it in the group. (In the end, he moved out of our home without even discussing it.) I eventually began leading the weekends with Len from Montgomery, Alabama who loved conflict and provoked it and then looked to me to handle the fallout.

In 1994, Larry and I were at a conference in Mexico where Danaan and Jerilyn had built a retreat for themselves out of an old chicken coop. When we arrived early, Jerilyn put us all to work cutting up vegetables for the meal she served the first arrivals. Afterward a group of us went out to a bar to chat. Danaan asked me, "Have you ever been partnered with a strong man?"

Remembering Eric, I said, "Yes, once. But he told me that he couldn't marry me because I would want a say in where we lived. He was right."

When I told Danaan this, I was thinking of the day in Atlanta sitting on a green hillside outside the airport between connecting flights in the mid-eighties when Eric answered my question, "Why didn't we ever make it work? We have been friends through so many years."

Danaan acknowledging the male privilege of being in charge and prioritizing his own career, "Oh, yes, men do want to be the decision-makers. It makes it hard for two strong people to be in relationship." Later we ended up in an airport in Amsterdam together and I got to see how he and Jerilyn solved their problems: she wanted to see something outside the part of the airport we were in. He was concerned that she would miss their flight. He told her, "You go and explore but I will be on that flight whether you get back in time or not."

That gathering in Mexico was a turning point for me. Growing up, the one group of people my mother had no tolerance for were Germans. I shared some comment that came from that bigotry with a German man, Martin, at the gathering.

He said, "Germans feel so guilty about what happened under Hitler, it makes it hard for them to be fully themselves. We feel so bad about ourselves because of guilt about the war."

It had never occurred to me that young Germans felt guilt that constrained them as much as the fear that constrains Jews. Martin's mother had been born the same time as I was, at the end of the war. Surely I couldn't hold him responsible for what had happened in his grandfather's generation. This was something I had never considered.

It turned out that Martin, as I, was involved in Reevaluation Counseling (RC)—an international organization that uses listening partnerships as a tool for social change by teaching peer counseling and empowering people to take charge of their lives. This has helped me heal from a challenging childhood and helped me to be connected, resilient and hopeful about the future and what can be created when we work together.

One of the patterns I had explored in RC is that of Jews who feel that we cannot trust anyone. Jews in RC use a contradiction (a statement which addresses the core message holding us back) which is, "For the long term survival of my people, from this moment on, I will act as if everyone is eager to be my warm, close and dependable friend and ally." Everyone wants warm, close and dependable allies, but it is especially a challenge for Jews to believe that people want to be our allies with our history of betrayal, as I have learned by listening to many Jews over the years of doing RC.

Another German I met in Mexico was Julianne. She organized a gathering for Earthstewards in Berlin in 1994, after the wall came down. We did a ritual celebration at the site of the defunct wall and planted "Peace Trees." I got to see Danaan work with the group in very powerful ways. Danaan's skill as a facilitator was the most evident that week in all the work I did with him over the years. The tensions between East and West Germans turned out to be a focal point, especially when we planted the Peace Trees. There was also an issue with an African facing his resentment toward Europeans for colonialism. Danaan handled it all without ever discounting or avoiding the feelings.

Danaan's death in November of 1996 figured in the ending of my relationship with Larry. I wanted to go to Seattle for the services. Larry wouldn't. Knowing that we would no longer have a significant role together in Earthstewards took a big benefit away from being married to Larry and, I believe, signaled the end of the relationship even though it took some additional time to die. It was wrong from the start, based on a false premise that he would get along with Sasha, (he didn't) and now we had hardly anything in common.

The second time I went to Berlin I stayed at Julianne's apartment for a few days. We visited various places in the city, but weren't able to enter the synagogue as I would have liked. It was guarded because of fears that it might be damaged as it had been during the war.

She also arranged for me to present to a group of her peers who were teaching conflict resolution. I used my favorite exercise where I set up the group into two cultures which are instructed to interact, but can't because they have been given contrary instructions. The participants loved the exercise. When I explained the five styles of conflict resolution I said, "Winning where the other person loses doesn't work. After all, we beat the Germans in World War I and they have hardly bothered us since then." I got a slap on the hand for that one! It's a line from a Tom Leherer song and I had never realized how prejudicial it is.

When I left Julianne's home, I travelled to Aachen where there was a contra dance weekend. I thought it was amazing to do this form of traditional American dance in Germany. I ran into a man I had known in Asheville. He was a German who had been married to an American and they had taken EP:W&M from me and Larry when they were living in Asheville. I spent a day wandering around the city with another man I picked up in a church I was touring. He was very handsome and I was no longer married, but I knew that I was just using him as I had in the past when I had travelled alone. He ended up figuring in the Dark Feminine play I later did as part of my healing journey around my relationships with men.

From here, I went to Hanover where there was a world's fair. I stayed with three different Servas hosts there. One was an unmarried couple, another was a family with children and the third was a single man. Both of the latter two had separate apartments in which they hosted guests. They were all very different from each other and I was able to experience Germans as varied as any Americans. I used a letter of introduction which started with the statement that I am a Jewish

American and got to see how little they were willing to interact with that information. Their behavior reminded me of how uncomfortable white people in the U.S. are with black people. The single man did help me to find a synagogue on Saturday. There I met a lot of refugees from the former Soviet Union who wanted to make their way to the U.S. It was strange to be in Germany, speaking with people in Russian! In Hanover, I also saw a beautiful Christian church where the central symbol of Christ was NOT on the cross. It was much more comfortable for me.

Martin picked me up in Hanover and we went to Bergen-Belsen, a former concentration camp. We saw many mounds under which were buried thousands upon thousands of Jews and others who had been persecuted by the Nazis. Most of the structures were gone and I found it rather stark and unemotional. But since both Martin and I had experience with RC, we took the opportunity to exchange listening time with each other and I could see that he was very moved by the experience. He went on to do programs that brought Jews and Germans together both in the U.S. and in Germany.

From there, Martin drove us to a friend's house in the Netherlands where we were going to an Earthstewards gathering. It turned out that this friend lived in Hooghalen, the town where Jews were held during the war before being transported east to be killed. Over a hundred thousand Jews were incarcerated at Kamp Westerbork in Hooghalen. When we arrived, there were already some other Earthstewards staying with this woman. One was a Serbian man who couldn't understand why we were still struggling with the history between Jews and Germans when his country was in the middle of war right at that time. Of course, that war was also driven by a long history of intergroup conflict. Whose truth?

The next morning, Martin, the Serbian and I, rode bikes over to the museum dedicated to the remembrance of the terrible things which had taken place in that town. The museum was very powerful for me. We began by watching a film in which a young Dutch woman tells the story of her Jewish friend who was taken from her and sent to the camps never to return. Then we walked into the main room where there were piles of shoes and suitcases which had been left on the site when people were moved east. Finally there was a wall of photographs of individuals. When the frame of the photo was opened it triggered a voice which told of the role the person had played during the war – a farmer, a train switchman, etc. The last frame held a mirror and when the frame opened, it asked, "What would you have done?" I could not answer that. I still wonder if I would have had the capacity to live like Anne Frank for months and months or if I could have sustained myself on faith like Viktor Frankl. Would I have been a collaborator or a resistance fighter? If I were not Jewish, would I have risked my life to save Jews? If I were a Jew during the war, what would have become of me?

The three of us went into the café which was part of the museum. We sat at a small table and took time to listen to each other's feelings. The Serbian man didn't understand much, but he was able to give good attention. When it was my turn, I just bawled. Looking around at these two men, one German, I realized that they had come to this place to support me in working through my feelings about the war, Germans, and my own safety in a world which despite all appearance is really benign and filled with people who would love to be my friends and allies if I would only let them and stop resisting out of fear of the future looking like the past. I cried and sobbed and all the other patrons in the café disappeared. What a contradiction! It was transformative. I wish I could hold on to the reevaluation I had at that time every day. I would like to experience every person I meet as my warm close and dependable friend and ally.

That trip as a whole was a watershed for me in moving through the inherited (epigenetic) fear that was passed on to me as a Jew about my lack of safety in the world. Certainly, all my travels have had an impact on my life, just as my years working with students from other countries have changed and challenged my point of view on the world. These relationships have shaped my thinking and deepened my commitment to working toward all people being free of the oppressions which face us in the world today – not to become like me, but to become what each is meant to be.

Martin and I became good friends. In 1996, we lead an EP:W&M workshop together in Tbilisi. On that trip, I was the guest of an American NGO and stayed with the staff member who had arranged for me to come. It was an amazing time. I got to lead three of the workshops I love the most: Essential Peacemaking, Prejudice Reduction and Conflict Resolution.

Without Danaan, I would never have experienced so much. Thank you Danaan for the world you opened to me. I miss you.

"You never find yourself until you face the truth."

- Pearl Bailey

CHAPTER THIRTEEN

IN MY FIFTIES AFTER DIVORCING MY THIRD HUSBAND, Larry, I took the opportunity to reevaluate my relationships with men. There were several pieces to this, but the most profound was the experience with Healing Theater. Healing Theatre brings your story to life by weaving together personal story, ritual theater and world mythology. At the same time, I was writing out my sex history for doing amends in Overeaters Anonymous and in the process had contacted Joseph again. His response to me figured in the play we created.

The four of us women who participated in the play called "The Dark Feminine" told our personal stories alongside the mythical stories of four archetypes. We created a performance that expressed and told the story of how our lives expressed the beauty and pathos of the goddesses Ereskigal, Cerridwen, Baba Yaga and Pele. I was Pele, Goddess of Fire and Anger, hot lava flowing down the volcanoes of Hawaii. I told the story of my relationship with Joseph. I recognized the ways I had used men to contradict the hurtful messages from my childhood and at the same time created more hurt for myself.

Olivia Woodford, the creator of the process, took the words we used in our work sessions and sculpted them into a play. She had us respond some times in the voice of the goddess and sometimes from our own experience. In writing the play, she alternated the scenes in which we were ourselves working on our issues with scenes where we played the Dark Goddesses.

In one of our work sessions, we were asked to look at our shadow side. I drew a picture of the Hollow Man and described him as, "Grim, old, dark, closed, hunched, lonely." I believed the "hollow man" was my father, and myself when I was at my most scared. These were the words I used to describe the Hollow Man,

"Not really here; don't count; trying to keep balance in boat of life; spineless; much work to hold up the body—a big hole—back can't support shoulders, let alone head. People are scary—mean—staying away is best—they hurt you—the world is unsafe; nobody notices. My philosophy is to run and hide to be safe. Hollow man can't imagine why anyone would want to connect to him. He wants someone to care for him and love him."

Olivia said, "He's real, vulnerable. If he began to trust, he would be really sad. If this part of you were allowed to matter Kathryn would be energized. Resistance takes energy. It is an old message you can't be sad, can't be lonely. The General is the opposite, the motivation. You use "The General" for motivation to overcome the torpor of feeling so empty, like your dad.

Kathryn says to the dad, shadow side, "Shape up. Change. Let me mold you into something."

This causes the Hollow Man to feel guilty. He can't cope and gives up.

At that point, Olivia asked, "What does the "Hollow Man" need?"

I answered, "I need to own the Hollow Man—spend time doing nothing, unmotivated, stop trying to motivate Sasha. [I need to] find interest in the Hollow Man, [explore who he really is]. [I need to] tell Sasha he is not guilty for being autistic, [and recognize] it wasn't dad's fault that he was blacklisted—really Mom was just as responsible." [This was the first I had realized this and a big transformation in my thinking about my father. I began to appreciate the good qualities I have been able to write about him.]

We then drew a picture of our best selves. I drew a big heart with feet, red lines radiating out. The words I used were "warm, open, glowing, available, generous. When I speak with clarity, well grounded (not flamboyant) I am most persuasive."

The play Olivia wrote had four parts: the introduction, an exploration of our addictions used to avoid our feelings and feel as if we were in control of life, the playing out of our hurts and resolution where we each took our power back. We rehearsed the play for weeks and then performed it over two weekends to invitation-only audiences. Our performance space was a small black box theater that holds only fifty people. We used simple props and costumes. When we were playing goddesses we had a certain piece of clothing which distinguished us from when we were playing ourselves.

In the play, Pele was filled with jealousy, anger and resentment toward women for stealing "her man." My anger was with Joseph. When I had contacted him he had shown interest at first and then made sure I knew he wasn't thinking of resuming our intimate relationship because I didn't look the part for him. He could only be monogamous with "tall, slender, beautiful women." I received that email while I was in Germany just before visiting the concentration camps.

In the process of writing and rehearsing the play, I sent Joseph back all his poems I had saved and burned the letters we had exchanged. I sent him back the poetry he had written and a book of poetry he had given me with an inscription assuring me we would be friends forever.

As Pele, Goddess of the Volcano in Hawaii, the play had many telling lines about my anger. Pele said, "I am bereft of the acknowledgement I deserve. Humans forget to honor us." I describe my wrath as hot and molten as I writhe on the couch.

In the part of the play where each of us inspects our addictions, I tell the story of my interaction with the German man I had picked up in Aachen. I say, "I behave with men in ways I wouldn't at home: irresponsible, indulgent and risky. I devour men, disrespect them. Feel I have conquered; take advantage of their vulnerability. Later when I look back, I realize I have disrespected myself as well. I feel ashamed." I had again acted out my attempt to contradict the hurts of being called "fatso" by finding a handsome man to flirt with. It took repeating this line many times before I got the full impact of it.

It was a shock to me when I realized for all my thinking my sexual behavior was "liberated" it was really just a new form of sexism taking advantage of men's normative sexual behavior to make myself feel more powerful; to no longer feel fat and ugly.

In the role of Pele, I say, "Men are all hypocrites, promise the stars and abandon and betray you. They are weak, easily seduced; just looking for another fuck. I spread myself and consume. I am hungry for life; for justice. I don't trust, am arrogant. I bring my passion from the inside and spread it over everyone. I want you to adore me, revere me or suffer the consequences." This reflected thoughts I had never been able to express before, but seemed an accurate representation of my feelings much of the time. As in Lifespring, I recognized how I used arrogance as armor. The passion I am talking about here is not just sexual passion, but passion for justice which can also be overwhelming to other people.

Toward the end of the play, I performed the invocation to the east as Pele: It is a place of new beginnings, a fresh start. I call on us "to live more in harmony with Her and our own dreams." At the end of the play when we are coming to resolution, (as Pele) I say, "I am radiating power, heat, passion, sexuality. Firmly rooted in the belly of the earth, I spread myself and consume everything. This is my great orgasm. I want a man who enjoys his body, relishes touch, texture, taste; graceful, powerful. I draw them to me. I know all about anger. I am practiced. It oozes and spills from my pores; hot consuming, uncontrolled."

Again as Pele, I describe myself as "the Goddess of Passion

and Lust. The old is swept away; we clear away anything that stands in the way of my full expression." I implore, "Release me from all beliefs that have held my heart closed. [Addressing Joseph] In 2000 on Rosh Hashanah, I burned all your letters. I spewed a 'fury of words.' You think you can have whatever you want because you look good. The fire transforms. I am open to transformation. New birth comes from the ashes. Spill over us in rich abandon; flood us in rich hot fecundity. [Referring to the four Goddesses] We are aged, deep, wise and fruity like a fine wine. Help us to contain the fire in our loins and not be burned."

In the end of the play, I affirm, "I am a passionate woman of flowing vulnerable power. These men welcome me to share the emotional, hurt, angry, vulnerable place." I tell the story of being at an Earthstewards workshop with a number of men whom I have known for some time in various settings. I show that they are able to handle my anger without being upset and to honor me despite my having strong feelings. This seems to me to affirm the possibility of having a relationship with men where I can be my full self and still be accepted and loved.

After many rehearsals of my lines, I felt complete and able to move on to a healthier partnership which I have now achieved. I learned in co-creating that play that I had misused my sexuality, playing on men's weakness shaped by society to make them susceptible to getting involved in sex when they, too, really want intimacy. I wanted a different relationship. I wrote a wish list that first of all "he chooses me." I want someone whose values are similar to mine. "We can talk about anything we feel about each other, conflict is accepted as part of the relationship...can see that when I am angry I want to be closer and will embrace me, not run away or push me away or shut down. Willing to engage deeply and feel; to let our relationship catalyze old wounds and then heal them; willing to stay present while I take on what comes up for me." The play was truly healing, repeating the lines in the play I had written over and over until I got the message.

Before Healing Theater, I tried Radical Forgiveness, a workshop led by Colin Tipping. This was also a powerful experience and helped me to connect the hurt I was feeling from ending my third marriage. I saw the hurt as being a reflection of what I had experienced when I lost the relationship with my father. The book by that name helped me in coming to understand that it was my interpretation of the events that was causing me hurt, rather than the events themselves. It was only in the workshop as I dissolved into tears while beating a tennis racket against a plastic covered cushion and screaming my frustration that I really got how my whole history with men had been colored by the sense I had a child that I had been deserted by my father, even though he stayed present in form. When the leader played a piece of music that says "I will never leave you" (which happens to be written and sung by Jim Meyer, a Meher Baba follower), I felt the comfort I had lost when my father shut down after losing his job.

Having done all this personal growth work, I am blessed now with having a partner who is willing to work on our relationship and remember that we love each other even when it is difficult. I wonder what I might have accomplished if I hadn't started out by losing the support of my father when he retreated after losing his government job. I saw the movie The Intern with Robert de Niro and thought, "What might I have achieved if I had had that sort of encouragement from a man whom I trusted?" First and foremost, I might have chosen a more supportive life partner earlier in my life.

Perhaps my struggle to see a positive image in my own reflection began with the poem I memorized in 9th grade, Sand Dunes by Robert Frost. At the end it says "and be but more free to think for the one more cast off shell." I feel that as life has gone along, I have cast off so many shells, ways of thinking, people left behind, movement from place to place, many homes I have loved. And with each experience, I have grown wiser, more aware, more able to think. I feel sad sometimes thinking of those I have left behind; writing this memoir has made me aware of how many people I have loved only to have the cords that bind us attenuate to nothing. It feels sad. But my life has become so much more of what I want it to be. I can't regret the changes. Some of the most important changes came around my shift from seeing the world primarily through politics and economics to having spiritual and psychological beliefs that complement my understanding of the world.

My parents were atheists which seemed reasonable since they were Marxists. My father suggested that my brother should be bar mitzvah and my mother just laughed. While I was living with my parents, I never entered a synagogue that I can remember except for Saturday night dances for high school students. During those years in New York City, I envied my Greek Orthodox friend Steve Karatheodoris because he had a clear religious faith. I thought it would be wonderful to know what you believed, to have the support of a belief system.

So my early memories regarding personal growth and commitment to an understanding of something greater than myself were of yearning and disappointment.

My mother insisted I see a psychiatrist when I came back from my European trip after college. I found the man she chose oppressive and didn't do it for very long. There was a small group of young adults and one of the boys thought that black people didn't have red blood! No one interrupted this uninformed statement! When I complained about how controlling my mother was, the psychiatrist told me I should stop accepting gifts from her, like the wonderful sheepskin coat she had just bought me. Of course, she was also paying him for seeing me. Was that a gift?

Whose truth?

When I was in graduate school, I went to a conference in Boston sponsored by Esalen. The only thing I remember about it was an exercise where we walked around the room with our eyes closed and noticed that we were so aware of other people even without vision that we didn't run into anyone even in a crowded room. This was the beginning of my interest in personal growth and humanistic psychology.

I wrote to my former supervisor after the conference:

"One of the things I found exciting about it was that I was not really learning new things, but being reinforced in the new realizations which I have been having: that I can really enjoy being with myself, that things can be a matter of choice. I feel much more clearly centered, and as if I know who I am and rather like that person, [more] than I have ever felt before. Which is not to say that I don't have my downs and need other people to help me. But I feel that it is much less intense and much more dependent on me and not the outside world. I feel a strength which comes from relinquishing control, without retreating from responsibility."

This was the beginning of my understanding about the difference between being willing and willful. I didn't have that language yet, but learning to let go and trust that things will go well even if I am not "in charge" has been an important part of my path to healing. As a Jew, this is particularly difficult as we tend to have patterns of feeling that if things don't go well, we will be blamed. This was reinforced by my mother who held me responsible for making everything go well, as she held herself responsible that way.

Everything about my time in Kenya was intensely growthful. Not only did I connect with nature in new ways, but I also connected with religion in a new way. When I got close to Celia, the woman who was a missionary for the Baha'is, she affirmed our common values without insisting I join in her practice of them. Baha'i is a tradition which honors the multiplicity of paths to God. However, they believe they are the pinnacle of paths to God. They embrace principles of equality between genders and races as part of their creed. These values matched mine. I just haven't been able to say that there is only one right path to an experience of a higher power. I so wanted to belong, but I knew I couldn't actually join them because I couldn't live within their rules: being married is not a prerequisite for me to having sex.

When I was working for the Quaker school in Kenya, I found a lot to agree with there also, especially the decision making by consensus that comes from listening in silence to an inner voice. There didn't seem to be much liturgy and no ministry and that worked for me as well.

Living in Kenya was a life changing experience for me. It became clear to me that for there to be such beauty that was not made by the hand of man, there had to be a power greater than humans. We do not make the sky so beautiful, the amazing animals which coexist on the savannah and the mountains covered with snow year round on the equator. Rather than being a dark continent for me, Africa was a place of enlightenment and from there I went on to explore many religious and spiritual paths.

I did a great deal of reading in Kenya starting with Assagioli's *Act of Will*. His theory of psychosynthesis had a great deal of influence on my thinking. He talked about the different aspects of oneself and how to get them to cooperate with each other. I had time to think and consider what I really believed. I challenged my beliefs and explored possibilities. I went beyond the either/or I had learned from my mother and discovered both/and thinking. I read a lot in Kenya, from *Art of Loving* to *Zen and the Art of Motorcycle Maintenance*. I also had a lot of time for introspection. I grew up into being responsible for myself in new ways as I took on responsibility for others.

When I came back from Kenya, I spent a month as an intern in a personal growth center: The New England Center for Personal and Organizational Development in Amherst, Massachusetts. This center was run by Jack Canfield (of *Chicken Soup for the Soul* fame) and Jack Rosenblum. I experienced many different modalities of personal growth work from gestalt to Feldenkrais. I met interesting people and was asked to stay and become their administrator. I didn't feel ready for this task and chose to go back to Atlanta and finish my Master's thesis.

The most transformative event for me was having a baby. It was a spiritual experience. I was astounded by the changes in my body and my emotions. Again an experience of being out of human control, while something magical happened. My son smelled entrancing. I thought he was the most delicious thing I could imagine. I was stunned into prideful delight that this being could have emerged from my body. I said, "Look what I did!" But it really wasn't me who did it. It was not something over which I had any control or about which I made decisions. Once begun, the process took over from me and I was just the vehicle. I became willing.

I also dabbled in various religious practices. I had lots of interaction with Western Sufis from weekend workshops to Dances of Universal Peace. I even spent a day with Pir Vilayat. He talked about not letting the experience of the body take over while I sat on the floor pregnant. It didn't capture me. I spent time in the Unitarian Church, the Quaker Meeting and with a Unity congregation. They were all interesting but none actually stuck. I was looking for community as much as I was looking for a spiritual path. I was still seeking belonging and having difficulty noticing that people liked me and welcomed me.

Over the years I have participated in many different kinds of personal growth activities. I have done the complete series of both Insight and Lifespring Trainings. These are personal effectiveness trainings that were developed in the 70s and were popular in the 80s. In the process I learned a great deal about who I am and how to become more of what I can be. At the end of many of these trainings, people give you feedback on cards. Some of the things said about me most often were: that I am supportive of others, warm, loving, care about the world, have wisdom and passion. These are not qualities that I would have expected for people to see. Over time I have come to accept that they are accurate descriptions of me. People often mention that they like my broad smile and feel that I am optimistic. This is very much in contrast with my own experience of the pain and covering numbness I feel when I am reminded of my Amagansett experiences, the hurt and fear I can rarely access.

I began personal effectiveness training in the mid 80s. I planned to go to the Association for Humanistic Psychology annual conference in Washington. My friend from my masters program, Terri, had just taken Insight training and thought it was great. She told me that Jack Canfield was leading an Insight training at the conference so I decided to take it. I was hooked. It combined the spiritual awareness I was seeking with the exploration of psychological underpinnings that also attracted me.

In one of the earliest Insight Trainings I had profound experiences. These are notes from my journal at that time, "My goal in this seminar is to uncover the child within me and accept and nurture her, and whatever irrationality she may present. To be playful and silly." I wanted to experience joy.

I decided to allow myself to let go and receive nurturance from others. I was afraid of repeating the experience of abandonment by someone I counted on to love me. I called my 'limiting character' 'Armored Arrogant Arnold.' I recognized that I was not letting the world see my vulnerable, scared self that felt helpless; I defended myself by being unwilling to hear negative criticism.

The workshop leader said, "Who did you take care of as a child?" Out of my mouth came, "My mother." It caused me to rethink my conversation about my mother who was dead by then. I also remembered that my mother had told me she had gone to NYC to have an abortion after Rick was born. As I thought about it in the workshop it seemed to me that's when she came back determined to make her hers, exclusively.

Further, I got a new perspective on singing. I was feeling so good during one of the breaks, I was singing to myself as I danced around the room. A man said, "You have a lovely voice." What a huge contradiction to the many times as a child I was told I was tone deaf. I went back to Atlanta and began taking voice lessons! Whose truth?

As a response to a prompt from the trainer, I wrote,

"Dear Mom,

"I want to be free. I forgive you for not wanting me to have a child; for making inordinate demands on me after I did; for being too busy to be nurturing with me when I was small, for demanding my involvement with you when we lived in Amagansett to keep you occupied; for driving a wedge between me and daddy; for cheating on daddy; for trying to tell me how to run my life; for disapproving of all my boyfriends except Joseph who was cruel to me; for being nasty to Howard; for dying and leaving me.

"I want you to know that I love you anyhow and I miss you and I appreciate all the qualities and things you have given me, including a sense of my own self worth."

"Dear Dad,

"I want to be free. I forgive you for going numb and not being present for me when I was growing up, for letting Mom run you off, for not being strong enough to set and maintain limits on me, for not creating good warm times as a family, for criticizing me for gaining weight.

"I want you to know that I regret I didn't allow us to connect when I was a teenager and you did come more alive. I appreciate your support when I decided to marry David. I enjoyed playing tennis with you. I wish I had been able to get more from your intellect.

"Love,

Kathy"

Over and over I asked to experience JOY. I wanted to feel assured that I was accepted and to be able to tell when I am loved and loveable. I was struggling with my weight and promising exercise and to give up chocolate. I noticed that when things didn't work the way I wanted, I got dismissive. I committed to expressing my power more gently.

For my "stretch" I played Isadora Duncan in a flowing sheer pink dress and danced and spoke in Russian, affirming my commitment to the work I was doing in exchanges with the Soviet Union. I came up with the powerful affirmation, "I am an abundant and receiving woman creating love in the world." This has carried me through to today where I do actually experience myself in this way, at least some of the time.

Parallel with my involvement with Tbilisi, I was opening up to my own power and efficacy through my work with the Insight Training. One day, I was sitting on the brown corduroy chair in the living room by the window of the octagon house looking through the mail. I remarked to Howard, "Here's a newsletter from Lifespring. It's a program like Insight. I wonder how they are different." Reading on I said, "Oh, they are doing trainings in Moscow! If they can do trainings in Moscow, perhaps they can do them in Tbilisi. If I get involved, maybe I can influence them to go to Georgia." So began my sojourn with Lifespring.

I still had work to do to fully own my own life. I wrote in my notebook at the end of my first Lifespring training,

"Dear Kathryn,

"You have spent the last year getting clear about what you want to do with the rest of your life now that your role as a mother and wife has gotten smaller as a priority and time commitment.

"How have you integrated your skills (facilitation, training, conflict resolution) with your interests (embracing diversity, Tbilisi) and your values (living simply in a natural environment, travel, community) to create a lifestyle of leading (regardless of others' opinions) and contributing to a world that works for everyone?

"I acknowledge you for moving through your fears, empowering yourself, learning and appreciating yourself regardless of what others say. I acknowledge your power and self-assurance and the willingness to take risks. Welcome home. Welcome to your true potential.

"Love,

Me"

Another love letter to myself after a Lifespring training says,

"Dear Kathryn,

"I love you. You are a beautiful, grateful and contactful person. There is joy and enthusiasm available just for being you – open, loving and warm.

"You can sing and dance and smile and others enjoy it, get pleasure just from you doing that. You don't have to do more.

"If people enjoy you and say so you don't have to do anything but accept it.

"Once you accept others as they are there is nothing more you should do. The rest is up to the process.

"Again, I love you. You are a loving, radiant being.

"Love,

Me"

I continued to take Lifespring workshops. At the Advanced Lifespring in early 1991, I noted the following:

"Shut down when I got feedback. Wasn't willing to let people see me hurt, instead got angry. I felt 'not enough.' Inadequate to mother Sasha, to bring in money either for myself or for the Tbilisoba event, to have a satisfactory marriage with Howard. 'No matter how much I give of myself, I never feel I do an A+ job. I could always do more, do better.' (My mother in my head.) I commit to 'creating a breakthrough for myself by opening my heart and experiencing my fear, pain and despair and allowing others to nurture me in my pain.'"

I realized that others couldn't hurt me by their negative feedback because I said much worse things to myself about my inadequacies. I decided that Howard and I had chosen each other to mirror our own self hate. We wanted to make the other as miserable as we each already felt about our self. It was not the kind of loving relationship I wanted or deserved, but it took many more years, another marriage and Healing Theater before I could figure that issue out.

I asked myself, "What do I honor and accept from my parents?" I recognized that mom, "Gave me strength to believe in myself and vision to draw me into commitment." And from dad, "You gave me acceptance and taught me compassion. You are a gentle man, tender and caring."

I continued to take these workshops and eventually I enrolled Howard in one in the fall of 1991. It was an amazing time as I had just completed the Tbilisoba event and I was feeling powerful, in spite of the way I was treated by Carleton Parker.

When I was deeply engaged in the work as a volunteer in Lifespring, the leader asked me if I was married.

I said, "Yes."

He said, "You won't be for long."

Clearly he saw that I was growing in ways that would separate me from my husband. As it turned out, I enrolled a large portion of the participants in the next Basic Training, including Howard. He got involved with a woman he met there and I said, "I've had enough of your philandering."

He said, "I'm not giving up this friendship."

I said, "Move out."

It was just before Christmas and we decided to have Christmas together as a family. His sons came up to North Georgia and we did the regular exchange of presents with the three boys. Immediately after, he moved into the apartment he had found while I was staffing the Intimacy workshop with Lifespring. He shared it with the woman he had met in his Lifespring training.

It was ironic that I was at the Lifespring Intimacy workshop while Howard was looking for an apartment. The frame for the workshop was, "You will have the power to create intimacy in the face of the normal human tendency toward separateness." At the time, I wondered if this was possible for me.

Lifespring said, "The barriers to intimacy are image management, believing 'this is not IT,' and thinking I should already know how to be intimate...To achieve intimacy, one needs to have a beginner's mind and be comfortable living in the mystery. Given our present paradigm, the best we can do is for two solitudes to come together and comfort one another. We need to create a new paradigm."

One of my beliefs I uncovered in that workshop was that "I am not worthy because I wasn't valuable enough to my father for him to maintain our intimacy despite his pain." I concluded at that time that "I can't trust men. They leave me. They abandon me." I recognized that my early feeling of separation from other girls my age came from being called "Fatso" and not having allies who defended me from that.

I continued to participate in the Lifespring programs and

in the spring I took the Lifespring Masters program. This was immediately after Howard had moved out and a few months after the Tbilisoba event. The opening question I asked myself, "When will I value myself enough to be valued by others? How many times do I need to be taught the same things before I learn them?" I answered, "My purpose for being in the Masters Course is to learn neutrality, to be able to accept what comes without losing my equanimity. At stake: being able to maintain a loving intimate relationship, being able to create significant results in the world and not getting stuck on obstacles like Carlton Parker and Sasha's fourth grade teacher, Ellen Ivey."

In my notes I wrote, *Steps to Mastery*:

1. Must be present with the experience (not a concept; feelings, thoughts and bodily sensations) [This meant that I had to get out of my head.]

2. Experience my experience: distinguish myself from my experience. Practice this distinction in language [This meant that I would stop saying "I am angry" and say "I am feeling angry."]

3. Communicate my experience such that others get it [Again, not vomit my anger on people, but use language to define my feelings and where they come from.]

4. The willingness to be responsible for everything [Not make excuses that someone else made me feel a certain way; rather to accept that it is my own beliefs that cause me to interpret what happens in a way that results in my feeling the way I do.]

All these principles have turned out to be the things I now teach when I teach conflict resolution. At the time, I noticed that when I was pressed to feel something uncomfortable, I felt anxious, and wanted to take ACTION, to move, to sleep, to eat, to run, to be held. All ways to not have to feel my anxiety. It became clear that these behaviors were not helping me to deal effectively with my feelings but rather creating increasingly negative outcomes.

I noticed that I confused "responsibility" with "duty." I acted out of obligation rather than response ability. I tried to control and manipulate the situation to make myself more comfortable. I found fault and took credit. This new awareness gave me a place to work from to be able to develop more positive responses leading to better outcomes, but it still took a lot more time than just the days in workshops.

To remind myself to continue to focus on joy, I posted this quote from G. B. Shaw, "True joy in life is to be used by a purpose declared by you to be a mighty one."

I named my purpose which became my "dedication" in Earthstewards, "to allow love to manifest by celebrating diversity and working through conflict, thus dissolving fear." It was based on the principles of honesty, respect, abundance and love, which have been with me ever since that experience.

The result I sought was "an intimate committed passionate relationship based on mutual respect and honest communication."

The work I did in Lifespring was life changing for me. I addressed both the personal issues of my relationships as well as the professional issues of who I wanted to be in the wide world. It was during this time that I learned my all time favorite quote which comes from W.H. Murray, a Scottish mountaineer who climbed Mt. Everest,

"Until one is committed, there is hesitancy, the chance to draw back. Concerning all acts of initiative (and creation), there is one elementary truth the ignorance of which kills countless ideas and splendid plans: that the moment one definitely commits oneself, then Providence moves too. All sorts of things occur to help one that would never otherwise have occurred. A whole stream of events issues from the decision, raising in one's favor all manner of unforeseen incidents and meetings and material assistance, which no man could have dreamed would have come his way." And then, quoting Goethe, he wrote, "Whatever you can do, or dream you can do, begin it. Boldness has genius, power, and magic in it. Begin it now."

I stayed involved with Lifespring as long as they were in Atlanta. I staffed workshops for a long time after I had completed the series. Adding Revaluation Counseling (RC) to Lifespring gives me on-going support for the insights I had during the years with Lifespring. Each provides an opportunity for me to feel emotions and reflect on choices.

RC gives me an on-going reminder of my goodness. The underlying philosophy posits that everyone is essentially completely good, loving, brilliant and zestful. It is only our distresses which are laid in early which get in the way of expressing our commitment to a deeply connected life. The way to return to the essential person is through discharging the hurts and distresses which have corrupted one. The person in the role of counselor is there to remind the person in the role of client of their goodness and to hold trust that the person clienting can come up with good solutions for herself.

RC also believes in a benign universe which is neither trying to help or harm us. Our distresses come substantially from the hurts past generations have experienced from oppression which get passed on to the next generation and from the oppression of a hierarchical society. (This is now being confirmed by the field of epigenetics.) The insights into the ways groups are oppressed have helped me to be both more accepting of myself and more tolerant of others.

It has taken thirty years of doing RC for me to begin to be able to notice that people like me and want to be with me. I am pleased that today I can tell that there are people who are glad to be around me and who accept me as I am.

I probably wouldn't have gotten as involved with RC if I hadn't taken the National Coalition Building Institute (NCBI) training. This is a prejudice reduction model based on the principles of RC, specifically that people can change when they are allowed to release their feelings through the expression of them. RC theory postulates that when we have feelings, they stay with us until we have the opportunity to discharge them. Discharge may take many forms of physical expression: laughing, crying, yawning, shaking, etc. When we have an opportunity to release these feelings physically, they no longer are unaware influences on our thinking and action.

Just after Howard had moved out, a flyer for NCBI landed on my desk advertising a "prejudice reduction and conflict resolution workshop." I had taken mediation training before leaving Atlanta and had done some reading on conflict resolution. I had even offered a class at the library after reading *Getting Together*. (*Getting Together: Building a Relationship as we get to Yes* by Roger Fisher and Scott Brown) It was revolutionary for me to understand that doing the same bad behavior as my opponent (revenge) was not in my best interest.

Although I didn't know it at the time, it was the beginning of the next stage of my life. After the workshop, Thee Smith invited me to be his right hand and demonstrated what it means to be an ally. I got more involved in RC which I had learned years before and began to focus on issues of identity. I also met Raye Rawls who eventually invited me into her business teaching mediation.

Before Howard and I divorced, I started reading the books from the Harvard Negotiation Project, *Getting to Yes*, etc. My first aha was the value of the assumption that people have good intentions. If someone is hurting you, look for how it is making them feel more comfortable and safe, rather than assuming they are "out to get you." Unfortunately, Howard and I were too far into our power struggle for these new techniques to work.

Using the tools I gained from my reading and some post

separation couples counseling, Howard and I were able to negotiate an amicable parting. The judge who interviewed us before granting our divorce asked if we would be willing to share our skills with others who were seeking a divorce as it was clear that we had worked through our issues and were making the best decisions for our son. However, living together again was not an option. I am pleased to say that we are each with new partners and are able to spend time together at the beach where Howard lives so that Sasha can join us for a week from time to time in the summer. Unfortunately, Sasha doesn't like the beach and that is becoming more difficult.

❧❧

There are several ways in which I have come to my present beliefs and attitudes. Certainly RC and Lifespring have been a big influence. I have also sought a more traditional spiritual path. Nothing has ever felt completely harmonious for me. Perhaps the most influential has been Western Sufism. The worship service acknowledges the value of multiple traditions and ends with honoring "all those known and unknown who have brought the light of truth to the planet." I also love the Dances of Universal Peace which have come out of this tradition. I have gone to several week long workshops which combine contemplative practices with the dances in a beautiful setting on the Pacific coast of Mexico. I find no difficulty in using the word "Allah" to express a benevolent higher power.

I learned to be able to use the word "God" in a 12-Step program where I could see that people had many meanings of the word and I didn't have to worry that their meaning was mine or vise versa. In Overeaters Anonymous I got the freedom to use the word "God" and not think that others would misunderstand me.

After Howard and I parted, I began spending time at the Meher Baba Spiritual Retreat Center in Myrtle Beach, SC. I have continued to go there at least once a year and often more. Although I am not able to say that Meher Baba is God incarnate, I do find a peace in that place. I have found that I am completely able to use the word "baba" to mean "god" and that I get to mean whatever I want when

I do. Again it is in the obvious majesty of nature in the woods and by the ocean and lake there that I find my closest connection to a power greater than human beings. I take time to write when I am there as the natural environment inspires me. This is a piece I wrote on one visit:

"The sun rises pink and peach over the lake, the sky streaked and brilliant dispelling the blackness that reigned for hours unblemished by electric lights. Now I can see the dark outlines of trees not bare in winter, still decorated by their evergreen leaves in this southern climate that doesn't fear breakage from heavy snows. This is the last virgin forest on the east coast...This coastal forest was preserved initially by the wealthy and now by the devoted over strenuous objection. Thanks, Baba, had you not sought such a refuge for rest and re-creation, I would not have this sanctuary to sustain and renew me.

"The lake with its boat house reflects the peace and serenity I miss in the wide world. Even the ocean in Myrtle Beach is generally quite pacific, sometimes more like the bay on Long Island than the ocean. But the shells spelling out the words "I am the ocean of love Meher Baba" always remind me of the expansive love which is available to me if I only open to it. Blue sky at the ocean; gentle waves lapping rhythmically are soothing to the soul. Even when it is overcast and the sea and sky blend into one another, there is a calm that prevails...

"I came at first for the communal meal preparation under Mina and I stayed for the respite and kind acceptance of conversation around a table in the Refectory. I continue to come for the soft cushion I can sink myself into while I explore my inner landscape among the virgin forest and ocean calm. Paths that are raked daily by devoted followers who find peace and harmony in their service to the Master."

Another time at the Center, which feels more like "home" than any other place I have been, I wrote,

"Sitting on the porch of a cabin at the Meher Baba Center in the cool morning with a towhee calling "drink your tea" and a frog croaking his discordant tune. Sun shines bright off the calm lake reflecting the spring green of the trees and I anticipate the pleasure of a swim in the brisk ocean later after walking through the densely green lined path. Here is a place where I have found God in nature, much like I did living in Kenya. Where the land has not been disrupted by the hand of man, but only tended here and there. I can see the grace that shaped the complexity we call nature. Here I can relax into those strong arms I found at the Christian retreat center near Barnardsville. In a circular building, high on a hill of undeveloped forest, I walked into a room that fully nurtured me and I cried. Even in the image of Christ, I felt safe as a Jew. The bench runs along the wall and carved wooden arms become my backrest. In the wall across from the entrance, the carving makes it clear that it is a representation of Christ. Nonetheless, it is welcoming and reassuring."

Funny how Christianity represents God as a bearded White man. Both the predecessor Jews and subsequent Muslims abjure representing god in any visual way. Perhaps if they did not have this prohibition we could see that there are vastly more possibilities for appearance. After all, all the "Abrahamic" religious came from Semitic people, dark skinned and patriarchal. Or God could be represented as Meher Baba as the folk do here, clearly a brown skinned man, pictured at many ages from a young Christ-like figure to a very heavy man in a pained body holding his alphabet board as he refrains from speaking. Personally, I don't believe God takes form, only avatars who have deep personal charisma and represent a deeper knowing.

I have sought that deeper knowing in many forms, personal effectiveness training, therapy, RC, Twelve Steps, Healing Theater, and on. But the closest I ever feel to God is in nature, where the hand of man has little disturbed what man cannot make. Now as we set off to rearrange what God has provided with genetic modification and nanochips, we must be sure our consciousness has grown large and subtle enough so that we do not create unintended consequences with our hubris that destroy life on this planet.

I will always identify as a Jew, but find most Jewish practice (and certainly anything in Hebrew) difficult. I do love Passover and always celebrate it as often and with as many other people as possible. I am finding a home in a Christian church without being put off by the feelings that come up when Christ is spoken as the name of "God." Living in a Christian hegemonic society, that name is particularly difficult for me as a Jew to use. I was thrilled when the pastor agreed for me to lead a Passover Seder and sixty eight people attended with interest and appreciation!

Danaan told a story that made great sense to me. He said that once upon a time there was a well of knowledge and people came from all over to drink from that well. As time went on, houses of worship were built around the well to make it easier for people to access the knowledge. Eventually it grew crowded and the houses surrounded the well. People could only access the well through the houses of worship. Then the houses closed their back doors so that people could no longer gain direct access, but could only learn through the interpretations they heard in the houses of worship. It seems to me today that the best way to access knowledge (truth) is by experiencing it through as many windows as possible, as many different points of view as one can access.

In Eric Weiner's book *Man Seeks God*, he writes, "Paradox is a prerequisite for spiritual truth." What a confirmation of what I have been thinking in my life. One of my favorite teachers is Jean Houston who talks of her encounters with Teilhard de Chardin who said that just like the atmosphere encircles the earth, so does the noosphere, a stage of evolutionary development dominated by consciousness, the mind, and interpersonal relationships. De Chardin argued the noosphere is growing towards even greater integration and unification. I am seeking that integration and unification. I am seeking what seems to be universally true from all the spiritual paths I have traversed. Yes, there are paradoxes, but that doesn't mean I am not viewing Truth from many different perspectives.

෫ഗ

Despite having been raised to pay attention most to the politics and economics of society, it is the miracle of living things that most delights me. Some years ago my partner and I were staying at a hotel in Puerto Vallarta, Mexico before going to a Sufi meditation retreat. The first morning we were looking at brochures of tourist activities and I saw one for a dolphin adventure. Immediately we went to the hotel desk to ask about arrangements. The steep price almost dissuaded me. Karl encouraged me, seeing the light in my face. As soon as we had made the commitment, I noticed the retreat leader in the lobby. Surprised he was at the same hotel, I ran up to greet him, glowing with delight. He was completely charmed, remembered our last encounter in Washington DC and congratulated me on choosing to follow my delight in his dry, wry way. "So you will swim with dolphins and dive into your soul."

We arrived at the dolphin facility quite early for our scheduled time, eager to go in. The last interaction between people and dolphins was just ending. The staff took a lunch break and we walked around, watching visitors interact with a walrus and some large iguanas. As we entered a dolphin area where the guests were leaving, a handler was walking along the side of the pool. A dolphin leaped out of the pool with half its body on the concrete edge trying to reach the handler, who brusquely indicated by hand gestures and sounds that the dolphin should stay in the pool.

After taking a boat across open water, we got into our safety gear and were instructed on proper behavior in the pool. The large group was divided into groups of six to seven, and each assigned a dolphin and a handler. We had a male dolphin and a male handler. All the staff were young and rather blasé about their work.

I was thrilled to have the opportunity to be close to this 900 pounds of magnificent creature. In the water, I arranged myself to have as much opportunity as possible to touch him as he swam around and around our group of two men, three children and me. The handler had us take turns feeding a fish and hugging with a kiss on the cheek from the well trained animal. But the really exciting part was when we each got a turn to ride the dolphin. He flipped on his back and swam close. I took one hand on his dorsal flipper and pulled myself across like mounting a horse, grabbing the other flipper with my second hand. Belly to belly, arm to arm, he arched his huge muscled body to propel us forward at 30 mph, undulating below my body. What a thrill! My face beamed. I was flying through the water. I could have kept going for miles, but we only had seconds before the camera snapped a photo and I was told to release the fins. The dolphin swam on alone.

This was not the end. We were lined up against the wall of the pool, two groups together. The two dolphins then swam back and forth the width of the pool leaping gracefully in front of us together, a sight I have seen in the freedom of the ocean but never imagined seeing so close by.

Leaving the pool we changed back into dry clothes and went to view the photos. Although seriously overpriced, we chose one of each of us to bring home the memory of that exaltation. They hang on the bedroom wall at the foot of the bed, where I can see my glowing face as I go to sleep and when I awaken every day.

Ever since living in Amagansett, I love being in water. I seek opportunities to be by the ocean. "The ocean of love" is written in sea shells when you step out onto the beach at the Baba Center. The unmoving ground of being and we the waves that play upon the surface, twisting this way and that, currents flowing north or south from day to day. Always ebbing and flowing with the movement of sister Moon. But generally taking up the same space on the planet, unless and until we change it through global warming. Am I really a dolphin?

River flows into the ocean. I love rushing rivers, waterfalls tumbling over rocks. Floating on a raft or paddling hard through white water. Meeting waves like ocean waves only here they are in response to the large boulders below. Water rushes downhill, meets rock, splashes back, swamping raft. We crash through to the other side, avoiding the rock, rushing on to the next. Down, down, always down toward the sea where all the water merges, no longer distinguishable fresh from salty.

River confined by banks. Redefining banks. Changing the shape of the land, some lose, some gain. If the river is our boundary, our boundaries are as fluid as the shape of the river. You can never step in the same river twice. The water is always changing even when the banks remain the same. These images of the natural world are where I find god, Great Spirit, a power greater than myself or any human being. Mysteries that can only be explored with eyes closed and heart open.

ωςος

I also believe that my work has been part of my spiritual path. The NCBI training taught me skills which allowed me to intervene in situations where there was mistreatment of people because of the groups to which they belong. This started my long term commitment to eliminating racism. At first, it grew out of my commitment to the acceptance of cultural differences. Later on I understood racism was a more powerful piece of the puzzle. From many years of working with people from different cultures, I was very aware that when people who are from different backgrounds embraced one another, I was very moved. Much of this comes from living in Amagansett and being bullied in ways that I wouldn't wish on my worst enemy and then finding acceptance from people who are vastly different in background from me.

Living in the South, I have come to believe that the key issue of social justice is racism. Moving to Atlanta after a year in Kenya, many of my friends were African Americans. When I was working with my friend Gerald, an African American with whom I led NCBI training, I said something about "cultural differences." He said, "Kathryn, you can't talk about cultural differences in the South. Both white and black Southerners share a culture, food, speech. But race is the overriding issue. The power differential is what matters here."

One of my sayings from NCBI is, "I love taking risks and making mistakes." This is the way to learn. If I don't take risks, I will never discover what I don't know that I don't know. I took Gerald's correction to heart and have worked to eliminate racism ever since. I have seen a great deal of change with regard to this issue over the many years I have been involved although we are still not where I would hope to be someday.

In 1991, I experimented with setting goals. I met several large ones and I also learned a lot about unintended consequences. For many years before that I had the motto that I was "learning to steer downstream." That year I was deeply involved with the Lifespring Leadership training and I practiced goal setting intensely.

I had made decisions before like deciding I wanted a child after returning from Kenya at age thirty. I had, in that instance, explored alternatives, living in a communal house with children, considering a lesbian relationship, etc. It seemed to me that however one got there, the birth mother ended up being the responsible parent when relationships fell apart as they seemed inevitably to do. So I chose marriage and a man who had already proven his commitment by keeping his two sons when their mother left Atlanta for Washington, DC. This was a willful decision and the outcome didn't look like I anticipated.

In Lifespring I shifted from willful to willing. Lifespring taught me that success might not look like I expected, but that I could create the outcomes to which I aspired. In the Advanced training, Stuart, our trainer had teased and taunted me about hiding out on a mountaintop contemplating my navel. Despite having spent the last five years arranging exchanges with the Soviet Union when we meditated to a series of speeches by MLK and JFK, my heart broke open and I was sobbing with the feeling that I had not lived up to my potential and made the contribution to the world that I was here to make. Having grown up in a family where tikkun olam (the Jewish phrase for "repair of the earth") was the way faith was expressed, I have a deeply embedded need to be in service to the greater good. I knew then that I had more work to do in the world.

At the same time, I could see that some of my willful decisions had not turned out just the way I wanted. I had a son, but he clearly had special challenges. I had my dream house, but the community wasn't accepting of Sasha and thus my plans for his education weren't working out. Even living in my beautiful off the grid octagonal house wasn't working so well.

Reviewing my mother's accomplishments and seeing that they didn't bring about lasting change has led me to believe that I can't push the river. Laws got changed, but behavior didn't. Being willful can lead to unsatisfactory outcomes. I need to be willing to steer downstream. I can make my contribution to the upward trend, but for every step forward, there is push back and often the progress is hard to point to. I have learned to lead from the middle, operate on the cutting edge, build relationships over time and not to set goals that are, in the end, in the hands of God, on the timetable of the trees. Thus I have spent twenty five years volunteering with an organization called "Building Bridges" which helps white people understand white privilege. I can see that times have changed and I believe that the work of Building Bridges has contributed to that.

I have some of the love notes I wrote myself, "God is creating an unprecedented future. Love comes to me easily. I trust in God, Love and Myself in loving myself."

❧❧

Teaching conflict resolution through The Mediation Center and American Friends Service Committee for 20+ years has been a personal growth/spiritual path as well. I continually have to reevaluate myself in order to understand the beliefs that underlie my feelings in response to someone else's behavior. Patterns that were established when I was a child may be hard to change, but taking time to look at what is going on inside me, asking myself what beliefs are generating these feelings, allows me to respond rather than react when I see behaviors I find unacceptable. I am increasingly able to listen to people who differ from me without feeling I need to force them to change. I generally don't believe I can change people with information. I truly believe that for people to change, they need to have new experiences and let the feelings emerge creating new beliefs. Reflection on oneself in groups allows each of us to see ourselves more clearly.

Teaching is a way of learning and the years I spent teaching mediation and conflict resolution were a direct outgrowth of what I had learned in Kenya: that either/or was a dead end and that if I wanted to see progress around issues that matter to me, I had to learn how to find the common ground and build on that. I still believe that compromise is not the best solution, but that collaboration is possible: win/win can be achieved by listening for one another's real needs and finding creative ways of meeting those needs. I find the work around dialogue and deliberation to be fascinating. Watching people use good facilitation skills, from a place of neutrality and understanding delights me. I can see that my early interest in finding ways of governance that take into account the needs of everyone are possible, if not easy. I still believe that with contemporary technology we can reframe solutions until they are acceptable to everyone involved.

&

Figuring out whether I am willful or willing has never been easy. Now I am learning to discern by sitting in quiet at the Meher Spiritual Center. I feel peace sitting by the lake, listening to the in and out breath of the ocean over the forested dunes. The sun is shining dappling the carpet of pine needles through the leaves. Birds share their multiple unique melodies. I treasure the lack of human voices that allows me to hear all these sounds of nature, feel the play of the breeze touching my skin. Notice the seabirds drifting on currents of air. They are willing, not willful. They seek their next meal relaxedly.

When they see what they are seeking, they are determined and committed. I want to imitate them.

Although I haven't gone to Esalen (an experience on my bucket list), I have taken part in many opportunities to participate in personal growth workshops along the way. I have been to the Omega Institute in Rhinebeck, NY. I particularly liked the one I took with Robert Gass. When my present partner was willing to do couples' work, it was natural for me to choose to work with Robert and his wife Judith Ansara. We took the workshop at Omega and then followed them for Deepening In Love back at the same location in Mexico where I had done the Sufi weeks. It was a wonderful celebration of our commitment to each other.

March 2, 2010 journal,

"When I'm there, I'll be where I want to be. I will have resolved my issues to the point that I can write about my early life in a way that is engaging and not self-deprecating. I'll be able to deal with white men in suits without being afraid of their judgments or disapproval. I'll no longer be afraid to spend money or travel wherever and whenever I want. I will be able to use my life energy to make a positive difference in the world without feeling pressured by inner voices that say I'm never doing enough.

"When I am THERE I will be where I want to be. I will be satisfied, content, not edgy or anxious.

"Where is the there I am searching for? It is not a place, but an internal state. It is not a destination, but a journey. Contentment is available at every moment. It is an attitude.

"People say 'adjust your attitude' as if it is a switch that can be flipped, a new object that can be bought or an experience had just by signing up and putting your money down. It is true that I can focus my mind (sometimes) where I want and some thoughts bring me pleasure and others bring me pain. But attitude adjustment doesn't come with the flip of a switch. Attitude reflects what is going on in my life. It is not independent of circumstances."

"I remember when Larry left how angry I was. I kept begging for someone to change the story so I could feel differently about it. But I was so ashamed of not being able to work it out with him since I was the 'great conflict resolver' and all I could feel was fury. And no one could change the story for me till I read about 'the identity conversation.' Now I find myself speaking with total neutrality about how I split up with Larry as if it held no emotion at all—and I am the protagonist—not him. Being at cause in one's life is immensely empowering. So much unhappiness comes from feeling "at effect." That is what is shown in the video *Unnatural Causes*. People become sick and die from feeling they cannot be in charge of their own lives.

Then there are the Twelve Steps sayings that say that God is in charge; God is my pilot. Even within that, I get to be responsible for my choices. Yes, some things are outside my power – things I cannot change; some things are within my power and I need courage to change them but the most important part is to know the difference! What is within my power to change and how can I move to actually change those things?

"I will truly be THERE when I can clearly discern what is within my power and have the courage to make those things match my best judgments as to how they should be."

This was the spring when I started the Stand Against Racism. I got seventy-five groups to sign up. I had left Building Bridges when we hired an executive director with whom I couldn't work with mutual respect. The Stand Against Racism, a program of the YWCA, turned out to be a place I was able to make a big difference. The second year of the program we had the greatest number of groups signed up of any city in the country. When I left we had spawned another program in the community which works to ensure employment and promotion for people of color.

Today my efforts are primarily around eliminating racism, teaching white people about white privilege and supporting black people's leadership and empowerment. I have a deep concern about the environment and climate change, but feel that my best role there is to help environmental organizations become more inclusive and equitable.

The years of my life are many fewer ahead than behind and striving must be balanced with care of the body and soul. Too many factors are already decided and my most impressive successes are already achieved. What lies ahead is to communicate what I have learned to others so that they may continue to carry on toward those still distant goal posts. I am pleased with having several younger people whom I have mentored or taught who are continuing the work.

"The past is not simply the past,
but a prism through which
the subject filters his own changing self-image."

- Doris Kearns Goodwin

CHAPTER FOURTEEN

I HAVE READ THAT IT GETS HARDER AND HARDER TO WRITE about one's life the closer it comes to the present. I believe that is so. The view at a distance is clear in that experiences are honed down into small bits of memory. What is close is still confusing and multilayered. It is strange to say that what happened twenty years ago is recent, but when you get to seventy years of age, time becomes foreshortened and twenty years seems very recent. Especially since for the first time in my life, I have stayed in one place. I have lived in Asheville since 1994.

Yes, I took a break from 2002 to 2007 and went to Maryland, but for the most part, I have lived in Asheville for these last twenty-five years. It is sometimes hard for me to understand all the changes that have taken place, the friends gained and lost, the projects fulfilled or not. When did this or that take place? What was the order of things? It has been a time of stability and continuity, very different from the previous stages.

Yes, there was still international travel, stressful relationships with men, challenges with Sasha, and much joy. I was married and divorced for the third time. I lived through cancer treatment and created a meaningful career. I have spent countless hours contra dancing with a wonderful community of people. I have invested myself in the RC community and I have done nationally recognized work in conflict resolution and mediation, even having the opportunity to lead training in other countries: Georgia, Japan, Hong Kong and Costa Rica. I have contributed to anti-racism work in Asheville and come to know some wonderful people who care about inclusivity and equity. My son is living on his own in Baltimore and completed a bachelor's degree.

☙☙

For me, Asheville has been the best place I ever lived. I had a role in the community which gave me access to people of all kinds, both those in positions of responsibility and those who were struggling. As staff of The Mediation Center responsible for setting up trainings and doing special projects, Dee and I had many opportunities to get involved in interesting conflicts in the community and to be called upon to work with many different groups.

I was on the committee that set up community wide dialogues called VISION dialogues. It was an organization of top leaders in the community trying to resolve the differences between the city and county to bring more development to Asheville. Both of these activities drew me into the field now called "facilitation of dialogue and deliberation." This developed my love of finding both/and solutions, recognizing the spectrum of possibilities rather than duality. It also has meant that I have to recognize that the people I cannot resolve conflict with are those who are stuck in a position and unwilling to look at their underlying needs and consider others' needs.

My years at The Mediation Center were the best work experience of my life. I learned a tremendous amount about myself, about conflict resolution, about being part of a team. We wrote manuals for teaching conflict resolution and mediation. We learned and taught facilitation skills. We disagreed and learned how to resolve our differences using the skills we were teaching. I loved working with Dee and felt I had a true teammate. When we got to the third executive director of the Center (who was not trained in mediation) things fell apart. She was chosen for her administrative skills, but she didn't share our values. She told me to stop trying to get her to use reflective listening!

She came on just as I was completing radiation treatment

for breast cancer. I was not in a good place. I fell into depression. I was living alone having moved Sasha into his own house about a mile from me. Having a boss who tried to bully me into doing what she imagined was possible was not acceptable. I started applying for work elsewhere. Asheville has few opportunities for someone with my skills, so I was looking to move, still knowing that Asheville was where I wanted to retire and spend the rest of my life.

I got a call from Baltimore inviting me to have a phone interview with American Friends Service Committee (AFSC), a Quaker organization, like Friends World College. The interview went well and they invited me to come up for a face to face interview. I only knew one person in Baltimore. It turned out that she worked for the Maryland Department of Commerce. When I asked her what the opportunities would be for Sasha to learn computer game design she told me that the state was making a big investment in this field because Hunt Valley, a suburb of Baltimore, was experiencing a great explosion of small game design companies. I knew this was where we needed to move. And I did.

Again, for the first month, I lived in someone else's house while I searched for a place to live. Once settled myself, I found a house for Sasha that he could afford that was near my office. He has lived there since 2002.

While in Maryland, I joined up with a wonderful man with whom I have built a house that I love back in Asheville and created a life that works for us both. I attribute this to all the work I have done on myself.

࿇

Recently, I saw the movie "The Young Marx" about how Marx and Engels got together and the Communist Manifesto was written. The scene in which Engels takes over the League of the Just and turns it into the Communist League made me aware of the essential tension which has run through my life. The Society of the Just is represented by statements about how all men are brothers and Engels with his background firmly fixed in Hegelian dialectic reminds the crowd that they are not "brothers" with the wealthy capitalists. The proletariat does not have the privileges of the bourgeoisie which takes advantage of their labor to make themselves rich. This tension between a spiritually based unity of humans and a political/economic dichotomy or duality pervades my experiences. It is much like the dichotomous truth that race is a meaningless social construct and at the same time it definitely defines the lived experience of everyone on the planet at this time.

Stamped from the beginning by the hypocrisy of American rhetoric of equality and justice for all, I have struggled with the tension between the vision of my parents who believed the rhetoric and fought for the principles the U.S. claims to stand for, and the reality that they are hollow promises. It is interesting to me to read blacklisted actor, Jeff Corey's ,memoir where he writes, "I owed full and unqualified allegiance to my flag and to our Constitution, which has given hope and encouragement to the world. I wanted them to know that I believed loyalty is measured by deeds and devotion to one's neighbors and by active participation in civic and charitable functions, not by a devotional fetish that required the mechanical affixing of a signature to a meaningless loyalty oath." (*Improvising Out Loud: My Life Teaching Hollywood How To Act* p. 71) He was raised to believe in the vision of America as a land of opportunity for all. Despite the fact schooling taught us to believe this vision, I recognize that many in my generation which came of age in the sixties have lost all faith in the hope that we can even approximate that allegiance. The 1950s repudiated all expectation that our government as constituted would ever support the creation of an inclusive welcoming home for all people. The 1960s confirmed the disparities, but still then almost all children (close to 90 percent) were able to grow up to earn more than their parents. For children born in 1984, who are now in the labor market, this fraction has fallen to 50 percent.

I can't align myself with the idea that all that is needed is for us to believe that all people live in a brother/sisterhood. Even in families, some succeed and dominate; we don't necessarily love each other and help each other. I am largely estranged from my family of origin; not because of hard feelings, but because of lack of contact. They don't reach out to me; I don't reach out for them. I may speak to my brother once a year. Yes, we grew up in the same family, but otherwise, we have nothing in common. Many of the people I know have moved and created families of choice rather than birth. Our family wasn't really the same for him as for me, as he was born at the moment of change.

Have I realized my mother's expectations? I don't think so. I am not active with any political party. Perhaps this is part of the disillusionment I experienced and she didn't come to even with her disappointments in government. She still thought that electoral politics could make a difference. I have more doubt about that. I hope we won't have to have violent revolution to make things change, but change is coming, I believe, one way or another. When a man like Donald Trump can be elected president, this system is too broken. He points a spotlight on America's shadow side. By the same token, I recognize that some may feel that way about having elected a black man president. I had a very enlightened Sufi master tell me that he thought it was wonderful that we had elected someone who didn't look like "an American." How could he think that a black man looked less like an American than I?

Not only are we divided in our beliefs, but we also don't come from the same knowledge base. Our schools have been resegregated largely by charter schools, where government funding is used to maintain separate and unequal education. No longer are we all reading the same information; instead we have separate tracks that purport to present the "news." And they have very little in common except their extremism. Having studied Hegel in college, I base my understanding of how society works on the dialectic between thesis and antithesis bringing about a new synthesis. I eagerly await this new synthesis and hope it comes before I die.

I was blessed with many opportunities to travel the world and learn from different points of view. I have been able to see that there is not one Truth that everyone can see, but a small piece of Truth in the center of a large ball and we all stand on the outside looking in. To learn more about what Truth looks like, I have looked through the windows of many people from many perspectives and many different lands and cultures. I have explored Truth from many angles and believe that it is impossible to grasp. I am uncomfortable with people who think they know Truth and insist that everyone should see it the way they do. I think that the language police who tell us that things must be said a certain way are losing sight of this multiplicity. I think that they alienate more than they enlighten. Truth is in the eye of the beholder, truly.

I continue to use my skills and knowledge to help people deal with conflict and understand racism. I use what I have learned in my own life and experience and share that with others. I enjoy sharing my skills and experience around conflict resolution with others who are interested. I don't have the last word. I am always listening to others and learning.

Times have changed and white people seem ready to accept that implicit and structural racism is still with us and create the underlying instability in the foundation of this country. At the same time, I find many whites who are drowning in guilt and willing to accept behavior from black people they would never accept from a white person. We need to follow the lead of people who have been marginalized, but that doesn't mean we give up discernment.

Asheville is a "progressive" place, which still struggles with the racism that is all around us: in education, medical care, housing, and policing. I say it is a very diverse white town, even with thirteen percent African American population. We have the new white retirees who love living near the mountains and the multigenerational white mountain people who have been living in these hollers for more than a hundred years. A friend says that Asheville is where people stand out to fit in. But it is not a place that has gone beyond where we are as a nation with regard to race and the economic disparities are exacerbated by race which shows up in every aspect of life.

The other end of the continuum is spiritual. Asheville is where old age meets new age and you can find every alternative health practitioner imaginable and every approach to spirituality. I have owned my Jewishness and can see the history of anti-Semitism which has plagued my life and was an element in the purges of the 1950s. At the same time, I don't find a home in any of the Jewish congregations. I have found a spiritual home with the United Church of Christ, as long as they let me be a Jew. Their inclusiveness has made me feel welcome and the historical and political basis works for me. I love that the pastor says that God is still speaking to us and we must listen for the contemporary word.

I have explored the extremes of political action for social change and spiritual enlightenment which recognizes the oneness of all – both human and the natural world. I see people standing in each position. Some say we should just get out there and act to make the world as it should be (mother's position). Others in this community of multiple spiritual paths say that we don't need to notice what is off in the world, just hold the vision that we are all one and all the differences and divisions will go away. I see this most when we talk about the issue of race: either race isn't real and then we should be color blind, or race is the most relevant factor in our contemporary inequality and we must focus on it. I believe that race has no biological basis but a huge sociological impact. Both/and.

I have grown to believe that the future must be determined by a combination of both the choices humans make (can we reverse climate change?) and the recognition of the relationships we depend on – both human to human and human to something greater (nature, a higher power, whatever). Too often I see people taking one position or the other: either we are going down the drain and must protest in large numbers or we are just part of the flow and should sit at home and meditate. I have come to believe that we must both heal ourselves with reflection on our personal interactions and also share with others our vision of a righteous world. My exploration of the technology of working with groups to build agreement and community seems like a path that combines the personal and spiritual with the political. I have long been attracted to Barbara Marx Hubbard's vision of consciously created culture that responds to the needs of all.

So, how do I see my life as a process? The wanderer became a tree planted in the soil of Western North Carolina. The wounded child became a warrior. The abandoned daughter found love. Even my mother's voice in my head has subsided for the most part. The only thing that has stayed the same is my fear of my government; only the details and players have changed. I believe we have to search for the good within it and continue to shine a light on the people and policies that take us far away from the freedoms our founding fathers fought for more than two hundred years ago. We have to learn how to mediate our way through the difficulties. I know from my work, that this can be achieved. It just takes courage to sustain it.

Even when things don't go well and I don't feel appreciated or understood, I know that this is home. My partner and I have built a new and better dream house. We are able to travel to interesting places together. I have worked out my early hurts around the loss of my dad and found a man who accepts me as I am. My son is settled. If I am not completely happy with how he lives, he says he is, although he acknowledges that he is sometimes lonely.

Even as I write, I see that the weeping cherry in front of our house thrives, blooming beautiful pink blossoms that harbinger spring. I look out my window and see the crest of the hills where the Blue Ridge Parkway runs. I still love early mornings and I watch the sun rise over the monitor as I write and the sky turns from grey to blue on a clear day. Even when it is grey, I can drive along familiar roads and be awed by the beauty of the mountains, perhaps not as majestic as Mt. Kilimanjaro but snow showing through the brown trunks of bare trees in the winter and warm green in summer, brilliant reds, yellows and oranges in the fall.

I love watching my garden grow. The strawberries, like the ones in Chevy Chase, capture the sun and explode in a burst of sweetness in my mouth when I bite into them. The purple iris spring by themselves out of the ground complementing the purple of the house. Arranged in a spiral to match the spiral rainbow of the stained glass window which casts its colors around the living room in the afternoon sun, the flower garden reminds me that life is not a straight line. We continue to see the world from new perspectives as we wind our way up the spiral staircase of the lighthouse, searching for truth. So I have.

I hope this book demonstrates that.

ACKNOWLEDGEMENTS

I WANT TO THANK ALL THOSE WHO HAVE MADE THIS BOOK possible.

First, those to who I have told my tale and they said, "That's an interesting story. You should write a book."

Then, those who have supported me in actually doing that. Most significantly, Emily Corey who has edited it and designed it for publication. Also, Julie Schneyer who read most of it and made suggestions. Members of the various classes I have taken in memoir writing and those teachers: Victoria Fann and Clive Matson most recently. Other friends who have read it: Judith Beers and Ferris Fakhoury. Clare Hanrahan who invited me to her writers' group and has consistently said, "You can do this."

Most of all, I want to thank my life partner, Karl Katterjohn, who has been my greatest cheerleader and supporter throughout the years I have struggled with what I want to say and how I want to say it.

Made in the USA
Columbia, SC
30 May 2020